Unsettling Opera

Unsettling
Opera

Staging Mozart, Verdi, Wagner, and Zemlinsky

David J. Levin

The University of Chicago Press | Chicago & London

David J. Levin is associate professor of Germanic studies, cinema and media studies, and theater and performance studies at the University of Chicago. He is the author of *Richard Wagner, Fritz Lang, and the Nibelungen* and the editor of *Opera through Other Eyes*.

The University of Chicago Press, Chicago 60637
The University of Chicago Press, Ltd., London
© 2007 by The University of Chicago
All rights reserved. Published 2007
Printed in the United States of America

16 15 14 13 12 11 10 09 08 07   1 2 3 4 5

ISBN-13: 978-0-226-47522-6 (cloth)
ISBN-10: 0-226-47522-0 (cloth)

Library of Congress Cataloging-in-Publication Data

Levin, David J., 1960 –
   Unsettling opera : staging Mozart, Verdi, Wagner, and Zemlinsky / David J. Levin.
      p. cm.
   Includes bibliographical references and index.
   ISBN-13: 978-0-226-47522-6 (cloth : alk. paper)
   ISBN-10: 0-226-47522-0 (cloth : alk. paper)
   1. Opera—Dramaturgy.   2. Opera—Production and direction.   I. Title.
   ML3858.L48 2007
   792.502′3—dc22

                                                           2006031476

ML 1700 LEV

CONTENTS

FIGURES

MUSICAL EXAMPLES

In June of 2004, within a single week and a few blocks, two of Berlin's three major opera houses presented new productions of operas that I discuss in the following pages: at the Staatsoper, Verdi's *Don Carlos,* and at the Komische Oper, Mozart's *Entführung aus dem Serail.*[1] These were striking productions—but striking in very different ways. Philipp Himmelmann's production of *Don Carlos* (in the four-act, Italian version) was insistently heterogeneous, alternately realistic and surreal, abstract and topical, chamber theater and grand spectacle. It was organized around a single, sleek table that assumed a variety of functions during the course of the performance—a dining-room table for the royal family; an ironing board for Elisabeth, newly domesticated as the Spanish queen; a desk in King Philippe's private study; an impromptu bed upon which Philippe seduces Princess Eboli (see figures 1 and 2). Of course, a table exudes a kind of fixity—it is a set place for, say, the family to gather at mealtimes or for the king to attend to his business. This production was interested in querying that fixity—or rather, the production was alert to the ways in which Verdi's piece queries the appearance of fixity.

1. Verdi's *Don Carlos* (in the four-act, Italian version, thus spelled *Don Carlo*) was presented at the Staatsoper Unter den Linden in Berlin in a new production by Philipp Himmelmann, with sets by Johannes Leiacker and costumes by Klaus Bruns. (During the course of his career, Verdi prepared a number of different versions of *Don Carlos* for a number of different venues. In order to avoid confusion, and unless otherwise noted, I have chosen to employ the French spelling of the title and character names.) The Berlin production featured René Pape as Philippe, Ramón Vargas as Carlos, Dalibor Jenis as Posa, Norma Fantini as Elisabeth, and Nadja Michael as Eboli; Fabio Luisi conducted. Mozart's *Die Entführung aus dem Serail* was presented at the Komische Oper Berlin in a new production by Calixto Bieito with sets by Alfons Flores and costumes by Anna Eiermann. The cast featured Guntbert Warns as Pasha Selim, Maria Bengtsson as Konstanze, Valentina Farcas as Blonde, Finnur Bjarnason as Belmonte, Christoph Späth as Pedrillo, and Jens Larsen as Osmin; Kiril Petrenko conducted.

Figure 1 Transactions at the table, no. 1: affairs of state. King Philippe II (René Pape, *right*) and Posa (Roman Trekel) in act 1 of Philip Himmelmann's production of Verdi's *Don Carlos* at the Staatsoper Berlin. Photo © Monika Rittershaus.

Figure 2 Transactions at the table, no. 2: affairs of the heart. King Philippe II (René Pape) and Princess Eboli (Nadja Michael) at the outset of act 3 of Philip Himmelmann's production of Verdi's *Don Carlos* at the Staatsoper Berlin. Photo © Monika Rittershaus.

Figure 3 Guess who's coming tp dinner? Don Carlos (Jorge Pita), Queen Elisabeth (Norma Fantini), King Philippe II (René Pape), and Princess Eboli (Nadja Michael) at the royal dinner table, with heretics before them, emissaries from Flanders to the right and left; and the populace and clerics behind them in Philip Himmelmann's production of Verdi's *Don Carlos* at the Staatsoper Berlin. Photo © Monika Rittershaus.

One of the most striking and characteristic gestures of this production was its predilection for stage pictures that combined and juxtaposed dramatic contexts, such as when a domestic scene (a formal dinner at the royal family's dining-room table) appeared incongruously in a public space (the church plaza where Verdi locates the auto-da-fé of act 2). The royal family appears to be at dinner inside, and yet it is surrounded on three sides by an assembly of clerics and the populace. Seated at the very front of the stage, their hands tied behind their backs and their backs to the audience, is the group of heretics, their bodies bearing traces of the whippings to which they have already been subjected (see figure 3). At stake in Verdi's scene is a crosscutting set of conflicts—private and public, personal and political. The production realized this simultaneity transparently and with theatrical verve. The sheer scenic invention of the Staatsoper production provided an implicit formal counterpoint to the dramatic bleakness of Verdi's piece. But that scenic invention ultimately proved compelling because it was, in a double sense, so illuminating.

In a general sense, the production's scenic invention offered an especially cogent account of the excess of expressive means that characterizes opera as a genre. The contradiction attending that formulation—a cogent account of excess—is indeed no contradiction at all. Rather, it is one of the characteristics of a successful production that it does not simply alert us to but in-deed clarifies an opera's specific incongruities, the precise terms of its contra-dictions. In a more specific sense, this production illuminated and clarified the piece's dramaturgical stakes. Thus, the multifunctional table offered a "place-setting" for the tensions that suffuse this piece. Each figure in *Don Carlos* brings very different desires to the table, which serves as a forum for these dif-ferent desires—and for their different forms. For example, the family's de-sires conflict with those of the individual or, for that matter, the state; the church's desires clash with the king's wishes; the queen's desire (say, to main-tain appearances, to repress her personal inclinations in favor of her familial responsibilities) clashes with Carlos's (to defy and denounce all appearances and give voice instead to his lasting and true desires). Each of these desires—and their disposition—found expression at the table, in various and distinct approaches to it, behaviors at it, or departures from it. As Norbert Elias has observed, the table constitutes an overdetermined space for the expression of sublimated power relations, a privileged site for the expression of abstract qualities (such as breeding or class) and kinship relations (such as those be-tween siblings, between parents, or between family members and guests).[2] There is always a subtext, largely unspoken, to events at the table, and this subtext is often about power. Who serves whom? Who sits at the head of the table? Who controls the conversation? Who monitors the manners? Who stays and who leaves? And *Don Carlos,* I argue in chapter 5, charts the over-whelming pressures of sublimation, the toll it exacts and the lyricism it pro-duces. By setting their production around the multifunctional table and then doing exceedingly interesting things with that variegated setting, Himmel-mann and his collaborators, including a first-rate cast of singer-actors, offered an account of *Don Carlos* that was at once complex, moving, and illuminating.

In contrast to the state of permanent mutation that characterized the set for the Staatsoper *Don Carlos,* the setting for Calixto Bieito's production of *Die Entführung aus dem Serail* at the Komische Oper was mutated and then fixed. The Komische Oper production was set in an utterly bleak and brutal under-world of sex, drugs, and cruelty (see figure 4). Bieito and his collaborators lo-cated the piece in a specific and recognizable world—one that was largely un-familiar to productions of this piece, but nonetheless immediately familiar to a contemporary audience. The production, like the setting, was overtly top-ical and programmatically shocking: there was a great deal of gore here, a re-

2. See, e.g., pt. 4, "At Table," in Norbert Elias, *The Civilizing Process,* trans. Edmund Jephcott with notes and corrections by the author, ed. Eric Dunning, Johan Goudsblom, and Stephen Mennell (Oxford: Blackwell, 2000). Originally published in German as *Über den Prozess der Zivilisation: Sozio-genetische und Psychogenetische Untersuchungen* (Basel: Haus zum Falken, 1939).

Figure 4 Fear factor. Konstanze (Maria Bengtsson) blindfolded and disoriented in the netherworld of sex, drugs, and violence into which she has been abducted in Calixto Bieito's production of Mozart's *Die Entführung aus dem Serail* at the Komische Oper Berlin. Photo © Monika Rittershaus.

lentless insistence on the brutality and misery of the underworld into which Mozart's emissaries from the world of privilege had strayed.

This depiction of contemporary society's underbelly was as monotonic as it was unsentimental. To cite an example from near the beginning of the piece: Osmin, the overseer of the pasha's harem, caught up with and raped a young prostitute, then sang his entrance aria while showering in a glass (which is to say, a see-through) stall. And from there things simply got more explicit, more vicious, more depraved. The exoticism of Mozart and Gottlieb Stephanie's "Turkey" took on a stridently contemporary, strikingly grue-some appearance. The Ottoman "seraglio" was located beneath the very bot-tom rung of the social ladder. In the Komische Oper production, that place is shown to be at less a geographical than a psychological remove: instead of be-ing far, far away, the underworld on stage emerged as a place very proximate to the world of privilege that it mirrored in distorted form.

If the Staatsoper production of *Don Carlos* was erratic, it was aptly, pre-cisely erratic, traversing the heights of intimacy and the depths of emotional violence charted by this most emotionally erratic and exhausting of Verdi's pieces. Bieito's production of *Die Entführung* at the Komische Oper was very different indeed. There, the terms of dramatization were clearly, program-matically oppositional, but in a limited sense. The Komische Oper's *Ent-führung* was singularly dark and claustrophobic, emphatically unresponsive to emotional and situational modulations in Mozart's piece. This is not to say that Bieito's production was oblivious to the terms of Mozart and Stephanie's piece. Far from it. As at least one critic noted, Osmin's words in the piece are consistently and surprisingly violent.[3] In their very first encounter, in act 1, scene 2, Osmin promises Belmonte a merciless beating, describes Pedrillo as a scoundrel who deserves to be skewered and whose neck ought to be broken, and threatens to hang them both. These threats precede his famously sadistic ditty "Solche hergelaufne Laffen"—a ditty that Osmin repeats in the course of the opera: "Erst geköpft, dann gehangen, dann gespießt auf heiße Stangen; dann vebrannt, dann gebunden, und getaucht; zuletzt geschunden" (First beheaded, then hanged, then impaled on hot spikes, then burned, then bound, and drowned, finally flayed). And Osmin is not alone in his recourse to extremely violent language. The pasha threatens Konstanze with "Martern aller Arten" (tortures of all kinds), a threat taken up by Konstanze in her famous aria of the same name: this and similar textual moments have conventionally been disregarded as merely comical window-dressing. In the account provided at the Komische Oper, the world of the pasha and Osmin, the world of the harem is anything but picturesque (see figure 5). But in substituting a world of claustrophobic bleakness for the more conventional world of picturesque inanity, Bieito and his collaborators merely replace one form of scenic constriction with another: although the terms of constriction may differ, the fact of scenic and dramaturgical homogeneity does not. I am less impressed by the achievements of such a production. Not because it is not striking (Bieito's production was nothing if not striking) or even moving (some of the singing in the Komische Oper *Entführung* was transcendent and some of the dramatic images electrifying), but because it ends up illuminating too narrow a swath of the piece.

✳   ✳   ✳

It comes as no surprise that both of these productions were controversial. Surprising, though, is the fact that they were controversial for the very same reason. As Shirley Apthorp harrumphed in the *Financial Times:* "It's penis week in Berlin opera. Philipp Himmelmann has made the same discovery at the Staatsoper Berlin that Calixto Bieito made at the Komische Oper on the weekend: a few grams of exposed male reproductive organ can dominate a full evening of opera. Instant scandal!" [4] Apthorp lambastes the auto-da-fé in the

---

3. See Alan Riding, "Definitely Not Your Mother's Mozart," *New York Times,* July 10, 2004.

4. Shirley Apthorp, "The Critics: *Don Carlo* Staatsoper Berlin," *Financial Times* (London), June 28, 2004, Arts, p. 9. Writing in the *New York Times,* Jeremy Eichler was a bit more restrained in airing the very same suspicion: "In many quarters opera still maintains an image as genteel and civilized entertainment, but that stereotype was long ago jettisoned in this thrill-seeking city. Directors here,

Figure 5 "Martern aller Arten." Pasha Selim (Guntbert Warns) forces Konstanze (Maria Bengtsson) to watch as Osmin (Jens Larsen) mutilates a prostitute (uncredited in the program book) in Calixto Bieito's production of Mozart's *Die Entführung aus dem Serail* at the Komische Oper Berlin. Photo © Monika Rittershaus.

Staatsoper *Don Carlos* as especially egregious: "At the height of the auto-da-fé, naked heretics (wouldn't they burn better with clothes on?) are doused in petrol and then hung by the feet above the royal dinner-table. Flanders flambé. It's enough to guarantee some demonstrative exits and a storm of boos." In a "Critic's Notebook" piece in the *New York Times*, Jeremy Eichler zeroes in on the auto-da-fé with just as much relish and a bit more detail:

> Over the course of this lengthy scene, the king feasts serenely on a banquet as five bound infidels lie naked and quivering in front of his table. Executioners

---

it seems, seldom meet an opera that a little sex and over-the-top violence can't fix." Eichler, "Berlin Tarts Up Opera With Sex and Violence," *New York Times,* July 21, 2004, section E, 5.

Figure 6 Flanders flambé? The heretics dangle, the security agents raise their lighters, and the crowd protects itself from the sparks to come at the very end of act 2 in Philip Himmelmann's production of Verdi's *Don Carlo* at the Staatsoper Berlin. Photo ©Monika Rittershaus.

duct tape the mouths of the captives and then slowly douse them with gasoline. They are strung up by their ankles and hoisted high in the air, spinning precariously as they go. The executioners spark their lighters, raising them up toward their dangling prey as the curtain falls. The persistent question is why? Why this flight into such sadistic realism in a production that otherwise allowed for suggestion and subtlety?[5]

Eichler's question is merely rhetorical. He follows it with the predictable speculation: "It's as if Mr. Himmelmann did not trust that the work would be sufficiently dramatic without such a harrowing spectacle. Or perhaps he knew such a stunt would draw press attention, which it has" (see figure 6).

Polemics aside, the question "why?" is one that neither of these reviews is particularly interested in pursuing. Yet it is a question well worth considering. So: why this flight into such sadistic realism in a production that otherwise allowed for suggestion and subtlety? Perhaps because that is precisely what Verdi's piece calls for? After all, what is an auto-da-fé if not a "harrowing spectacle"? It may well be that we have grown accustomed to a decorative

5. Eichler, "Berlin Tarts Up Opera," 5.

rendering of the scene, but the picture that emerges from Verdi's score is *utterly* harrowing. True, he composed a grand, festive scene—but what transpires in that scene? The assembled masses alternate wildly between a thirst for the spectacle of public execution and a heartfelt pity for the victims. But that is not all. In the midst of this scene, and in the center of the spectacle, Carlos challenges his father's, the king's, authority, mounting an impromptu Oedipal insurrection—and gains the sympathy of the people, only then to be disarmed by Posa, his erstwhile best friend and confidant. In short, the "stunt," the "harrowing spectacle," is not Himmelmann's invention, but Verdi's.

Which is not to say that anything goes. As I will argue in the course of this book, we need to be able to judge productions. But more important than the need for judgment is the need for solid ground upon which to form that judgment—and the presence (or, for that matter, the absence) of bare skin hardly suffices. By focusing on sex and nudity, these reviews overlook the real achievements of these productions—and their real shortcomings. Denunciation here serves as a shorthand for disregard. What we need instead is a variegated vocabulary with which to assess productions, be they of familiar works or unknown ones; be they experimental, like the two Berlin productions discussed above, or conventional, like two productions of Wagner's *Meistersinger von Nürnberg* that I discuss in chapter 2.

Surely one place to look for an answer to Eichler's "why?" is the score of the opera in question. And indeed, it provides all kinds of answers. This is not to say that the only appropriate seat in the opera house is a score-reading stall in the upper balconies. But one way to approach challenging productions is to reflect upon their relationship to the piece being rendered. This necessitates a certain nimbleness of interpretation, a willingness to modify and renew our sense of meaning and reference. Over the course of the last thirty years—and most intensely over the last decade—it has become clear that a new production of a work offers more than a neutral or uninflected platform for singers; it can afford an opportunity to explore and revise our musical and dramatic assumptions about a piece. Any production can unsettle opinions that had become settled.

This, it seems to me, is a good thing. But in order to chart the shifting meanings proposed by each production (and to answer the question "why?" that each production will necessarily pose), we need a nuanced analytic vocabulary and method. This book seeks to provide a variety on both counts—a variegated vocabulary and a variety of critical methods. Surely the vocabulary and methods proposed here will not appeal to all. But that is as it should be, and if this book stimulates others to propose additional methods and a more refined vocabulary, then it will have achieved a good part of its goal.

* * *

I have presented work from this project to a variety of audiences (in Berkeley, Berlin, Chicago, Essen, Evanston, Iowa City, Ithaca, New York City, Palo Alto, Princeton, Salzburg, Tempe, and Toronto) and have profited enormously from their feedback. Earlier versions of my discussion in chapter 2 of Wagner's *Die Meistersinger von Nürnberg* appeared in *Cambridge Opera Journal* 9, no. 1 (Fall 1997): 47–71, and *New German Critique* 69 (Fall 1996): 127–46. An earlier version of chapter 5 appeared as "'Va Pensiero'? Verdi and Theatrical Provocation," in *Verdi 2001*, edited by Fabrizio della Seta, Roberta Marvin, and Marco Marica (Florence: L. S. Olschki, 2003), 463–75. A number of colleagues have been kind enough to read through and comment upon sections of this manuscript. Of these, I want to offer special thanks to a small number of colleagues at the University of Chicago who formed an exceedingly productive working group—Deborah Nelson, Danilyn Rutherford, Sandra Macpherson, Jacqueline Stewart, Jacqueline Goldsby, and Danielle Allen. I owe heartfelt thanks to my colleague Eric Santner, who provided an extraordinarily detailed and characteristically penetrating reading of the manuscript at a very early stage and remained a generous interlocutor throughout the process of the book's preparation. Michel Chaouli likewise provided wonderfully thoughtful assessments of the book at various stages of its gestation. Beyond that, a number of colleagues and friends offered generous support and astute criticism as I pursued this project, including Carolyn Abbate, Heidi Coleman, Martha Feldman, Philip Gossett, Tom Gunning, Miriam Hansen, Berthold Hoeckner, Gundula Kreuzer, Hanna Leitgeb, Janel Mueller, Roger Parker, Pamela Rosenberg, Warren Sack, Michael P. Steinberg, Martin Stokes, John Urang, Marc Weiner, David Wellbery, Abigail Zitin, and two exceedingly thoughtful anonymous readers for the University of Chicago Press. I owe profuse thanks to Benjamin Fink for heroic assistance in preparing the manuscript for publication. Barbara Norton was a helpful and sensitive copy editor; John Urang did a wonderful job preparing the index; Randy Petilos and Erik Carlson at the University of Chicago Press were especially helpful in navigating the book through production. Additional thanks are due to Jasen Loverti, Jon Ryan Quinn, and Catherine Sprecher-Loverti for research assistance provided during the book's preparation. Laura Macy, editor-in-chief of the Grove Dictionaries of Music, generously granted permission for the use of the plot summaries that appear in the appendix. Permission to reproduce the plot summary for *Der König Kandaules* was generously provided by the Vienna Volksoper. For sage professional advice and support, my thanks, as always, go to my brother, Tom, and my parents, Evi and Walter. Walter Lippincott was an early and enthusiastic supporter of this project, and Alan Thomas of the University of Chicago Press lent the manuscript his trademark blend of editorial acumen and straightforward judgment. Finally, my greatest debt is due my wife, Claudia, and our two children, Eliza and Nicholas, who endured my interminable trips to rehearsals, performances, and, ultimately, a library study (accessible, thanks to the insane generosity of the University of Chicago Libraries, twenty-four hours a day, 365 days a year) with an endless reserve of humor and good cheer.

DRAMATURGY AND MISE-EN-SCÈNE

"The Text is experienced only in an activity of production."

Roland Barthes, "From Work to Text"

. . .

This is a book about opera in performance. It seeks to address a particular and familiar phenomenon in opera production: what happens when operas that are more or less comfortably ensconced in the canon—works by Mozart, Verdi, or Wagner—are thoroughly rethought and dramatically recast onstage. And beyond asking what a particular staging does to our understanding of a particular opera, I want to ask what stagings do to our understanding of the genre more generally. That is, although a stage production can unsettle a work that was thought to be settled, I will argue, opera itself is unsettled, and that stage performance, at its best, clarifies this condition and brings opera in its unsettledness to life.

In a sense, the academic terrain from which this project emerges is also unsettled. Over the course of the past generation, musicology in the United States has reinvented itself. In 1985, the preeminent musicologist Joseph Kerman bemoaned the state of musicology in the United States—its isolation from, even hostility to, developments in related fields of humanistic inquiry such as textual theory and cultural analysis.[1] In the wake of Kerman's critique,

1. "We do not have musical Arnolds or Eliots, Blackmurs or Kermodes, Ruskins or Schapiros. In the circumstances, it is idle to complain or lament that critical thought in music lags conceptually far behind that in the other arts. In fact, nearly all musical thinkers travel at a respectful distance behind the latest chariots (or bandwagons) of intellectual life in general, as we shall see many times in the following pages. Semiotics, hermeneutics, and phenomenology are being drawn upon only by some of

and under the banner of the new musicology (admittedly, no longer so new), academic work in musical studies came to consider questions of textual indeterminacy or inscribed power relations alongside more traditional questions of compositional form, structure, history, and analysis.[2]

From early on, opera played an important part in this disciplinary transformation. In the introduction to *Analyzing Opera: Verdi and Wagner*, a collection of essays from a seminal conference at Cornell in 1984, Carolyn Abbate and Roger Parker outline a new conceptual framework for opera. Their framework clearly draws upon some of the critical discourses that, to Kerman's mind, would help to invigorate musicology.

> Opera is peculiar, its clash of systems can produce incongruities and extravagant miscalculations. At a time when organicism is no longer an adequate interpretive metaphor and when musical scholars tend more and more to reject positivism in criticism as well as history, opera is becoming a central area of investigation. This is hardly a surprise. Analysis of opera often reveals the imperfect, the ambiguous, the illogical. If it shows us how to recognize such qualities, perhaps it can also teach us to face them without uneasiness or fear.[3]

There are two important points here. The first, implicit in Parker and Abbate's polemic, involves the focus of their proposed reforms. In formulating their program in the context of a reconsideration of Verdi and Wagner, Abbate and Parker—and the new opera studies—signaled a determination to

---

the boldest of musical studies today. Post-structuralism, deconstruction, and serious feminism have yet to make their debuts in musicology or music theory." Joseph Kerman, *Contemplating Music: Challenges to Musicology* (Cambridge, Mass.: Harvard University Press, 1985), 17.

2. See Ruth Solie, ed., *Musicology and Difference: Gender and Sexuality in Music Scholarship* (Berkeley: University of California Press, 1993), or, more recently, Georgina Born and David Hesmondhalgh, eds., *Western Music and Its Others: Difference, Representation, and Appropriation in Music* (Berkeley: University of California Press, 2000), a collection that, in the words of the editors, "take[s] initial steps in the direction of exploring the relations between structured inequalities of race/class power and the history, theory, and analysis of music" (Born and Hesmondhalgh, introduction, 8.) Although Kerman's critique undoubtedly served to coax musicology out of its isolation, Carolyn Abbate has argued that the costs of doing so may have been far greater than originally understood. "While Kerman's aim was to divert musicology towards criticism and hermeneutics and away from composer biography, archival history, and strict formalism, something important was foreclosed when old music criticism became new music criticism. And the something was not just Cecilia Bartoli or Martha Argerich but real music: the performances that were to remain in large part as marginal to criticism or hermeneutics as they had been to formalism, biography, history, or theory. See Abbate, "Music—Drastic or Gnostic?," *Critical Inquiry* 30 (Spring 2004): 506.

3. Carolyn Abbate and Roger Parker, "Introduction: On Analyzing Opera," in *Analyzing Opera: Verdi and Wagner*, ed. Carolyn Abbate and Roger Parker (Berkeley: University of California Press, 1989), 1–24, at 23–24.

engage canonical works in novel ways. This is not to say that recent work in musicology has been uninterested in discovering new works. But from its inception, the new musicology has been especially interested in rediscovering familiar works by subjecting them to new critical approaches.[4] Which brings us to the second point of Abbate and Parker's polemic. It is hard to overstate the importance of their notion of opera's characteristic peculiarity, imperfection, ambiguity, and logic—in terms of its distance from the reigning critical paradigm in musicology of the mid-1980s and in terms of its impact on subsequent critical discussions.

In the wake of this wholesale reconceptualization, opera has undergone a series of signal transformations—first, from "work" to "text," and more recently, from text to performance.[5] In Roland Barthes's account, the work is a holistic item, a respectable, desirable object in cultural commerce; the text, on the other hand, is mobile, plural, and furtive, resistant to ready encapsulation and commodification. Reconceived as a text (and, as I will argue here, as a text *in performance*), opera has emerged as an agitated or unsettled site of signification, one that encompasses multiple modes of expression and necessitates new modes of reading. Of course, opera's musical text, the score, had long been conceived in terms of such mobility and furtiveness. But until quite recently, the intellectual nimbleness with which musicologists conceptualized the instability of opera's musical text had only rarely extended to its performance text.[6]

As musicologists ventured into unfamiliar territory to explore new modes of textual and cultural analysis, a number of their newfound interlocutors—in history, gender studies, and literary studies, among others—

---

4. This is true for many branches of recent musicological research—for example, a number of scholars interested in postcolonial studies have focused upon the nineteenth-century operatic canon. See Ralph P. Locke, "Constructing the Oriental 'Other': Saint-Saëns's *Samson et Dalila*," *Cambridge Opera Journal* 3, no. 3 (1991): 261–302; Locke, "Reflections on Orientalism in Opera and Musical Theater," *Opera Quarterly* 10, no. 1 (1993): 49–73. On *Aida*, see Edward Said, "The Imperial Spectacle," *Grand Street* 6, no. 2 (Winter 1987): 82–104, later published as "The Empire at Work: Verdi's *Aida*," in *Culture and Imperialism* (New York: Knopf, 1993). See also Susan McClary, *Georges Bizet: Carmen*, Cambridge Opera Handbooks (Cambridge: Cambridge University Press, 1992).

5. According to Roland Barthes, "Over against the traditional notion of the *work*, for long—and still—conceived of in a, so to speak, Newtonian way, there is now the requirement of a new object, obtained by the sliding or overturning of former categories. That object is the *Text*." Barthes, "From Work to Text," in *Image, Music, Text*, essays selected and trans. Stephen Heath (New York: Hill and Wang, 1977); emphasis in original. See also Brigitte Scheer, "Inszenierung als Problem der Übersetzung und Aneignung," in *Ästhetik der Inszenierung*, ed. Josef Früchtl and Jörg Zimmermann (Frankfurt am Main: Suhrkamp, 2001), 91–102, esp. 95.

6. For an exceedingly interesting consideration of the textual status of the musical object and its relation to performance, see Carolyn Abbate, *In Search of Opera* (Princeton, N.J.: Princeton University Press, 2001), 50.

took up an interest in opera.[7] Over the past twenty years, musicologists and scholars from a host of other disciplines have developed a shared set of concerns and an increasingly nuanced vocabulary with which to consider them. As a result, a growing number of publications on opera have approached the genre from a variety of unfamiliar perspectives (including poetics, philosophy, politics, psychoanalysis, film theory, medical history, and gender studies, among others), discovering new instances of "the imperfect, the ambiguous, [and] the illogical," and proposing new ways of conceptualizing those discoveries.[8]

As new critical paradigms were making their way into musicology

7. See, e.g., Herbert Lindenberger, *Opera: The Extravagant Art* (Ithaca, N.Y.: Cornell University Press, 1984); Jeremy Tambling, *Opera, Ideology, and Film* (New York: St. Martin's Press, 1987); Catherine Clément, *Opera, or the Undoing of Women,* trans. Betsy Wing (Minneapolis: University of Minnesota Press, 1988); Arthur Groos and Roger Parker, eds., *Reading Opera* (Princeton, N.J.: Princeton University Press, 1988); Paul Robinson, *Opera and Ideas: From Mozart to Strauss* (Ithaca, N.Y.: Cornell University Press, 1985).

8. See, e.g., essays published in the *Cambridge Opera Journal* as well as the following, listed in order of publication date: Michel Poizat, *The Angel's Cry: Beyond the Pleasure Principle in Opera,* trans. Arthur Denner (Ithaca, N.Y.: Cornell University Press, 1992); Wayne Koestenbaum, *The Queen's Throat: Opera, Homosexuality, and the Mystery of Desire* (New York: Poseidon Press, 1993); David J. Levin, ed., *Opera Through Other Eyes* (Stanford, Calif.: Stanford University Press, 1993); Stanley Cavell, *A Pitch of Philosophy: Autobiographical Exercises* (Cambridge, Mass.: Harvard University Press, 1994); Jeremy Tambling, ed., *A Night In at the Opera: Media Representations of Opera* (London: John Libbey, 1994); Corinne E. Blackmer and Patricia Juliana Smith, eds., *En Travesti: Women, Gender Subversion, Opera* (New York: Columbia University Press, 1995); Linda Hutcheon and Michael Hutcheon, *Opera: Desire, Disease, Death* (Lincoln: University of Nebraska Press, 1996); Jeremy Tambling, *Opera and the Culture of Fascism* (Oxford: Clarendon Press, 1996); Richard Dellamora and Daniel Fischlin, eds., *The Work of Opera: Genre, Nationhood, and Sexual Difference* (New York: Columbia University Press, 1997); Herbert Lindenberger, *Opera in History: From Monteverdi to Cage* (Stanford, Calif.: Stanford University Press, 1998); Gary Tomlinson, *Metaphysical Song: An Essay on Opera* (Princeton, N.J.: Princeton University Press, 1999); Marcia Citron, *Opera on Screen* (New Haven, Conn.: Yale University Press, 2000); Heather Hadlock, *Mad Loves: Women and Music in Offenbach's* Les contes d'Hoffmann (Princeton, N.J.: Princeton University Press, 2000); Linda Hutcheon and Michael Hutcheon, *Bodily Charm: Living Opera* (Lincoln: University of Nebraska Press, 2000); Mary Ann Smart, ed., *Siren Songs: Representations of Gender and Sexuality in Opera* (Princeton, N.J.: Princeton University Press, 2000); Jeongwon Joe and Rose Theresa, eds., *Between Opera and Cinema* (London and New York: Routledge, 2002); Simon Morrison, *Russian Opera and the Symbolist Movement* (Berkeley: University of California Press, 2002); Slavoj Žižek and Mladen Dolar, *Opera's Second Death* (London and New York: Routledge, 2002); Carolyn Abbate, *In Search of Opera* (Princeton, N.J.: Princeton University Press, 2003); Wendy Heller, *Emblems of Eloquence: Opera and Women's Voices in Seventeenth-Century Venice* (Berkeley: University of California Press, 2003); James Treadwell, *Interpreting Wagner* (New Haven, Conn.: Yale University Press, 2003); Linda Hutcheon and Michael Hutcheon, *Opera: The Art of Dying* (Cambridge, Mass.: Harvard University Press, 2004); Lawrence Kramer, *Opera and Modern Culture: Wagner and Strauss* (Berkeley: University of California Press, 2004); Mary Ann Smart, *Mimomania: Music and Gesture in Nineteenth-Century Opera* (Berkeley: University of California Press, 2004); Michael P. Steinberg, *Listening to Reason: Culture, Subjectivity, and Nineteenth-Century Music* (Princeton, N.J.: Princeton University Press, 2004); and Michal Grover-Friedlander, *Vocal Apparitions: The Attraction of Cinema to Opera* (Princeton, N.J.: Princeton University Press, 2005).

(mostly, but not only, in North America and the United Kingdom), a similar wave of innovation was sweeping across the stages of a number of the world's opera houses. Since the late 1970s, opera production (mostly, but not only, in Europe) has undergone a thoroughgoing transformation akin to that outlined by Abbate and Parker. In the wake of Patrice Chéreau's centennial production of Wagner's *Ring* at Bayreuth in 1976, a number of opera houses began to rethink a more or less settled sense of opera as routinized spectacle—exploring, gingerly at first, the genre's "peculiarity," and seeking to render the "incongruities" that result from its "clash of systems."[9] Of course, this is not the first time in history that operatic stage practices have been challenged and refashioned.[10] Since its birth in the waning years of the sixteenth century, opera has seen the pendulum swing from the primacy of drama or words to the primacy of song or music; from a preference for mythological events to one for historical and even quotidian events; from the predominance of grand spectacle to a preference for dramatic integrity.[11] As it turns out, the project of reimagining opera, undertaken by a number of opera houses since 1976, bears remarkable similarities to the project of the new musicology: both share a commitment to rethinking central works of the repertoire combined with an interest in previously unexplored formal conditions and thematic relations.

What, we might ask, has been the effect of this coincidence of innovation? On the one hand, the new opera studies have had a noticeable effect on the new mise-en-scène: a number of houses have freely incorporated recent academic work in their production protocols (dramaturgical materials employed in preparing new productions) and in their program books. In Europe, and especially in Germany, opera houses often prepare extensive program books to accompany and elaborate upon new productions. Beyond

9. See Tom Sutcliffe, "A Repertoire of Classics," in *Believing in Opera* (Princeton, N.J.: Princeton University Press, 1996).

10. For a cogent overview of the history of opera stagings, see Roger Savage, "The Staging of Opera," in *The Oxford Illustrated History of Opera*, ed. Roger Parker (Oxford: Oxford University Press, 1994), 350–420.

11. The inflection of such oppositions has important implications for the politics of operatic history. See, e.g., Lorenzo Bianconi and Giorgio Pestelli, preface to *Opera Production and Its Resources*: "[The German historical tradition] interpreted the history of opera as a succession of goal-oriented, connected events, and it resorted to a series of antitheses (melodrama/music drama; closed form/open form; bel canto/harmonic expression; convention/adherence to nature) as keys to the comprehension of opera's evolution. That scheme led, however, to eliminating Italian opera from the historical map or at least to marginalizing it as an incongruous mixture of heterogeneous elements, some of which were deemed noteworthy but only insofar as they contributed to the predetermined objective." Lorenzo Bianconi and Giorgio Pestelli, eds., *The History of Italian Opera*, pt. 2, vol. 4, *Opera Production and Its Resources*, ed. Bianconi and Pestelli, trans. Lydia G. Cochrane (Chicago: University of Chicago Press, 1998), xi–xii.

listing the cast and production team, these *Programmhefte* often include historical and interpretive materials, such as the libretto, historical documents, critical essays, a director's or dramaturg's statement, and associative materials, such as paintings, photographs, prose, or poetry.[12] The program books extend and embed the interpretive work done in the production, affording a further forum in which to elaborate the ideas presented onstage.

How have the new opera studies engaged with the reconceptualization of opera on so many of the world's stages? Strangely enough, they have not. Academic writing on opera has not ignored questions of performance. But for the most part, these questions have been historical. Since the mid-1990s we have gained an increasingly detailed understanding of historical performance practices and of the social conditions in which opera has been performed.[13] But what we do not possess—what musicologists and non-musicologists alike have tended to shy away from—is a sense of how stage performance can shape and even alter our understanding of opera.[14] Carolyn Abbate puts it polemically in the preface to *In Search of Opera:* "That musical works acquire alternative histories—identities constituted by licentious or excessive performances and (for opera) adaptations and stagings—is a threat many scholars regard with horror: one need only look at reactions to radical mises-en-scène."[15] This sense of horror is especially strange, because contemporary critical concerns resonate in and with contemporary developments in operatic stage production. Put otherwise, contemporary develop-

---

12. On the program book in German theater, see Martin Esslin, "The Role of the Dramaturg in the European Theater," in *What Is Dramaturgy?*, ed. Bert Cardullo (New York: Peter Lang, 1995), 43–48, at 46.

13. See, e.g., Mark A. Radice, ed., *Opera in Context: Essays on Historical Staging from the Late Renaissance to the Time of Puccini* (Portland, Ore.: Amadeus, 1998); Anselm Gerhard, *The Urbanization of Opera: Music Theater in Paris in the Nineteenth Century,* trans. Mary Whittall (Chicago: University of Chicago Press, 1998); Lorenzo Bianconi and Giorgio Pestelli, eds., *Opera on Stage,* trans. Kate Singleton, The History of Italian Opera, Part II: Systems, vol. 5 (Chicago: University of Chicago Press, 2001); John Warrack, *German Opera: From the Beginnings to Wagner* (Cambridge: Cambridge University Press, 2001); and Downing A. Thomas, *Aesthetics of Opera in the Ancien Régime, 1647–1785* (Cambridge: Cambridge University Press, 2003).

14. Some important exceptions only reinforce the rule. See Martha Feldman's observation that "it hardly needs saying that attention in musicological studies to experiential dimensions of music and efforts to try merging them in our present horizons with textual ones are rather recent. At issue now is not just 'what was produced?' and 'for whom?' but 'how did the "who" affect the "what" and the "what" the "whom"'? Increasingly we are aware that modes of production—complicated and extremely variable in themselves—converged with different local histories and conditions of experience over the course of the century to make seria many things to many people." Feldman, "Magic Mirrors and the *Seria* Stage: Thoughts toward a Ritual View," *Journal of the American Musicological Society* 68, no. 3 (Fall 1995): 423–84, at 426.

15. Abbate, *In Search of Opera,* xi.

ments in opera production have come to intersect with contemporary critical concerns in opera studies, yet that intersection has never been mapped. This book provides such a map.

Or maps. Although I plan to account for the development and achievements of what the popular press has termed "deconstructive stagings," my interest here is primarily theoretical rather than historical. I am less interested in proposing a comprehensive survey of such stagings than in exploring some key terms—for example, text, translation, voice, and performance—with which we might understand them. This study will focus upon some of the most familiar works by some of the most familiar composers. A few of the productions discussed here will no doubt be familiar to some readers, either by virtue of their notoriety (such as Peter Sellars's stridently anachronistic production of Mozart's *Le nozze di Figaro* [*The Marriage of Figaro*]) or their resolute lack of it (such as Wolfgang Wagner's thoroughly conventional Bayreuth production of Wagner's *Die Meistersinger von Nürnberg* [*The Mastersingers of Nuremberg*]). This book seeks to account for productions that, in important ways, unsettle our conception of these particular works and of the genre more generally, irrespective of whether that particular staging has gained notoriety. I wish to introduce the reader to a cross-section of modes of stage production, conventional and unconventional: decorative, political, self-referential, and abstract. In addition, I intend to sketch a variety of analytic modes (multiple ways to examine the operatic text) and examine a variety of analytic objects (consideration of these texts in, beyond, and prior to performance). Finally, I hope to suggest just how much we stand to gain in analytic range and explanatory power by attending to the reconceptualization of opera that has been taking place in our midst, onstage.

In selecting the productions that I will discuss here, I have been guided not only by a sense of their interpretive achievement and theoretical significance, but also by a pragmatic consideration, namely, their availability in recorded form, on video or DVD—that is, their availability for my readers to experience via the mediation of a TV or computer screen. I am willing to risk—and will seek to account for—the complications (there are some obvious losses but also some gains) occasioned by that mediation in order to focus our attention on the fact and consequences of mise-en-scène. For although I do not deny the importance—let alone the pleasures or oddities or, for that matter, the personal and theoretical significance—of experiencing opera live, in the opera house, the familiar insistence on liveness as a necessary prerequisite for interpretation has effectively forestalled any sustained consideration of operatic mise-en-scène. The insistence on presence has effectively absented mise-en-scène as an object of discussion, since the ephemerality of opera onstage has foreclosed a nuanced consideration of its interpretive gambits and achievements.[16] We can speculate about interpretation onstage, but absent a detailed record of that interpretation, our speculation will have a hard time emerging from a deeply impressionistic hole. (This, it seems to me, is the absence that enables the rhetoric of presence.) In an important and influential article, "Music—Drastic or Gnostic?," Carolyn Abbate has argued that live performance is a precondition for an encounter with music's carnality, materiality, and ineffability. In Abbate's view, live performance—and a critical practice that is alert to it—presents a challenge to conventional musicological (and indeed, academic) criticism. The "eventness" of live performance cannot be held in one's fingers, as Abbate puts it, and as such, it cannot be grasped by conventional hermeneutics. In lieu of marshaling an abstract work's meaning and measuring its interpretive value (which Abbate, following Vladimir Jankélévitch, dubs academic "gnosticism"),[17] she proposes an alternative practice, a radical (or "drastic") musicology that listens to music in performance, and in so doing, is open to the manifold embarrassments, personal and professional, that might result:

> Rather than bringing out souvenirs and singing their praises or explaining their meanings one more time, I want to test the conviction that what counts is not a work, not, for example, Richard Wagner's *Die Meistersinger von Nürnberg* in the abstract, but a material, present event. This entails seeking a practice that at its most radical allows an actual live performance (and not a recording, even of a live performance) to become an object of absorption.[18]

This is a compelling project and one with which I sympathize. But I am troubled by the fine print, that our absorption in the work's performance (its

16. In the first chapter of *In Search of Opera*, Abbate suggests that operatic works can be understood as souvenirs of live, ephemeral performance: "What, then are operatic 'works'; what is 'Parsifal,' or 'The Magic Flute'; what role do works play in discourse about opera? One answer is that the works are *souvenirs*. Not a postcard or a piece of porcelain, nor a program book with color pictures and a cast list: they are not tangible, and you cannot put them in a drawer. Yet perhaps musical works, imagined objects, are mementos nonetheless, a reminder (though, unlike porcelain, not evident to the sense) that can stand for an embodiment, and what was once experienced in present time" (51). Abbate returns to and probes this point in her "Music—Drastic or Gnostic?," 506, 513. My argument here has a lively prehistory in theater studies. For a clear and compelling account of the arguments for and against the privileges of liveness, see chapter 7, "The Ontology of Performance: Representation without Reproduction," in Peggy Phelan, *Unmarked: The Politics of Performance* (New York: Routledge, 1993), and the first two chapters of Philip Auslander, *Liveness: Performance in a Mediatized Culture* (New York: Routledge, 1999).

17. Jankélévitch's argument appears in Vladimir Jankélévitch, *Music and the Ineffable*, trans. Carolyn Abbate (Princeton, N.J.: Princeton University Press, 2003).

18. Abbate, "Music—Drastic or Gnostic?," 506.

eventness and materiality) is limited to live performance, that it must not extend to recordings. Abbate's reasons are clear: she is intent on minimizing mediation, on opening herself (and having us open ourselves) to "the state that the performance has engendered in us." But surely that state is itself the product of mediation? And surely it is less the fact of mediation but rather its function to which Abbate objects? Recordings, in this line of reasoning, are unwelcome because they serve the hermeneutic cause of documentation, fixing for critical scrutiny that which (in live form) is otherwise ephemeral, experiential, drastic. This makes good sense. And yet, there is no reason why we couldn't be transported by a recording as by a live performance: it is, I think, a question of openness and approach. We are certainly not barred from encountering, in the course of experiencing an opera on DVD, "musical performance's strangeness, its unearthly quality as well as its earthy qualities, and its resemblance to magic shows and circuses." [19] It is true: an opera in the opera house and an opera on television are two different things. But I do not think that one of them has a lock on strangeness, transcendence, or materiality.

There is another, important component of Abbate's argument that I find myself disagreeing with. It involves what I would call the "either/or-ification" of her claims. I am troubled by the notion that the eventness of a piece is to be understood in contradistinction to its hermeneutic aspirations, that the work understood as a material, present event is to be understood as "not" the abstract work, as in: "I want to test the conviction that what counts is not a work, not, for example, Richard Wagner's *Die Meistersinger von Nürnberg* in the abstract, but a material, present event" (506). The terms of my hesitation are perhaps best elucidated by turning to the very example Abbate cites. In the song contest in act 3 of *Die Meistersinger,* Wagner is intent on having us learn much the same lesson that Abbate would impart. The song contest famously pits Beckmesser's outmoded, bureaucratic, rule-bound singing against Walther's feisty, innovative, outsider-artist talents. In order to win Eva, who is the contest's designated trophy, each contestant must win the hearts and minds of the Folk. The scene on the festival meadow in act 3 distinguishes between modes of performance, inflecting Beckmesser's attempt to produce the song as utterly in thrall to mediation (he tries desperately to read the song he would perform) in contradistinction to Walther's song, which is inflected as a product and document of cultivated inspiration. The risks of Abbate's either/or-ification are beginning to emerge: the "actual, live performance" in Wagner's Nuremberg (like the onstage city itself) is not actual but virtual. Not just because the song contest is staged, but because it is staged to solicit and model precisely the sort of

19. Ibid., 508.

romantic absorption in eventness that Abbate seeks out. If I might anticipate an argument I will make at greater length in chapter 2, it strikes me that Abbate's argument, like Wagner's work, derives its punch from the emergence of a good object and the absenting of a bad object. Thus, Wagner's piece suggests that Walther is not just a wonderful singer and a proper object of absorption, but is *not* a bureaucratic singer, *not* an improper object of absorption. And in case we don't get it on our own, the chorus (standing in here for the Folk and for us) articulates the terms of differentiation. In Abbate's argument as in Wagner's piece, the material, present song is juxtaposed to the abstract, mediated work; our delighted absorption in the former is a by-product of our failure to be absorbed by the latter. The point is that Wagner's juxtaposition is at once apt and overdetermined. I want to argue for an equal-opportunity openness to both the experience and the terms of absorption.

I would amend Abbate's proposal, suggesting that we allow for live performance *and recordings* to serve as the objects of *all manner of* absorption, critical and experiential. In short, I want to have it both ways: I want to be transported and to think about where we are going.

Clemens Risi proposes a useful model for imagining this interplay when he suggests that our experience and perception of opera in production encompasses sense and sensibility, *Sinn* and *Sinnlichkeit,* the intellectual pleasures of representation and the unpredictable emanations of presence:

> Since the directors' theater finally entered the world of opera around the 1970's, the audience's perception of opera performances has been characterized by two tendencies. On the one hand, producers and audiences derive intellectual pleasure from wrestling with new modes of reading and interpretation. On the other hand, we find moments that are formulated and experienced as something that cannot be described as the presentation of anything concrete (representation). Rather, they elicit first and foremost intensive responses and corporeal reactions to what has been experienced. These moments are frequently characterized by irritation, an interruption of understanding, intensity, a sudden consciousness of perception or time. They lead to a feeling of bodily participation (presence).
>
> In each performance, the relationship between representation and presence, sense (*Sinn*) and sensibility (*Sinnlichkeit*) determines the act of perception. In the process, representation and presence in no way cancel each other out. On the contrary: sense and sensibility, *Sinn* and *Sinnlichkeit,* are co-determinate, conditioning one another.[20]

---

20. Clemens Risi, "Sinn und Sinnlichkeit in der Oper: zu Hans Neuenfels' *Idomeneo* an der Deutschen Oper Berlin," *Theater der Zeit* 6 (June 2003): 38–39 at 38.

In my mind, Risi's co-determination of representation and presence in the opera house extends to the experience of performance on DVD. Indeed, DVDs of opera in performance can offer both an object of analysis and one of absorption, and I hope to account for both their "gnostic" and "drastic" appeals.[21] Thanks to recording technologies, we can be absorbed and attempt to delineate the terms of absorption; furthermore, we can focus upon the particularities of interpretation and argue about their implications. In this way, I hope to jump-start a discussion of how we might read opera's performance text and what we might gain in doing so.

Given the vagaries of the term "text," I want to be clear about the claim I am making. I am not claiming that operatic performance is best understood in terms of its textual components, such as the libretto or musical score.[22] Rather, I want to argue that Barthes's sense of the text corresponds in fruitful ways to opera's peculiar and defining surfeit of signifying systems—a surfeit that these productions render in interesting (or at least symptomatic) ways and, in so doing, to which they alert us. Thus, throughout this book, I will use the term "opera text" to designate opera's agitated and multiple signifying systems—for instance, the score, the libretto, stage directions—prior to performance. On the other hand, opera in performance, its "performance text," lends expression to this condition of agitation and multiplicity while at the same time partaking of it. This is not only true of certain select productions. Rather, every production (or performance text) takes up a position relative to the opera text. And although most performance texts reiterate a consensus about a given opera text (rendering it readily comprehensible by inflecting it in a recognizable relation to familiar forms of representation), some productions seek to render the characteristic agitation of the opera text. It is these latter productions—which we might, echoing Abbate echoing Jankélévitch, term "drastic" productions—that most interest me, insofar as they unsettle operas and opera, producing aptly startling accounts of pieces that are best, if rarely, experienced as startling.

21. I do so with reference to some of the very works to which Abbate turns—Wagner's *Meistersinger* as well as Mozart and Da Ponte's *Nozze di Figaro*. Abbate frames her argument in terms of an opposition between music as gnostic and as drastic. Echoing Jankélévitch, she characterizes as "gnostic" the hermeneutic orientation of musicology, its determination to make works signify, while a "drastic" engagement with music involves a turn toward music as event, as "ephemeral object, subject to instantaneous loss, but equally importantly as something that acts upon us and changes us." Abbate, "Music—Drastic or Gnostic?," 532.

22. In this, I am echoing a claim that Hans-Thies Lehmann makes for postdramatic forms of theater, namely that "staged text (if text is staged) is merely a component with equal rights in a gestic, musical, visual, etc. total composition." Lehmann, *Postdramatic Theatre*, trans. Karen Jürs-Munby (London and New York: Routledge, 2006), 46; *Postdramatisches Theater* (Frankfurt am Main: Verlag der Autoren, 1999), 73.

In her Ernst Bloch lectures of 1997, Lydia Goehr argues for a conception of classical music as "an imperfect practice." Her elucidation of this imperfection is quite close to my own sense of unsettledness:

> Motivating this argument is the thought that practices (musical, philosophical, or political) are desirably open when they are imperfect, and imperfect when they are critical, critical in the sense that practices survive their self-deceptive but necessary assertions of perfection by allowing strategies of conflict, criticism, and resistance constantly to keep them in check. The critical dimension arises, in other words, from the presence in a practice of competing conceptions that halt the absolutist pretensions of any single one.[23]

The productions I consider span the gamut between openness and closure: some of them acknowledge and even stage the "strategies of conflict, criticism, and resistance" that would warrant their openness; some are just as emphatically closed in their assertion of (a self-deceptive) perfection. In the course of this book, I will be making a case for the full variety of unsettledness and trying to account for its constitutive openness, a sense that opera in production can take many forms and signify in a variety of ways. It is less a prescription for how a production must look or how we must hear or read it than a plea for a pragmatic and theoretical openness in looking, listening, and reading.

In addition to inflecting these stage productions as texts, I want to explore their status as performative and theatrical. Here I will be relying on a distinction that Hans-Thies Lehmann draws between theater and drama—where the conventional grounding of drama in *fabula* and text contrasts with theater's more expansive and variegated expressive repertoire. In the chapters that follow, we will repeatedly encounter productions in which opera's performance text is inflected as more theatrical than dramatic. One of the most significant ways they do so is by seeking to lend expression to multiple, sometimes conflicting expressive registers. Rather than monological or even dialogical stagings, we can describe them as polylogical.[24]

There is no simple way to account for that polylogism. Since each opera and each production raises a distinct set of questions, each of the chapters that follow will engage a different set of questions and employ a variety of theoretical tools. In chapter 2, I consider the dramaturgy of performance

23. Lydia Goehr, "Conflicting Ideals of Performance Perfection in an Imperfect Practice," in *The Quest for Voice: On Music, Politics, and the Limits of Philosophy* (Berkeley: University of California Press, 1998), 135.

24. I borrow the term—which I expand upon below—from Lehmann, who in turn borrows it from Kristeva. See Hans-Thies Lehmann, *Postdramatic Theatre,* 32; *Postdramatisches Theater,* 46.

that is front-loaded into Richard Wagner's *Die Meistersinger von Nürnberg* in order to ask how it is performed—which is also to say, how Wagner's characteristic hostility to mediation is in turn mediated and then remediated—by three distinctly different productions of the work. In chapter 3, I explore work in translation theory in order to examine the logic of fidelity in Peter Sellars's production of Mozart's *Le nozze di Figaro;* in chapter 4, I employ the work of Mladen Dolar and Hans Ulrich Gumbrecht to account for the distinction between *singen* and *spielen* that animates a Stuttgart production of Mozart's singspiel, *Die Entführung aus dem Serail* (*The Abduction from the Seraglio*). In chapter 5, I propose a reading of Giuseppe Verdi's *Don Carlos* as an opera text that is thoroughly absorbed by problems of expression—and, by extension, of performance, dramatizing the allure and, at the same time, the functional impossibility of an unbridled expression. In chapter 6, I ask how and whether the arguments proposed in the book—arguments derived from and applied to canonical works—might apply to a piece that is in important senses already unsettled: Alexander Zemlinsky's *Der König Kandaules* (*King Candaules*), a noncanonical work that the composer left unfinished upon his death in 1942.

Beyond arguing for theoretical flexibility, I also want to suggest the value of analyzing different things: thus, in chapter 2, I compare different productions of the same piece; in chapters 3, 4, and 6, I analyze individual productions; and in chapter 5, I examine *Don Carlos* as an opera text, that is, prior to production. Unlike a more conventional map, which might chart previously unsettled or recently resettled territory, the maps drawn up here offer a contingent guide to previously settled territory that is becoming unsettled. There is, of course, a great deal of territory left unexplored in the wake of this project. This study will have succeeded if it encourages others to venture into that territory.

Staging Wagner in the Nineteenth Century

Although the contemporary landscape is unsettled and thus difficult to map, it is somewhat easier to trace the historical events that resulted in this unsettledness. Of course, staging has played an important role in the history of opera, dictating compositional choices and affecting public reception. However, the notion that staging is integral to both the interpretive work and the eventness of opera is relatively recent. Prior to the middle of the nineteenth century, newly composed operas were generally inserted into something of a production cookie cutter. Which is not to suggest that these were not distinct cutters, or that their products were not astonishing, elaborate, and even fanciful. But from the very start, the discourse of operatic production was one of particular, highly rhetorical, and circumscribed effects. The various waves of protest that arise in operatic history attest to the fact that new operas tended to enter into a formalized discourse of performance by which they were shaped. Thus, for example, a premiere in one of the new public opera houses of Venice in the 1640s required elaborate scenic effects (e.g., flying machines, intricately painted backdrops), breathtaking vocal acrobatics from the principals, and dizzying plot complexities. By contrast, for nearly a century between 1670 and 1770, an opera presented at the Académie Royale de Musique in Paris featured a combination of danced *divertissements,* heroic acting, a spectacular choral entrance, and the use of newfangled stage effects and machinery.[25] Prior to the middle of the nineteenth century, opera production throughout Europe was largely the province of impresarios, who oversaw the repertoire and assumed responsibility for casting, marketing, and, ultimately, for staging as well.[26]

One of the most important figures in the emergence of operatic staging as a locus of interpretation is Richard Wagner. As is well known, in his prose works Wagner repeatedly and forcefully argues that the institutions and norms of opera need to be rebuilt from the ground up. And in a characteristic literalization of the polemic, he then went about erecting an entirely new opera house and, with it, or so he announced, a new culture of opera, one that would redress the manifold shortcomings that Wagner felt he (as a conductor and composer) and his works (as the "artworks of the future" he had proclaimed them to be) had endured in innumerable provincial and metropolitan opera houses. The logic of the architectural plans for the Festspielhaus at Bayreuth is entirely revealing. To adapt vocabulary from cinema studies, we might say that with the opening of the Festspielhaus in 1876, Wagner sought to retool opera from a medium of attractions onstage and distractions in the auditorium to one of total absorption.[27] In the Festspielhaus, every seat was

25. See in this regard, Savage's observation that in the wake of Lully, "the Opéra was a machine which, without too much grinding of cogs, could mesh together heroic acting from the principals (more piquant and racy acting if it was an opéra-ballet), stirring contributions from the chorus (arranged rather statically in a U-formation around the stage once they had made their spectacular entry), dazzling effects from the designer, chic costumes from the wardrobe, and of course festive *fêtes* and diverting *divertissements* from those great Parisian specialities, the dancers." Savage, "Staging of Opera," 369.

26. See, e.g., John Rosselli, *The Opera Industry from Cimarosa to Verdi: The Role of the Impresario* (Cambridge: Cambridge University Press, 1984); Ellen Rosand, *Opera in Seventeenth-Century Venice* (Berkeley: University of California Press, 1991).

27. I offer a detailed account of Wagner's relationship to staging in chapter 2. On the cinema of attractions, see Tom Gunning, "Cinema of Attractions: Early Film, its Spectator, and the Avant-Garde," in *Early Cinema: Space, Frame, Narrative,* ed. Thomas Elsaesser with Adam Barker (London: BFI, 1990), 56–62. On Wagner's relationship to the aesthetics and politics of visibility, see Goehr, "Conflicting Ideals," 156–65. See also Jonathan Crary, *Suspensions of Perception: Attention, Spectacle,*

to offer an unimpeded sightline, the auditorium was to be plunged into total darkness during the course of a performance, and the orchestra pit was to be located largely beneath the stage, rendering both the conductor and the orchestra invisible to members of the audience.[28] Thanks to this programmatic erasure of visual impediments, very little stood between a member of the audience and events onstage. Very little, that is, except the events onstage themselves.

By the late 1840s, Wagner had become increasingly preoccupied with a dramaturgy of immediacy according to which viewers would be addressed directly and viscerally by events onstage.[29] He expressed his disdain for the prevailing norms of operatic staging with great frequency and vehemence. In Wagner's view, opera was a prime example of how the natural expressive inclinations of the Folk had been appropriated in the service of modern, urban, cosmopolitan culture. Music-drama had given way to spectacle; simplicity had been replaced by senseless complication; transparency had given way to opacity; in a word—a prototypically Wagnerian word—nature had been banished by culture. One such account is taken from the 1849 pamphlet "Art and Revolution":

> Opera has become a chaos of sensuous elements flitting by one another without rhyme or reason, from which one may choose at will what best suits ones fancy—here the alluring leap of a ballerina, there the *bravura* passage of a singer; here the dazzling effect of a triumph by the set designer, there the astounding efforts of an orchestral eruption. Do we not read every day that this or that new opera is a masterpiece because it contains many fine arias and

and Modern Culture (Cambridge, Mass.: MIT Press, 1999), 247–57. According to Crary, "One of Wagner's 'reforms,' incarnated in the design of [the Festspielhaus at] Bayreuth, involved the transformation of the nineteenth century theater into a construction of visibility that more rigorously structured the spectator's perceptual experience. His aim was to establish a 'theatron,' a 'place for seeing'" (250–51). See also Jo Leslie Collier, *From Wagner to Murnau: The Transposition from Stage to Screen* (Ann Arbor, Mich.: UMI Research Press, 1988), 30–34.

28. James Treadwell opens his extraordinary study of Wagner with a masterful account of the Festspielhaus's intentions and effects. See Treadwell, *Interpreting Wagner* (New Haven, Conn.: Yale University Press, 2003), 3–4. See also Beat Wyss, "Ragnarök of Illusion: Richard Wagner's 'Mystical Abyss' at Bayreuth," trans. Denise Bratton, *October* 54 (Fall 1990): 57–78, esp. 73–74. See also Evan Baker, "Richard Wagner and His Search for the Ideal Theatrical Space," in *Opera in Context: Essays on Historical Staging from the Late Renaissance to the Time of Puccini,* ed. Mark A. Radice (Portland, Ore.: Amadeus Press, 1998), 241–78; Friedrich Kittler, "Opern im technischen Licht," in *Tannhäuser,* Programmheft VII, Programmhefte der Bayreuther Festspiele 1989, ed. Wolfgang Wagner, 1–17 (translated in the same program booklet as "Operas in a Technological Light," 35–45).

29. William Weber locates the origins of Wagner's campaign in 1849, when the composer "mounted a large-scale social and intellectual redefinition of opera that was at once vicious in its musical politics and lofty in its philosophical statement." Weber, "Opera and Social Reform," in *Wagner Compendium,* ed. Barry Millington (London: Thames and Hudson, 1992), 153–58, at 154.

duets, and the instrumentation is extremely brilliant, etc. etc.? The aim which alone can justify the employment of such disparate means,—the great dramatic aim,—people no longer give that so much as a thought.[30]

Over the years Wagner gave that "great dramatic aim" a good deal of thought. In place of the unmotivated chaos of sensuous events—Wagner's polemical denunciation of "effects without causes"[31]—the Wagnerian artwork of the future aspired to unify cause and effect under the banner of "the great dramatic aim." As Wagner repeatedly pointed out, the actions of the singing actors onstage were of central importance to this project: if on the operatic stage of his day the singers reproduced a corrupt and cosmopolitan *culture*, on the stage of the Festspielhaus they would act and sing *naturally*.

The importance Wagner attributed to the integrity of dramatic events onstage had enormous implications for the history of opera production. In the short term, it once again ushered in an era of more "natural," less stilted acting.[32] Like any number of composers before him, Wagner insisted that his singers embody their roles while at the same time subordinating that embodiment to the work's larger "dramatic aim"—one that they would need

30. Wagner, "Art and Revolution," in *Richard Wagner's Prose Works*, trans. William Ashton Ellis (London, 1893; reprint, New York: Broude Bros., 1966), 1:44, translation modified; citations are to the Broude Bros. edition, hereafter cited as *PW*. Published in German as "Die Kunst und die Revolution," in *Gesammelte Schriften und Dichtungen* (Leipzig: E. W. Fritzsch, 1887–88), 3:20–21; hereafter cited as *GSD*. I offer a more detailed consideration of this passage and Wagner's overall dramaturgy of forms in David J. Levin, *Richard Wagner, Fritz Lang, and the Nibelungen: The Dramaturgy of Disavowal* (Princeton, N.J.: Princeton University Press, 1998). Among other places where Wagner formulates a similar critique of opera's cult of distraction, see "A Theatre at Zurich" (1851), *PW* 3:23–57, *GSD* 5:20–52; "Zukunftsmusik" (1861), *PW* 3:293–345, *GSD* 7:87–137; and "Public and Popularity" (1878), *PW* 6:51–81, *GSD* 10:61–90.

31. Wagner's works offer rich allegorical figurations of many of these concerns. Thus, for example, *Tannhäuser* stages and allegorizes the condition of sensuous elements flitting by without rhyme or reason. (In the late 1980s, David Alden prepared a production of the work for Munich that sought to render the overlap between the composer's aesthetic politics and his hero's predicament.) In Jo Leslie Collier's account, Wagner's *Das Liebesverbot* renders a "straightforward confrontation between Culture and Nature." See Collier, *From Wagner to Murnau*, 16–17.

32. The terms of Wagner's proposed reforms echo, in numerous respects, others that have been launched throughout operatic history. Thus, for example, in the preface to *Alceste*, Christoph Willibald Gluck pleads for the return to a simpler, more natural style of operatic composition and presentation. "When I undertook to write the music for *Alceste*, I resolved to divest it entirely of all those abuses, introduced into it either by the mistaken vanity of singers or by the too great complaisance of composers, which have so long disfigured Italian opera and made of the most splendid and beautiful of spectacles the most ridiculous and wearisome. . . . I believed that my greatest labor should be devoted to seeking a beautiful simplicity, and I have avoided making displays of difficulty at the expense of clearness; nor did I judge it desirable to discover novelties if it was not naturally suggested by the situation and the expression; and there is no rule which I have not thought it right to set aside willingly for the sake of an intended effect." See C. W. Gluck, "Manifesto of the 'Dramma per Musica,'" in Alfred Einstein, *Gluck*, trans. Eric Blom (New York: McGraw Hill, 1972), 98–100, at 98–99.

to intuit (in order to embody and express it) and that he would need to instill.[33] However, the rhetoric of this instillation (with its demand for a controlling arbiter of dramatic meaning) and the concomitant demand for the "natural" interpretation of a work prior to its presentation suggested the need for a new kind of director on a new kind of operatic stage. Initially, of course, that director was Wagner, and the stage was at Bayreuth.[34] But the logic of Wagner's proposed innovations echoes and extends an institutional shift that was sweeping across Europe during the course of the nineteenth century: the emergence of the stage director as manager and arbiter of stage action in many (spoken) theaters.[35] In Wagner's case, that emergence was directly associated with his personal campaign to wrest control of opera—its composition, staging, and reception—from the forces of culture and return it to its "natural" expressive intentions and affiliations.[36]

In the next chapter, we will see how the legacy of Wagner's particular preoccupation with a "natural" dramatic integrity led to the emergence of two opposing schools of opera production: a rear-guard protectionism on the one hand and what we might term an avant-garde explorationism on the other. Thus, to a significant extent, the battle over opera's disposition onstage in the late twentieth century—whether it would be deeply settled and familiar or markedly unsettled and unfamiliar—was waged over and through Wagner productions. The summer of 1976 in Bayreuth was surely one of the most important moments in that battle, not just because it marked the centennial of the opening of the Festspielhaus, but because it marked the premiere of Patrice Chéreau's production of the *Ring*, a production which, according to

33. For an eyewitness account of the terms of Wagner's insistence, see Heinrich Porges, introduction to *Wagner Rehearsing the Ring: An Eyewitness Account of the Stage Rehearsals of the First Bayreuth Festival*, trans. Robert Jacobs (Cambridge: Cambridge University Press, 1983), 2–3. According to Porges, "Every expression, every intonation bore out this principle of fidelity to nature." On Wagner's notion of the actor-singer's need for *Selbstentäusserung*, see Wagner, "Über Schauspieler und Sänger," *GSD* 9:157–230; "On Actors and Singers," *PW* 5:157–228.

34. See Lilli Lehmann's account of Wagner's work with Josephine Scheffsky (Sieglinde) in preparation for the first *Ring* festival at Bayreuth: "Wagner, no feminine figure, [acted out her role for her] with an overwhelmingly touching expression. Never since has any Sieglinde, in my experience, come near to matching him, even remotely." Lilli Lehmann, in *Bayreuth: The Early Years*, ed. Robert Hartford (Cambridge: Cambridge University Press, 1980), 48.

35. See Oscar G. Brockett and Robert R. Findlay, *Century of Innovation: A History of European and American Theatre and Drama since 1870* (Englewood Cliffs, N.J.: Prentice-Hall, 1973), 29. Brockett and Findlay link the emergence of the stage director with the ideology of the *Gesamtkunstwerk*. See also Arne Langer, *Der Regisseur und die Aufzeichnungspraxis der Opernregie im 19. Jahrhundert* (Frankfurt: Peter Lang, 1997), 89–91.

36. In fact, Wagner's inflection and critique of "culture" is not very far removed from what Adorno and Horkheimer, from a very different perspective, would later term "the culture industry." See Andreas Huyssen, "Adorno in Reverse: From Hollywood to Richard Wagner," in *After the Great Divide* (Bloomington: Indiana University Press, 1986), 16–43.

Annette Michelson, "constitutes a major stage in the renewal of performance as textual production within our culture."[37]

Staging Wagner in the Twentieth Century

In 1967 Pierre Boulez urged that Europe's opera houses be blown up.[38] But within a decade, Boulez was to be found on the podium at Bayreuth, conducting Chéreau's centennial production of the *Ring*.[39] The premiere of the centennial *Ring* in 1976 was something of a neutron bomb for opera production, one that left the opera houses standing but exploded some of their most settled practices.[40] The production signaled a new chapter in the postwar rehabilitation of Bayreuth as a forum for innovative production practices. (It is worth noting that this new chapter was produced by Wagner's grandson Wolfgang, who had taken over—and by some accounts, botched—the project of Bayreuth's postwar rehabilitation in the wake of his brother

37. Annette Michelson, "Bayreuth: The Centennial *Ring*," *October* 14 (Fall 1980): 65–70, at 65–66. The production elicited more than its share of grand critical pronouncements. In *Believing in Opera,* Tom Sutcliffe claims that the Bayreuth *Ring* of 1976 "was the moment when [the 'deconstructionist' revolution in theatrical interpretation] suddenly became palpable." See Sutcliffe, *Believing in Opera,* 103.

38. In this, Boulez was echoing a sentiment expressed by Wagner almost a century earlier. According to Boulez, "The new German opera houses certainly look very modern—from outside; inside they have remained extremely old-fashioned. It's nearly impossible to produce a work of contemporary opera in a theater in which, predominantly, repertory pieces are performed. It is really unthinkable. The most expensive solution would be to blow the opera houses up. But don't you think that would also be the most elegant solution?" See Felix Schmidt and Jürgen Hohmeyer, interview with Pierre Boulez, "Sprengt die Opernhäuser in die Luft!," *Der Spiegel* 40 (September 25, 1967): 166–74, at 172. An English translation appeared in the British journal *Opera* in June 1968; it was republished, with a reply by Rolf Liebermann, as "Opera Houses?—Blow Them Up!," in *Opera, 1950–2000: A Celebration of the First 50 Years,* ed. John Allison and Rodney Milnes (London: Opera Magazine, 2000), 32–41, at 37.

39. Richard Peduzzi designed the sets; Jacques Schmidt designed the costumes. The casts included, for *Das Rheingold*: Donald McIntyre as Wotan, Helmut Pampuch as Mime, Hermann Becht as Alberich, Hanna Schwarz as Fricka, and Ortrun Wenkel as Erda. For *Die Walküre*: McIntyre as Wotan, Schwarz as Fricka, Peter Hofmann as Siegmund, Matti Salminen as Hunding, Jeannine Altmeyer as Sieglinde, and Gwyneth Jones as Brünnhilde. For *Siegfried*: McIntyre as Wotan, Becht as Alberich, Jones as Brünnhilde, Wenkel as Erda, Manfred Jung as Siegfried, and Heinz Zednik as Mime. For *Götterdämmerung*: Jung as Siegfried, Becht as Alberich, Jones as Brünnhilde, Altmeyer as Gutrune, Franz Mazura as Gunther, and Fritz Hübner as Hagen.

40. See Jean-Jacques Nattiez, "Chéreau's Treachery," *October* 14 (Fall 1980): 71–100. Michel Foucault also wrote a brief review of the Chéreau production, which appeared in English translation as "19th Century Imaginations," *Semiotext(e): The German Issue* 4, no. 2 (1982): 182–90. For a more philosophical rumination on many of the issues raised by the Chéreau production see Nattiez, "'Fidelity' to Wagner: Reflections on the Centenary *Ring*," in *Wagner in Performance,* ed. Barry Millington and Stewart Spencer (New Haven, Conn.: Yale University Press, 1992), 75–98. Frederic Spotts describes the production as "the most sensational production since 1876." Spotts, *Bayreuth: A History of the Wagner Festival* (New Haven, Conn.: Yale University Press, 1994), 281.

Wieland's unexpected death in 1966.[41]) As I have already suggested, the importance of the centennial *Ring* extended far beyond the history and status of Bayreuth, lending impetus to a renascent movement to reform operatic stage production at a number of less renowned, less prestigious opera houses.[42]

In Michel Foucault's view, the centennial *Ring* staged an archaeology of Wagnerian mythology. According to Foucault, the production

> took Wagner seriously, even at the cost of having to show the opposite of what Wagner wanted to show. Wagner wanted to give the nineteenth century a mythology? Very well. Did he choose to assemble it from Indo-European legends? Fine. Did he thus want to give his epoch the world of images which it lacked? It is precisely at this point that Chéreau's "realization" intervenes.
>
> The nineteenth century was full of images which were the true reason for those great mythological reconstructions, which they changed and concealed. Chéreau did not want to elevate the bazaar of Wagnerian mythology into the sky of eternal myths, nor did he want to reduce it to concrete historical reality. He wanted to unearth those true images which lent power to the invented ones.
>
> Thus Chéreau dug out the images buried under Wagner's text. Desperate images: utopian fragments, machine parts, social types, the waste of luxury towns, children dragons, Strindberg scenes, the profile of a ghetto Jew. . . . In

41. See, e.g., Spotts, who notes that "the failure of the 1960 *Ring* [directed by Wolfgang Wagner] brought to a head anxieties about Wolfgang's work that had been deepening for years, not only among music critics but also within the Wagnerian inner sanctum itself. . . . Against this background it can be imagined what a staggering blow was Wieland's death to the Festival's admirers and, given Wolfgang's record as a producer, what deep apprehension it created about the institution's future." *Bayreuth,* 254–55. See also Nike Wagner, *The Wagners: The Dramas of a Musical Dynasty,* trans. Ewald Osers and Michael Downes (Princeton, N.J.: Princeton University Press, 1998), chaps. 16 and 17, 235–82, esp. 253–59. Although Wieland Wagner was first and foremost an enormously influential stage director, he was also a forceful exponent for a radical recasting—for what I have been terming an "unsettling"—of his grandfather's works. He outlined his aesthetic position in a number of articles and interviews, including "Überlieferung und Neugestaltung" (1951) and "Denkmalschutz für Wagner" (1958), both in *Wieland Wagner: Sein Denken,* ed. Oswald Georg Bauer (Munich: Bayreuther Festspiele, 1991), a volume accompanying the 1991 exhibit "Denkmalschutz für Wagner" at the Bayreuth Festival. The 1951 essay has been translated into English as "Tradition and Innovation," in *Penetrating Wagner's Ring: An Anthology,* ed. John Louis DiGaetani (1978; reprint, New York: Da Capo, 1991), 389–92. I discuss Wieland Wagner's position in relation to Wagner stagings in greater detail in chapter 2.

42. At the same time, and predictably, the centennial *Ring* at Bayreuth also produced a forceful counter-reformation: a number of houses declared their determination not to allow such innovations onto their stages, and several critics launched passionate and vitriolic assaults on this particular production and on the overall project of challenging conventional modes of operatic staging. See, e.g., A. M. Nagler, *Misdirection: Opera Production in the Twentieth Century,* trans. Johanna Sahlin (Hamden, Conn.: Archon, 1981).

a certain sense, [Chéreau] descends from Wagner's mythology to the bustling images which populated it and recreates for us a new myth out of them, while simultaneously showing their paradoxical splendor and disagreeable logic.[43]

In order to understand Foucault's claim, we need to locate Chéreau's production in the history of the Bayreuth festival.[44] The most important innovator at Bayreuth prior to Chéreau was undoubtedly Wieland Wagner, whose stagings of his grandfather's works in the aftermath of World War II produced at least as much controversy and invective as Chéreau's centennial production.[45] (In a 1951 press conference at Bayreuth marking the reopening of the festival after World War II, for instance, Wieland noted that "we have destroyed the 'Bayreuth Style' because Germanic gods are of no more interest to us. We want to get away from the cult of Wagner; our goal, on the other hand, is a cultic theater.")[46] Wieland Wagner is best known for having radically changed the look of the Wagnerian stage as well as the events that transpired upon it, excising much of the antiquarian bric-a-brac and conventional, grandiloquent stage business that had accrued to his grandfather's works in favor of a spare, abstract representation.[47]

As Foucault's claim suggests, Chéreau, in turn, revised the revision. Once Wieland Wagner had cleared away those layers of kitsch, Chéreau went about excavating and then rendering the aspirations that underlay them. When the centennial production first appeared, it was met with a ferocious outpouring of protest. Its inflection of the work as occupying distinct temporalities at the same time—such that Brünnhilde sported a conventional Valkyrie's helmet while Wotan, carrying a spear, was otherwise outfitted as a nineteenth-century industrialist—produced incomprehension and out-

43. Foucault, "19th Century Imaginations," 188–89.

44. The history of Wagnerian stagings—including those at Bayreuth—has been recounted from a variety of perspectives in a variety of works. See, e.g., Mike Ashman, "Producing Wagner," in Millington and Spencer, *Wagner in Performance*, 29–47; Dietrich Mack, *Der Bayreuther Inszenierungsstil* (Munich: Prestel, 1976); Oswald Georg Bauer, *Richard Wagner: The Stage Designs and Productions from the Premières to the Present* (New York: Rizzoli, 1983). For a condensed version of Bauer's book-length survey, see Oswald Bauer, "Performance History: A Brief Survey," in *Wagner Handbook*, ed. Ulrich Müller and Peter Wapnewski, translation ed. John Deathridge (Cambridge, Mass.: Harvard University Press, 1992), 502–23. See also Savage, "Staging of Opera," 386–401.

45. For a Wagner family tree, see Nike Wagner, *The Wagners*, xviii–xix.

46. "Wir haben den Bayreuther Stil demoliert, weil uns keine germanischen Götter mehr interessieren. Wir wollen weg vom Wagner-Kult, wir wollen jedoch hin zum kultischen Theater." Bauer, *Wieland Wagner*, 149.

47. See Geoffrey Skelton, *Wieland Wagner: The Positive Sceptic* (London: Gollancz, 1971). For a critical reevaluation of Wieland Wagner's career with particular reference to *Die Meistersinger von Nürnberg*, see Nike Wagner, "'No Change Will Come to Our Western Art': New Bayreuth as Waste Disposal Plant," in Nike Wagner, *The Wagners*, 103–30.

Figure 7 A conventionally clad Brünnhilde (Gwyneth Jones) pleads with Wotan (Donald McIntyre), clad as a nineteenth-century industrialist, in Patrice Chéreau's production of Wagner's *Ring der Nibelungen*. (The scenic design, not visible in this picture, suggests a Strindbergian drawing room.)

right hostility (see figure 7).⁴⁸ As Foucault notes, the disjunction served a more general (and by now, largely familiar) insight, namely, that Wagner's recourse to myth in the tetralogy enabled him to render, in duly mediated form, a number of contemporary concerns. What was unfamiliar and unsettling in the centennial production was its insistence on rendering the simultaneity of these registers—the recourse to a nationalized mythology as well as its nineteenth-century origins. The production, we might say, staged the dramatic vibrancy as well as the dramaturgical logic of that recourse. Chéreau sought to stage the cultural terms of Wagner's recourse to a "natural" mythology, and in so doing arguably reinflected the *Ring*'s performance

48. Tom Sutcliffe describes Chéreau's inflection of *Das Rheingold*: "Chéreau did not placard the stage in any obvious way. He introduced a range of references. *Rheingold* presented the gods as privileged members of a pseudo-eighteenth-century *ancien régime*. Wotan was an old pantomime pirate in a brocade waistcoat. His women were fashionable ladies of the 1870s and 1880s. Only Alberich and the Nibelungs looked in period and in class, with black or dark gray dust-coats standard for workers and foreman in factories for fifty years and more after the *Ring*'s first performance. The Rhinemaidens were Toulouse-Lautrec whores from Montmartre. The stage directions talk about the Rhine at the start of *Das Rheingold* and of sportful Rhinemaidens. Peduzzi set a primitive hydro-electric dam across the stage, with the gold in its bowels. Dry ice rushed through locks and over pistons. The Rhinemaidens toyed with Alberich. His head was up one of their skirts. Love, when he rejected it and empowered himself to steal the gold, was blatantly erotic." Sutcliffe, *Believing in Opera*, 112.

text, shifting its locus from drama to theater, from an exclusive engagement with the *fabula* to an account of the *fabula*'s imbrication with and emergence from a disparate group of registers—political, historical, musical, biographical, and architectural. Beyond signaling the vitality of such an archaeological dramaturgy for the project of rethinking Wagner, the centennial *Ring* also signaled a more general paradigm shift in staging practices, one that reflected a willingness to explore and even render (rather than suppress) opera's representational unruliness.[49]

The paradigm shift in production practices reflected by the centennial *Ring* recalled innovations that had taken place on the stages of many German opera houses prior to the advent of National Socialism. During the Weimar Republic, opera had served as a forum for extraordinary aesthetic and theatrical innovation. Much of the most adventurous work by many of Germany's most innovative directors, artists, and choreographers was to be viewed on the opera stage.[50] For example, between 1927 and 1931 at one of the most visible centers of operatic experimentation, Berlin's Kroll Opera, "stage directors without preconceptions were brought in from spoken theatre, and artists like De Chirico, Schlemmer, and Moholy-Nagy were given shows to design."[51] As Ernst Bloch put it, at the Kroll Opera "old works were presented as if they were new, and new works were presented as if in recognition that their contemporaneity was not of the cheap and easy sort."[52] With the advent of National Socialism, many of these innovators fled or were arrested. During the course of the Nazi regime and for years after its demise, a great deal of German opera production, retooled and rededicated to serve the national cause, reverted to the backwater that had so frustrated

---

49. Annette Michelson argued in 1980 that "this production of the *Ring* will stand as more than a chapter in the history of Bayreuth or, more generally, of performance; it is our conviction that it constitutes a major stage in the renewal of performance as textual production within our culture." Michelson, "Bayreuth: The Centennial *Ring*," 65–66.

50. See Vibeke Peusch, *Opernregie/Regieoper: Avantgardistisches Musiktheater in der Weimarer Republik* (Frankfurt am Main: tende, 1984); Walter Panofsky, *Protest in der Oper: Das provocative Musiktheater der zwanziger Jahre* (Munich: Laokoon, 1966); Hans Curjel, *Experiment Krolloper: 1927–1931*, ed. Eigel Kruttge, foreword by Ernst Bloch, Studien zur Kunst des neunzehnten Jahrhunderts 7 (Munich: Prestel, 1975); Susan Cook, *Opera for a New Republic: The Zeitopern of Krenek, Weill, and Hindemith* (Ann Arbor, Mich.: UMI Research Press, 1988). Cook's study includes an enormously helpful bibliography: see esp. "The State of Music and Opera in the 1920s," in *Opera for a New Republic*. For a detailed consideration of the politics of opera in Berlin during the Weimar period, see John Rockwell, "The Prussian Ministry of Culture and the Berlin State Opera, 1918–1931" (Ph.D. diss., University of California, Berkeley, 1972).

51. Savage, "Staging of Opera," 397.

52. Ernst Bloch, "Die Oper, ganz anders," in Curjel, *Experiment Krolloper*, 7: "Altes wurde dort aufgeführt, als sei es neu, und Neues als eine Ahnung drin, daß eine Aktualität nicht zu der billigen gehöre."

Wagner.[53] It is not surprising, then, that as a spirit of innovation returned to Germany's opera houses in the mid-1970s, it would be marked once again by a commitment to invite "outsiders" back into the opera house, to open opera production to innovators from a host of other fields and countries.

Many of these innovators came to opera from the spoken theater, which during the 1970s was undergoing a seismic shift of its own as it began to come to terms with the emergence of what Hans-Thies Lehmann has termed post-dramatic theater. In Lehmann's argument, post-dramatic theater encompasses a literary movement and a theatrical practice that sought to steer theater away from its familiar service as a vehicle for the (regularly scheduled) delivery of *fabula,* or an overarching, coherent dramatic narrative.[54] As a literary movement, it produced a series of experimental theatrical texts inherited from figures such as Samuel Beckett (and, in complicated ways, Bertolt Brecht)[55] and encompassing, in the German context, authors such as Peter Handke, Botho Strauss, Heiner Müller, and Elfriede Jelinek.[56] As a theatrical practice, it encompassed a host of innovative stage directors, many of whom were intent upon forestalling the rote reproduction of classical texts. Among many examples of this latter tendency that Lehmann cites are Robert Wilson, Tadeusz Kantor, and Klaus-Michael Grüber, each of whom evinced an interest in an alternative, heterogeneous theatrical discourse, in what Lehmann, citing Julia Kristeva, terms a performative polylogism.[57] As Lehmann points out, both the literary-dramatic texts of post-dramatic theater and its practitioners were interested in querying the presumed unity of theatrical signification, its reliance on the transmission of

53. See Michael Steinberg, *The Meaning of the Salzburg Festival: Austria as Theater and Ideology, 1890–1938* (Ithaca, N.Y.: Cornell University Press, 1990); on the situation in Bayreuth—where the innovators were by no means uniformly banished—see Jens Malte Fischer, "Wagner-Interpretation im Dritten Reich: Musik und Szene zwischen Politisierung und Kunstanspruch," in *Richard Wagner im Dritten Reich,* ed. Saul Friedländer and Jörn Rüsen (Munich: Beck, 2000), 142–64; for an exceedingly informative case study, see Gundula Kreuzer, "'Erzieher und Bannerträger an der Spitze des Volkes': Aspects of Verdi Reception in the Third Reich," in *Verdi 2001: Proceedings of the International Conference; Parma, New York, New Haven,* ed. Fabrizio Della Seta, Roberta Montemorra Marvin, and Marco Marica, 2 vols. (Florence: Leo S. Olschki, 2003), 1:295–306. On the situation in Italy, see Fiamma Nicolodi, "Opera Production from Italian Unification to the Present," in Bianconi and Pestelli, eds., *Opera Production and its Resources,* trans. Lydia G. Cochrane, pt. 2, vol. 4 of *The History of Italian Opera,* ed. Bianconi and Pestelli (Chicago: University of Chicago Press, 1998), 165–228, at 192–207; see also Eric Levi, "Towards an Aesthetic of Fascist Opera," in *Fascism and Theatre: Comparative Studies on the Aesthetics and Politics of Performance in Europe, 1925–1945,* ed. Günter Berghaus (Providence, R.I.: Berghahn, 1996), 260–76. Levi's account is primarily concerned with compositional aesthetics; it barely touches upon questions of staging.

54. See Lehmann, *Postdramatic Theatre,* 37.

55. Ibid., 32–33.

56. Ibid., 33 as well as 56.

57. On performative polylogism, see Lehmann, *Postdramatic Theatre,* 32.

a homogenized meaning. Opera, of course, was ripe for just such a query, so it comes as no surprise that theater practitioners—such as Chéreau, Robert Wilson, and Hans Neuenfels—who were invited into opera production in the late 1970s brought with them from the theater (and not just there) a nascent interest in querying the settledness of operatic representation.

The reintroduction in the late 1970s of unfamiliar faces into operatic production was accompanied by a set of significant structural shifts in production practice. During the final quarter of the twentieth century, a number of European opera houses abandoned the star system—a system by which the major vocal stars jetted from one opera house to the other, necessitating exceedingly short rehearsal times and producing, in turn, a routinization of production practices while reinforcing an ongoing contraction of the repertoire.[58] In place of the star system, these houses reestablished an ensemble of resident singers who were contractually bound to a single house and thus available for extended rehearsal periods.[59] The singers were integral to the particular character of the house and familiar with its aspirations. More important, their availability for extended rehearsal periods and extended performance runs provided the necessary preconditions for substantive dramaturgical and directorial innovation. Not surprisingly, the overwhelming majority of innovative productions created since 1976 (and most of those considered in this study) originated in houses dedicated to ensemble work.

In an important sense, then, these structural and institutional shifts enabled a series of interpretive shifts, giving life to a culture of dramatic and dramaturgical experimentation. But how might we describe the stakes of that experimentation? What *is* "dramaturgical innovation"?

Thinking Through Dramaturgy

Let us proceed with a relatively common experience for operagoers today: the curtain goes up on a canonical work and what appears onstage seems utterly unfamiliar. Thus, for example, we encounter Figaro (in a butler's uniform) and Susanna (wearing a skimpy maid's outfit) in a laundry room in

58. Roger Savage traces rejection of the star system to the Berlin Kroll Opera of the late 1920s and early 1930s. "Under Klemperer's musical direction and occasional theatrical direction too, the Kroll between 1927 and 1931 was concerned to abolish the operatic star system and to get away at the same time from what was felt to be the tired picturesqueness and irrelevant pomp and circumstance of so much traditional *mise-en-scène*" (Savage, "Staging of Opera," 397.) On contractions in the repertoire, see Savage, "Staging of Opera," 391.

59. Most theater historians argue that this shift from a star system to an ensemble system was first undertaken by George II, duke of Saxe-Meiningen, who insisted on the subordination of star actors to an ensemble and created the position of the stage director to direct the ensemble's work. See Helmut Schwarz, *Regie: Idee und Praxis moderner Theaterarbeit* (Bremen: Carl Schünemann, 1965), 15.

Trump Tower (in the first scene of Peter Sellars's production of *Le nozze di Figaro* from the late 1980s). Or, just when we thought the work was over, the curtain does not come down at all. Instead, Pasha Selim, the Turkish despot whose magnanimity has just been extolled in the concluding vaudeville and chorus of Mozart's *Die Entführung aus dem Serail,* steps forward (in Hans Neuenfels's Stuttgart production of 1998) and recites a grim poem by Eduard Mörike, penned some seventy years after the premiere of Mozart's work. Critics and audiences have all too often been confounded, uncomprehending, even angry.

Symptomatically, the vocabulary employed in the press in the United States—say, the *New York Times,* the *San Francisco Chronicle,* or *Opera News*—to assess these productions is often quite heated: melodramatic, stentorian, and Manichean, it tends to parrot the rhetoric of nineteenth-century grand opera. For its part, as I suggested above, academic criticism has not so much excoriated inventive stagings as failed to account for them altogether. As a result, we hardly seem to possess a vocabulary with which to assess what these productions do.

Journalistic accounts have tended to insist on the inherently suspect nature of any deviation from conventional (and often prescribed) representational forms (e.g., of setting, costuming, or situation). In an opinion piece on unconventional stagings in *Opera News,* Theodore Rabb, a professor of history at Princeton, laments that in the hands of many contemporary opera directors, "the venerable tradition of symbol and allegory has become little more than an opportunity for incomprehensible allusions, private fantasies and distracting 'concepts.'"[60] Rabb associates the resulting preponderance of inscrutability—and its critical corollary, a supposed reticence on the part of critics to denounce these productions—with "current academic fashion." The analogy is clear: in the academy, as in the opera house, obfuscation, self-indulgence, and interpretive willfulness are supposedly celebrated rather than challenged. (Although I disagree, Rabb has a point. But I wonder whether his point doesn't apply to any field of imaginative endeavor: in the opera house and in the academy, as in architecture, biotechnology, and aircraft design, we find plenty of evidence of experiments gone awry. A culture that relies on innovation does not just risk producing mistakes—it has to tolerate them.) To my mind, the intersection of contemporary stage production with contemporary developments in cultural and textual analysis seems especially promising—if not for the reasons that Rabb cites. Rabb's frustration is familiar enough, although his polemic (he calls for "fierce denunciation" in the face of such directorial "contempt") strikes me as misguided. The

60. Theodore Rabb, "Symbols Crash," *Opera News* (May 2001): 96.

difference between "using symbols to communicate" (Rabb's sense of what a good director does) and using symbols "to impose" (what a bad director does) is hard to determine. But if "the venerable tradition of symbol and allegory" is indeed venerable (which is by no means clear), then it is so by virtue of the artfulness of its recourse to mediation, something that inevitably risks baffling its audience on account of that very recourse. In its most extreme form, the anti-innovative-stagings polemic reverses the familiar German dictum about children: to many, opera is best heard and not seen. And when it is seen (in its familiar, assigned role as the stepchild of music), opera ought to be tidy and presentable rather than wild and unruly; it can be imaginative as long as it isn't intrusive; better settled down than unsettling.

I am skeptical of this position, in part because it disregards—or even suppresses—what I take to be a fundamental aesthetic condition of the genre: its constitutive representational unruliness, what Abbate and Parker term its "clash of systems." To quote Pierluigi Petrobelli's by now canonical observation, "In opera, various 'systems' work together, each according to its own nature and laws, and the result of the combination is much greater than the sum of the individual forces."[61] Of course, the question is how these systems work together and whether their working together is best understood as a function of laws or convention. Opera is compelling in part because it is so unruly. This unruliness results from the combination of so many disparate expressive forms as well as the disparate forms within those forms. It is not just that opera encompasses music, drama, poetry, song, dance, and stage spectacle, or that it juxtaposes and combines these forms in ever-changing configurations, but that it encompasses the expressive volatility that characterizes each of these forms. Despite the repeated efforts of composers to lasso these forms into a unified, corporate apparatus, the proliferation of expressive means necessarily unsettles opera, leaving it always in excess of itself, characterized by an extravagance that resists the very domestication that it invites.[62] There are multiple sites for this domestication—or, conversely,

61. Pierluigi Petrobelli, "Music in the Theater (Apropos of *Aida*, Act III)," in *Music in the Theater: Essays on Verdi and Other Composers,* trans. Roger Parker (Princeton, N.J.: Princeton University Press, 1994), 113.

62. Of course, opera history is dotted with various attempts to contain and refashion this unruliness, and indeed, at various points, the genre has been more or less tidy. But although the terms and gradations of unruliness have shifted over time (with Gluck, Wagner, and Pfitzner as—very different—avatars of order, and Rameau, Meyerbeer, and Bernd Alois Zimmermann as—very different—avatars of disorder), the fact of discursive surfeit, of a too-muchness of opera's representational means, has remained constant. That surfeit or unruliness finds various forms of expression in production onstage—even in its absence or, indeed, in its suppression. See Herbert Lindenberger, *Opera: The Extravagant Art* (Ithaca, N.Y.: Cornell University Press, 1984). One of the most forceful critiques of Wagner's corporatizing program is Antonin Artaud's notion of a theater as plague. See

for an anti-domesticating, liberating expression: the operatic stage is one. Since the emergence of the stage director (and in contrast to earlier periods in opera history), opera production has tended to constrict rather than to render this excess, settling opera by conventionalizing its representation and reference. In that sense, opera's settledness has been settled for quite some time. Indeed, the very threat of uncontrolled signification—a threat repeatedly and understandably associated with opera—has produced a performance practice characterized by the suppression of discursive disorder, the marshaling of signification as fixed and ordered. As I suggested earlier, an alternative practice—one that thrived in the Weimar Republic and that was revived most forcefully around the mid-1970s[63]—uncorks that disorder and stages the characteristic clashes of expressive systems, taking operatic staging as a complex and autonomous (rather than merely derivative or decorative) expressive form.

The distinction between modes of mise-en-scène corresponds to noteworthy differences in the conception and inflection of the operatic audience. Writing in the early 1960s, Theodor Adorno argued that opera fulfills an important function in contemporary culture, serving to reaffirm a generalized mode of "deconcentration" and, at the same time, serving as a marker of failed cultural aspirations—a recognizable (and recognizably invalid) calling card for those who can only aspire to membership in the club of bourgeois culture:

> The conduct of today's opera habitué is retrospective. He guards the cultural assets as possessions. His creed is a line to be voiced in a local dialect: "Still a damn good old opera, isn't it?" The prestige comes from the period when opera was still counted with the more pretentious forms. It attaches to the names of Mozart, Beethoven, Wagner, also that of Verdi. But it is linked with the possibility of a deconcentrated mode of conception that feeds on habit and maintains a state of universal semi-education. Opera, more than any

---

David Graver's observation that "in contrast to [Gordon] Craig, who wants to eliminate any authority within the theatrical performance that conflicts with or threatens to overshadow the director, Artaud cultivates multiple sources of authority as much as possible without dissipating the powers of the theatrical event." Graver, "Artaud and the Authority of Text, Spectacle, and Performance," in *Contours of the Theatrical Avant-Garde: Performance and Textuality*, ed. James Harding (Ann Arbor: University of Michigan Press, 2000), 43–57, at 48. There are some important exceptions to the corporatizing program, including John Cage and Bernd Alois Zimmerman.

63. We can find individual instances of innovative staging practices throughout modern operatic history. In *Believing in Opera*, for example, Tom Sutcliffe traces his "pre-history of modern operatic production in Britain," to the tremendous resentment caused by Peter Brook's stagings in the late 1940s of *Boris Godunov* and *Salome* (the latter with settings by Salvador Dali) at the Royal Opera House Covent Garden. See Sutcliffe, *Believing in Opera*, 19–27.

other form, represents traditional bourgeois culture to those who simultaneously fail to take part in that culture.[64]

The project of the new mise-en-scène is implicit in Adorno's critique. In his
account, The Great Composers have been—and continue to be—appropriated in the service of this deconcentration. But a number of the productions
we will consider suggest that those same composers can be reclaimed from
that appropriation, reconceived in a newly concentrated mode that is impatient with habit and invites reflection. This shifts the terms of prestige cited
by Adorno, from a residual cultural affiliation (where going to the opera
offers an experience of class) to a material cultural expression (where going
to the opera offers an experience of aesthetic complexity).

For many of the productions we will consider, dramaturgy and mise-en-
scène complement one another; indeed, they are arguably even coexten-
sive.[65] Dramaturgy is a German invention. Deriving from the pragmatic and
theoretical interests of Gotthold Ephraim Lessing, dramaturgy developed in
the course of the second half of the eighteenth century as a means of reflecting upon the particularity of drama.[66] By the beginning of the nineteenth
century, a number of German municipal theaters had created a position
whose function encompassed those of a resident playwright and literary
manager: when he wasn't writing plays, the dramaturg assessed and nur-
tured them, including foreign works (which he was expected to translate)
and works in progress, seeking to ensure that they would be executed most
effectively—which is also to say, most dramatically.[67] With the emergence

---

64. Theodor W. Adorno, "Opera," in *Introduction to the Sociology of Music* (New York: Seabury,
1976), 82. See also Peter Evans, *Sociology of Opera*.

65. In the course of his essay "Which Theories for Which Mise-en-Scènes?" Patrice Pavis cites
Juan Antonio Hormigón's definition of mise-en-scène as "the coordinated articulation of dramaturgical work and technical-craft practice." According to Pavis, in mise-en-scène "there is necessarily an
element of dramaturgical work (even if it denies its own existence), it comprises the systematizing
of practical actions realized in concrete terms by a 'technical-craft practice.'" In this book, I will be
interested in productions where that systematization is of particular theatrical and theoretical importance. See Pavis, "Which Theories for Which Mise-en-Scènes?," trans. David Williams, in Harding, *Contours of the Theatrical Avant-Garde,* 96–109, at 103. The quotation from Hormigón is taken
from *Trabajo dramaturgico y puesta en escena* (Publicaciones de la Asociación de directores de escena
en España, 1991), 63.

66. Lessing served as dramaturg for the National Theater in Hamburg from 1767 to 1769. For a
brief and amusing account of Lessing's career as a dramaturg, see Joel Schechter, "Lessing, Jugglers,
and Dramaturgs," originally published in *Yale/Theatre* 7, no. 1 (1975): 93–103; reprinted in Cardullo,
What Is Dramaturgy?, 27–41. For a capsule account of some of the important successes of German
dramaturgs in the first half of the nineteenth century, including Ludwig Tieck and Karl Immer-
mann, see Schechter, 38–39. For a documentary account of the early history of German dramaturgy, see Benno von Wiese, ed., *Deutsche Dramaturgie vom Barock bis zur Klassik,* Deutsche Texte 4
(Tübingen: Max Niemeyer, 1956).

67. See Esslin, "Role" 43.

of stage directing in opera at the conclusion of the nineteenth century and the contraction of the operatic repertoire that coincided with it, some of the burden of originality and the focus of attention in the opera house shifted from the composer and librettist to the conductor and director.[68] As the role of the director emerged, that of the dramaturg shifted as well. If the dramaturg was most likely to be found in a writer's salon in the eighteenth century, assessing and serving the playwright's production of new material, in the twentieth century he (and, more recently, she) was more often to be found in a theater or opera house serving the production of new interpretations. Today, the opera dramaturg—or, more precisely, the critically oriented opera dramaturg—tends to shuttle between a reading room, a conference room, and a rehearsal room, preparing an interpretation in the first, discussing and refining it in the second, and assessing its disposition in the third.[69] This is not to say that the task of reading is entirely functional. Indeed, the best dramaturgs are generally the most speculative readers, capable of an exploratory, dialogic engagement with the (opera) text, attentive, as Jankélévitch would put it, to both the drastic and the gnostic.[70] In this

68. For an historical account of the emergence of the operatic stage director, see Savage, especially "Continuities and Innovations: 1896–1966," 387–401. For a recent revisionist account of the history of the stage director in the spoken theater, with a particular emphasis upon developments in Paris, see Ehren Fordyce, "When Directing Became a Profession: The Emergence of the Régisseur, Mise en Scène, and Metteur en Scène in Early Nineteenth-Century Paris" (Ph.D. diss., Columbia University, 2001). For an exhaustive account of the emergence of the director on the operatic stage, see Langer, Der Regisseur.

69. In practice, the sequence generally works as follows: a dramaturg will prepare a preliminary reading of a piece and present it at an initial meeting of the production team (i.e., the conductor, director, set designer, costume designer) in order to launch a discussion of how the piece will be staged. Once a provisional conception has been hammered out, it is the dramaturg's responsibility to assess how the various proposals offered in response (e.g., for sets and costumes; for the inflection of characters and situations, etc.) relate to the production's overall conception. This process of assessment continues once the rehearsal process is underway. That is, the dramaturg collaborates with the director and other members of the production team, critiquing rehearsals and posing questions regarding costuming, lighting, and set design. In short, a dramaturg serves as a resident conceptual director.

70. See in this regard Zehelein's admonition: "When the task of reading is removed from the very center of the dramaturgy, when the artistic or the administrative leadership of an opera house subjects the task of reading to pragmatic imperatives, then what results is the institutionalization of dramaturgy or, even worse, the institutionalization of reading. This implies a form of reading dictated by pragmatism, be it by the supposed circumstances of the house, by considerations of casting, the limitations of the stage or technical considerations, the likelihood of the audience's getting it. All of these are considerations that a dramaturg must consider at some point, but if they become controlling too early on in the process, then what results is a manipulated reception of texts. This impedes an exploratory form of reading. At the outset, the most important stance is one of discovery, of probing, without immediately taking account of scenic imperatives and their conditions. Only an unmitigated exploration enables discoveries." Klaus Zehelein, "Dramaturgie und Intendanz: Aus Gesprächen mit Juliane Votteler," in Musiktheater heute: Klaus Zehelein, Dramaturg und Intendant,

sense, we can conceive of the dramaturg not just as a given production's "first (or privileged) spectator," but, before that, as its first reader.[71] This book considers the practical implications of this shift. In particular, we will consider the relationship between mise-en-scène and dramaturgy, between the fact of unsettling stagings and the dramaturgy of the particular operatic texts that are thus unsettled. It is only by recasting our conception of the ways that operas mean that we will be able to comprehend significant recastings of meaning in performance.

A Polylogical Criticism

Many of the issues raised in this book are germane to—even familiar from—discussions of theatrical performance. But opera raises the stakes and shifts the terms of those discussions on account of its characteristic surfeit of expressive means. That surfeit both simplifies and complicates the project of analysis. Although drama can make use of musical means, its range of expression is anchored in and sanctioned by words. Opera, like post-dramatic theater, has multiple sites where we can locate the origin of meaning and multiple channels through which that meaning finds expression. This multiplication also complicates our capacity to seize and fix that meaning. An example will help to explain what I have in mind.

In a chapter on Verdi's *Don Carlos* in *Opera and Ideas,* Paul Robinson offers a compelling account of the four principal characters in Verdi's opera, focusing on the intersection of their musical, political, and psychological profiles. At times Robinson encounters moments of what we might term "telling divergence"—that is, moments where the text of the libretto and the musical accompaniment seem to go in different directions. One place where they do so, in Robinson's account, is at the conclusion of the great bass duet between King Philippe and the Grand Inquisitor in act 4 of the five-act version of Verdi's work.[72] As the Inquisitor shuffles off, Philippe is given the lines "So the throne must always bow to the altar!" (Dunque il trono piegar dovrà sempre all'altare!).[73]

---

ed. Juliane Votteler (Hamburg: Europäische Verlagsantstalt/Rotbuch Verlag, 2000), 17–54, at 19–20; my translation.

71. On the dramaturg as the first spectator, see Zehelein, "Dramaturgie und Intendanz," 34–36.

72. During the course of his career, Verdi prepared a number of different versions of *Don Carlos* for a number of different venues. In order to avoid confusion, and unless otherwise noted, I have chosen to employ the title (*Don Carlos*) and spelling of character names from the original French version of the work, prepared for Paris in 1867.

73. At the time Robinson's study was published, *Don Carlos* was known primarily in its Italian version. The same line in French reads: "L'orgueil du Roi fléchit devant l'orgueil du prêtre!" All quotations from *Don Carlos* are taken from Giuseppe Verdi, *Don Carlos: Edizione integrale delle varie versioni*

Musical Example 1 A textual defeat, a musical victory. Philippe's words, sung at the end of his scene with the Grand Inquisitor (act 4, scene 2), suggest a thoroughgoing concession to the Inquisitor's power. On the other hand, the virtuosic two-octave display of range and the strong cadential motion in the music indicate that Philippe's strength has not yet been exhausted.

In Robinson's account, "Philip's utter collapse . . . seems registered in his final line, which he sings as the Inquisitor moves offstage, supported by his two Dominicans. . . . But as he had done in the middle section of the king's monologue, Verdi again disregards his libretto to transform this textual defeat into a musical victory."[74] Robinson's point is a good one: the musical articulation here would seem to suggest a force that conflicts with the literal terms of Philip's lines. My disagreement with Robinson involves his (repeated) use of the term "disregard."[75] By implication, had Verdi not disregarded the libretto,

in cinque e in quattro atti, comprendente gli inediti verdiani, ed. Ursula Günther, piano-vocal reduction with original French texts by Joseph Méry and Camille Du Locle and Italian translation by Achille de Lauzières and Angelo Zanardini as well as Italian translation by Piero Faggioni of unpublished verses, 2 vols. (Milan: Ricordi, 1980), at 2:453.

74. Robinson, *Opera and Ideas,* 207.

75. A bit earlier in the same chapter, Robinson makes much the same claim about Philippe's solo aria "Ella giammai m'amò!," which precedes his encounter with the Grand Inquisitor: "The morose utterances of the aria's first section are followed by a passage whose musical effect is exactly the opposite. As in the final phrases of the recitative, the text hardly seems to call for a change: *'Se il serto regal a me desse il poter, di leggere nei cor, che Dio può sol, può sol veder!'* [If the royal crown could but give

his music would have amplified or underscored it. This claim is symptomatic of a widespread sense that opera's signifying systems are tautological. Apparent divergences between musical logic and textual meaning have to be resolved, the "disregard" noted (almost always in deference to an attributed musical meaning). And yet, we could just as easily suggest that the music carefully regards the libretto and amplifies it by taking up a position relative to it. In such an interpretive model, opera is dialectical, its expressive means complex. By contrast, the implied model of unification—arguably a product of Wagner's interpretive legacy—allows for a modicum of complication between text and music but also tends to restrict the complications to that register. That is, although music and text can be seen to diverge, their divergence is rarely conceived as stageworthy. Stagings that would render the tension between opera's constituent elements are frequently denounced for supposedly dispensing with the very coherence that they in fact seek to achieve. A dialectical or polylogical staging may be unusual, but it is not necessarily incoherent, just as a conventional staging is not necessarily coherent by virtue of its conventionality. A polylogical staging may in fact bring us closer to what is at stake in a work than a staging that ignores or resolves contradictions in favor of an ordered, conventional presentation.

One of the tasks of dramaturgical analysis is to ferret out those stakes and assist in their expression during the course of rehearsals. Initially this is a philological task: reading the text in order to locate it in multiple contexts, including, for example, the generic conventions and historical conditions that informed the composition as well as its place in the composer's and librettist's oeuvres. Beyond the philological task is a more pragmatic and pressing one—of developing an interpretation for and with a production team. Dramaturgical analysis can take any number of forms—all the more so in the United States, where dramaturgy remains relatively unfamiliar, especially in the opera house.[76] For one, dramaturgy can pose the challenge of applied criticism, transplanting textual theory and analysis from the library and the classroom into the rehearsal room and onto the stage.[77] As the German theater dramaturg Herman Beil describes it:

---

me the power to read human hearts, which God alone can see!] But Verdi again *disregards* the libretto. If the text alludes to a power the King doesn't have, the music speaks boldly of the power he in fact possesses." Robinson, *Opera and Ideas*, 200 (emphasis added). The passage from *Don Carlos* can be found at *Don Carlos*, 2:438–39.

76. On dramaturgy in the United States, see Mark Bly, introduction to *The Production Notebooks: Theatre in Process* (New York: Theatre Communications Group, 1996), esp. 1:xv–xxvi. See also *Theatre Topics* 13, no. 1 (March 2003), which is devoted to dramaturgy.

77. See in this regard Martin Esslin's observation that "the absence of the Dramaturg, until relatively recent times, in the theater of the English-speaking world, was intimately connected with a commercial system which precluded the development of a long-term repertoire policy, as each

The dramaturg used to sit in a library and do research. The results of his work would then be made available to the director, who could proceed with them as he wished. That's not how it works anymore. The dramaturg has to learn along with everyone else. He has to hear what the director, designers, and actors are thinking, he has to move around within their imaginations. These long-winded early sessions can be wild and exciting. The dramaturg, of course, sets up the preliminary concept . . . then it gets thrown around and finally you get a tangible approach and a series of situations, what they have to express and how they have to be translated. But nothing is yet accomplished—for it still has to go into rehearsal and there the draft will undergo violent and decisive changes. There is the acid test: how can the actors play these ideas? That's why the dramaturg has to attend rehearsals to find the errors and strengths of the concept.[78]

Here, then, criticism and theory find an outlet in real life, or rather in the pragmatics of work in an opera house. Thus, as I hope to make clear in this book, opera in production can mean reading and staging these texts—and reading the stagings—in light of contemporary cultural and textual theory. This does not mean that opera ought to become hostage to the rote application of abstruse academic concerns. In reading opera texts and opera's performance texts, we animate the intersection of creative interpretation in the academy and onstage, adding vibrancy and substance to both.

Which is not to say that the language of dramaturgical analysis is fully developed. It seems clear that we will need a more nuanced analytic vocabulary, including a more variegated conception of mise-en-scène, in order to account for the dramatic and conceptual achievements of a given production. This need finds symptomatic expression in even the most subtle academic writing on opera. In his provocative essay "Reading the *Livrets,* or the Chimera of 'Authentic' Staging," Roger Parker repeatedly metonymizes mise-en-scène as what he terms "the visual aspect" of a production (or, in other cases, its "visual manner" or "the visual system").[79] I sympathize with Parker's project. If our conceptualization of opera in production has tended to privilege—even to fetishize—the aural, Parker would have us attend to all that is not specifically musical, which he gathers together under the

production was planned as a separate commercial venture unconnected to any previous ones except, perhaps, by the personality of the producer (Esslin, "Role," 43.) On the politics (and indeed, the dramaturgy) of repertoire planning, compare Reinhardt Stumm, "Dramaturgy in Stuttgart: An Interview with Hermann Beil," in Cardullo, *What Is Dramaturgy?,* 49–55, at 51.

78. Stumm, "Dramaturgy in Stuttgart," 51–52.

79. See Parker, "Reading the *Livrets,* or the Chimera of 'Authentic' Staging," in *Leonora's Last Act: Essays in Verdian Discourse* (Princeton, N.J.: Princeton University Press, 1997), 128, 130, 133.

rubric of the visual. But in Parker's account, the purview of the visible seems unduly narrow, encompassing the fact of mise-en-scène but not its conceptual exigencies: mise-en-scène is seen but is hardly seen to be worthy of more complex analysis. And yet, the visual system is not always only a fact, it is also a dramaturgical factor and needs to be seen as such. A final brief example from *Don Carlos* will help to explain what I have in mind.

In *Don Carlos,* the visual register is particularly important to the sense of constriction that pervades the work. Here we have a sense, much like in Richard Strauss's *Salome,* that there is a visual regime in place that would keep everyone and everything in view. Philippe's object in constructing and sustaining this regime is not so far removed from the Grand Inquisitor's object or, less obviously, the stage director's: all three would seem to be intent on making emotion visible, if in different ways. In the end, Philippe's "bright lights" regime, his determination to uncover the truth of his wife's supposed infidelity, will bring very little to light, or at least, very little of what he intended: in place of the supposed indiscretions of his new wife, Elisabeth, with Carlos, his son from a previous marriage, we discover Princess Eboli's indiscretions with the king, while the king is left in the dark—metaphorically and also quite literally—regarding his wife's affections. More than anything, the bright lights occasion a proliferation of insult and melancholy, such as when Elisabeth has to publicly comfort the countess of Aremberg, her lady-in-waiting, for enduring a very public humiliation by the king, who banishes her for having left the queen unattended (in act 2, scene 2, of Verdi's opera). The countess is sent packing for violating "the rules of the court" (as Philippe puts it, "Ignorez vous la règle de ma cour?"): in this case, the rule that the queen must be forever visible in order to keep track of her desire and, presumably, to keep it on track.[80] This scene of the countess's dismissal and her (and by extension the queen's) resulting humiliation alerts us to a problem in the opera text that we might otherwise overlook: that everyone in this piece seems to be watching, even if hardly anyone seems to be able to see much of anything. (The notable exceptions to this rule underscore its irony, because the Inquisitor, who sees all, is blind, and Posa, whose gaze penetrates all, only has eyes for the suffering in Flanders.) The logic of surveillance in *Don Carlos* is such that the transparency of objects appears to be inversely proportionate to the intensity of the gaze(s) trained upon them. But if matters are functionally as opaque as they appear to be transparent, then this condition, in turn, needs to be made visible—it needs to be staged.

80. *Don Carlos,* 1:198.

The dramaturgical disposition of *Don Carlos* presents a more elaborate visual system than that invoked by Parker. In my view, the mise-en-scène needs to engage the dramaturgy of the text, and criticism needs to illuminate that engagement. Why? Because the results, onstage and in criticism, might well be more complex and less predictable. And we might gain a clearer—a newly unsettled—view of a genre whose complexity and achievements in performance we have only just begun to map.

READING A STAGING/STAGING A READING

Wagner's *Die Meistersinger von Nürnberg* in Performance

In February 1929, the German National Party demanded a parliamentary investigation into "the transformation of the State Opera at the Platz der deutschen Republik [popularly known as the Kroll Opera] into a laboratory for Bolshevik art experiments." [1] The crisis in the Prussian State Parliament had become particularly acute in the wake of the Kroll Opera's production of *Der fliegende Holländer* (*The Flying Dutchman*), which had premiered a few weeks earlier on January 15, 1929, and which, according to the party, brazenly "mocked the spirit of Richard Wagner." [2] For anyone who has worked on Wagner or, for that matter, simply attended performances of his works, the sentiments come as no surprise. Indeed, the fact that they arose in the wake of Otto Klemperer's and Jürgen Fehling's modernist production (with sets by Ewald Dülberg) make them almost predictable. Klemperer, general music director of the Kroll Opera, and Fehling, a famous Berlin theater director, incurred the wrath of the National Party for violating a long-standing convention of Wagnerian stagings. [3] In the Kroll Opera production, the Dutchman's

---

1. See "Zensur der Inszenierungen," *Abendblatt der Frankfurter Zeitung*, 21 February 1929. Unless otherwise noted, translations are my own.

2. The anecdote is recounted in Peusch, *Opernregie/Regieoper*, 24. Production stills and several reviews of the Berlin production as well as articles concerning the storm of controversy that surrounded it can be found in Curjel, *Experiment Krolloper*, 252–59, 380–82, and plates 47–52. Additional stills can be found in Gerhard Ahrens, ed., *Das Theater des deutschen Regisseurs Jürgen Fehling* (Berlin: Quadriga, 1985), 130–33.

3. On Klemperer's and Fehling's work at the Kroll Opera, see Curjel, *Experiment Krolloper*; Mike Ashman, "Producing Wagner," in Millington and Spencer, *Wagner in Performance*, 29–47; Patrick Carnegy, "Designing Wagner: Deeds of Music Made Visible?," in Millington and Spencer, *Wagner in Performance*, 48–74. For a general account of Fehling's stage productions in the context of theatrical innovations during the Weimar Republic, see John Willett, *Theatre of the Weimar Republic* (New

Figure 8 The Dutchman's vessel, Kroll Opera, 1929. Ewald Dülberg's scenic design forged an abstract visual landscape for Fehling and Klemperer's modernist *Der fliegende Holländer*. Photo courtesy of Akademie der Künste, Berlin.

ship may be anchored in the mid-nineteenth century, but it is not permanently mired there. And that is precisely what enraged the National Party in Berlin, just as, almost half a century later, Patrice Chéreau would incur the wrath of countless like-minded Wagnerians in Bayreuth with his centenary production of *The Ring* (see figure 8).[4]

To Wagnerians in the late 1920s and 1970s, the Master's intentions were recognizable through the familiarity of his stagings. That familiarity derived from a conventionalized and literalist mode of interpretation. The audience—or at least, its contingent of Wagnerians—expected to join Daland in the recognition that he pronounces upon his initial appearance at the outset of the work, "Sandwike ist's, genau kenn' ich die Bucht" (It's Sandwike; how well I know the bay). His sentimental recognition within the framework

York: Holmes & Meier, 1988), esp. 156–57; a much more detailed account is offered in Ahrens, *Das Theater*.

4. For an example of the outrage produced by Klemperer and Fehling's production (and Chéreau's as well), see Nagler, *Misdirection*. The book contains a chapter excoriating the Kroll production as well as Chéreau's "ridiculous" *Ring*. For a recent restatement of the positions outlined in Nagler's book, see Ulrich Weisstein, "How to Stage or Not to Stage an Opera: Some Methodological and Historical Observations on a Performing Art with Examples Drawn from Weber's *Freischütz*," *Arcadia* 36, no. 2 (2001): 256–86. For a detailed (and much more sympathetic) discussion of Chéreau's production, see Jean-Jacques Nattiez, *Tétralogies: Wagner, Boulez, Chéreau* (Paris, Christian Bourgeois, 1983). For an abbreviated version of the argument, see Nattiez, "Chéreau's Treachery."

of the dramatic action is doubled by the audience's familiarity with the bay. That recognition forms an important component of the canonical status of Wagner's works: it is not so much the places (medieval Nuremberg, a bay in Norway, etc.) that are familiar, but rather their place in a collective fantasy.

Fehling and Klemperer displaced *Der fliegende Holländer* by recasting its naturalism and romanticism in modernist terms. Criticism of the production and the available documentation suggest that in crucial ways, Dülberg's sets rendered abstract what had heretofore been presented in explicitly naturalistic form, while at key moments Fehling's direction rendered quotidian and simple what had heretofore been presented in quintessentially romantic and hyperbolized form. In Dülberg's rendering, the Dutchman's vessel looks more like a spare, modernist allusion to a boat than a schooner with all the trappings. And in Fehling's account, Senta—the arch–Wagnerian heroine who abandons her small-town life and her small-town beau in favor of a doomed, visionary love with the brooding Dutchman—is less an embodied romantic fantasy of innocent German maidenhood than a modern, defiant, headstrong young woman. To understand the scandal that this rendering aroused, we need to return to the discussion of Wagner's relationship to operatic staging initiated in the last chapter.

In chapter 1, we noted that from early on in his career, Wagner emphatically sought to consolidate the expressive means of a genre that had come to be fully identified with a variety of distractions. In Wagner's mind, the culture of distractions was a product of—and found expression in—routinized performance practices. The resulting stagings, invariably as silly as they were spectacular, were for Wagner entirely adequate vehicles for a host of "senseless" effects in "senseless" works—works generally culled from the immensely popular French and Italian operatic literature. Against this penchant for purportedly unmotivated spectacle and display, Wagner aspired to a theater of total absorption.[5]

In Wagner's account, the culture of distraction produced a generalized (and from his perspective, a lamentable) culture of scopophilia—a pleasure in looking; and even then, the audience's gaze was rarely trained on the stage. Instead, members of the audience were to be found ogling one another, if they weren't asleep. And if they happened to turn their attention to events onstage, they would most likely find a string of bombastic scenic effects along with their musical correlatives, which Wagner disparagingly termed musical

---

5. On the juxtaposition of absorption and theatricality, see Michael Fried, "Absorption and Theatricality: Painting and Beholder in the Age of Diderot" (Berkeley: University of California Press, 1980). See also H. Martin Puchner, "Polyphonous Gestures: Wagnerian Modernism from Mallarmé to Stravinsky," *Criticism* 41, no. 1 (Winter 1999): 25–39.

"harangues." Wagner summarized the situation in his essay of 1873, "A Glance at the German Opera-Stage of Today":

A dull unconsciousness lies stamped on every countenance [in the audience at the opera house]: uninterested in all that transpires between the stage and the orchestra, the audience only awakens from its deaf sluggishness to cap the singer's inevitable "harangue" with a round of applause, if only to demonstrate that it had not so far forgot itself as to really fall asleep. Nary a face betrays a hint of expression, save that of curiosity about its neighbors: the merriest or most tragic scene may be transpiring on stage, not a muscle betrays even the faintest sympathy. It is "opera"; which has nothing to do with either merriment or tragedy, but simply—*opera*, and why doesn't the prima donna sing us something pretty? And for this they have now decked the theater with astounding luxury! The house is all aglow with gold and velvet, and the expansive, comfy easy chair [*Fauteuil*] appears to be prepared for the theater evening's principal enjoyment. From nowhere can one get a view of the stage that does not include a large slice of the audience: the flaming row of footlights abuts on the middle of the proscenium boxes; it is impossible to watch the prima donna, there in front, without having to take in the glasses of the "opera friend" who ogles her. One thus can find no dividing line to part the putative artistic action from those before whom it is set. The two dissolve into a single brew of a most repulsive mixture, in which the Kapellmeister twirls his baton as a magic ladle of the modern witch's cauldron.[6]

It is not clear which is worse: the fact that every face at the opera house is marked by "a dull unconsciousness" or that the institution of opera thrives upon that unconsciousness. In constructing the Festspielhaus at Bayreuth, Wagner would banish both the culture of distractions onstage and the preponderance of distractions in the auditorium.[7] Here, then, we witness the birth of music-drama out of the spirit of aesthetic absorption. Of course, the experience of absorption was not restricted to the audience; it was supposed

---

6. Richard Wagner, "Ein Einblick in das heutige deutsche Opernwesen," in *GSD* 9:279; "A Glance at the German Opera-Stage of Today," in *PW* 5:277; translation modified.

7. As I suggested in chapter 1, the design of the Festspielhaus at Bayreuth—including the submersion of the conductor and orchestra, the perfected sightlines afforded the audience, and the total darkness in the auditorium—lent material form to some of the key terms of Wagner's longstanding aesthetic campaign. Commenting on the disparaging inflection of "opera" in the passage quoted above, James Treadwell notes that in Wagner's argument, "opera has no content, aesthetic or theoretical or otherwise. It's just a word denoting what goes on in an opera house, the absolutely trivial and meaningless brand of entertainment to which all musical drama (whether *Don Giovanni* or *Le prophète* or *Lohengrin*) is reduced once it finds itself in the grip of German theatres." Treadwell, *Interpreting Wagner*, 227.

to emanate from the singers (Wagner termed them "singing actors") on-stage. So that his singers would embody this sense of absorption and educe it from the audience, Wagner demanded that they adopt a "natural" de-meanor onstage.

The term "natural" is one of the most highly charged in the Wagnerian lexicon: it denotes a prelapsarian—which is to say, a premodern—sense of all that is Germanic, simple, intuitive, rooted and "of the folk," as opposed to that which is modern, cosmopolitan (i.e., French and/or Jewish), com-plicated, academic, rootless, and cultured.[8] Wagner's various accounts of history—the history of language, of German culture, of opera and theater—recycle the same essential scenario: in the beginning, there was a natural or-der that thrived on the basis of natural bonds (between a word and a tone, or between an idea and its expression, or between a farmer and the soil); this state of natural affinities was shattered by the advent of modern culture; only a radical intervention will banish modern culture and reinstate the natural or-der. Here, for example, is a characteristic passage from *Opera and Drama*:

> But beneath the frosty mantle of its civilization the *Volk* preserves, in the in-stinctiveness of its natural mode of language, the roots by which it remains connected to nature's ground; and everyone may come by an instinctive un-derstanding of those roots, if he turns from the hubbub of our official-state-business language exchange [*unseres staatsgeschäftlichen Sprachverkehres*] to seek a loving view of nature, and thus makes these roots available to feeling, through an "unconscious" use of their *kindred* qualities.[9]

In Wagner's view, the proliferation of mindless effects on the operatic stage testifies to the predominance of an unnatural, cosmopolitan culture: the hubbub on the cosmopolitan operatic stage is not far removed from—indeed, it is a symptom of—the hubbub of our "official-state-business lan-guage exchange."[10] Wagner would change all that. And because, in his view, the advent of mindless effects had not simply coincided with the decline of

---

8. See Goehr, *Quest for Voice*, 66. See also Marc A. Weiner, "Reading the Ideal," *New German Cri-tique* 69 (Fall 1996): 53–83.

9. *Opera and Drama*, in PW 2:265; translation modified, emphasis in original. Published in Ger-man in Wagner, GSD 4:128. For a more detailed discussion of this passage as well as Wagner's ac-count of the origins of language, see David J. Levin, *Richard Wagner, Fritz Lang, and the Nibelungen: The Dramaturgy of Disavowal* (Princeton, N.J.: Princeton University Press, 1998), 44–51.

10. In his *Communication to My Friends* of 1851, Wagner formulates a similar thought in different terms, advocating the abolition of the position of Kapellmeister because he or she "must cater to a nightly entertainment, never energetically demanded, but forced down people's throats by the spirit of speculation and lazily swallowed by the social ennui of the dwellers in our larger cities" (GSD 4:305; published in English in PW 1:351.

German opera but had also brought down the German theater in its wake, he expected his works to resurrect both. The resurrection would take place once nature was reintroduced to the stage through and in his works. Wagner describes how, in the immediate aftermath of an unusually successful dress rehearsal just before the world premiere of *Die Meistersinger von Nürnberg* in 1868, he gathered together all of the staff and assistants and

> could assure them of my renewed conviction that, if the theater had indeed been ruined by the opera, it would, in any case, only be through opera that it would ever be raised again. . . . Those who in the past, when it was dubbed "opera singing," immediately felt a compulsion to fall into spasms of false pathos now by contrast find themselves encouraged to engage in a brisk and vivid dialogue with the utmost fidelity to nature. From this starting point, they attained, imperceptibly, the pathos of poignancy. To their own surprise, this had the very effect they could never achieve with the most spasmodic exertions.[11]

Here, the regeneration of art emanates concentrically from Wagner's artwork of the future. At the center of that artwork stands nature: Wagner's work is purportedly a natural outgrowth of a drive toward natural expression—one that will rescue opera and theater (which had previously been abducted into artifice) thanks to its inclination toward true, natural pathos. The "brisk and vivid dialogue" of Wagner's singing actors at that dress rehearsal attains its briskness and vividness on account of its "utmost fidelity to nature."

Over time, and especially in the wake of Cosima's jealous guardianship of her deceased husband's artistic legacy, the dialogical became scripted, the briskness slowed and the vividness faded. The naturalistic terms in which Wagner's aspiration to immediacy had originally found expression came to serve as the visible guarantors of that immediacy rather than its contingent form. By recasting Wagnerian naturalism in modernist terms, the Kroll Opera challenged the canonized rhetoric of this immediacy. If in 1843, when *Der fliegende Holländer* premiered, naturalism was a radical (and, at the time, unrealizable) alternative to an entrenched and generic operatic opulence, by the time the Kroll Opera staged the work in 1929, it had in turn become the entrenched and generic norm. With Dülberg's spare, modernist allusion to "shipness" and Moje Forbach's account of Senta as a liberated, modern

11. See Richard Wagner, "Über Schauspieler und Sänger," in *GSD* 9:211–12; "Actors and Singers," in *PW* 5:210, translation modified.

woman, the Kroll *Holländer* did not violate the aspiration to transparency so much as its codified form—a naturalized naturalism.[12]

The controversy surrounding the Kroll Opera production of *Der fliegende Holländer*—like Vsevolod Meyerhold's St. Petersburg production of *Tristan und Isolde* twenty years earlier or Adolphe Appia's production of the same work at La Scala in 1923[13]—lays bare a problem for any production, a problem that might be encompassed under the ungainly rubric of the politics of staging. In this chapter, I want to explore the politics of staging in and through Wagner, asking how *Die Meistersinger von Nürnberg* as an opera text conceptualizes and renders (or, if you will, stages) the scene of performance, and how various productions (as performance texts) in turn conceptualize and render that scene. Why start with Wagner? There are a host of reasons—some general, and some quite specific. As I suggested in chapter 1, Wagner's contribution to the history of operatic mise-en-scène involves an attempt to modify and discipline its forms by narrowing their range and consolidating their means.[14] But what is more interesting is that his works not only document this attempt, they often also render its terms. That is, Wagner's works often treat within the drama the conceptual and formal problems that they seek to remedy.[15] In *Die Meistersinger,* the work takes up as a dramatic (or diegetic) problem the particular concerns of Wagnerian performance: how to render a natural music-drama, one that educes a natural aesthetic concentration from the audience by providing that audience with an utterly compelling, completely natural aesthetic expression. *Die Meistersinger,* then, offers an especially appealing forum in which to launch our exploration of the problematics of opera in performance.

The results of Wagner's aspiration toward a natural expression onstage have been lasting and contradictory, as is reflected in the early formation and vitality of two diametrically opposed camps of Wagner production. The simultaneously regressive and progressive potential that, according to Lydia Goehr, marks Wagner's thinking about formalism also characterizes the

---

12. Indeed, the available evidence suggests that transparency was very much the object of this production. See Curjel, *Experiment Krolloper,* 52, on the production's concept and realization, as well as 252–59 for a cross-section of critical responses. As Heinrich Strobel writes in a 1929 edition of *Melos,* "The Dutchman wasn't de-romanticized, it was de-operacized" (Der *Holländer* wurde nicht entromantisiert, sondern entopert). Heinrich Strobel, *Melos* 7 (1929): 84, as quoted in Curjel, *Experiment Krolloper,* 258.

13. On Meyerhold's production, see his "Tristan and Isolde," in *Meyerhold on Theatre,* trans. and ed. Edward Braun (London: Methuen, 1969). On Appia, see n. 19 below.

14. See, in this regard, Langer, *Der Regisseur,* 179–84.

15. In the *Ring,* for example, the problems that dog the compositional and dramaturgical conception of the work (e.g., a preponderance of narration) will also undo the work's tragic hero. This is an argument that I set forth in *Wagner, Lang, and the Nibelungen,* chap. 2.

disposition of Wagner's works on the stage.[16] Indeed, the battle between that regressive and progressive potential—its emergence in visible and audible form—is joined in production, and the history of Wagner stagings serves as one of its most important chronicles. *Die Meistersinger,* as opera text, sets out the terms of battle; the mise-en-scène, as performance text, takes sides in the battle it chronicles.

Wagner's works have served for more than a century as vehicles for aesthetic campaigns headed in very different directions.[17] On the one hand, we have the traditionalists, who have hopped onto what they take to be the Master's bandwagon, one invariably headed straight back to the aesthetic grounds from which the works arose. This camp has produced a long series of consciously imitative, quasi-naturalistic productions (associated, most famously, with the second wave of Bayreuth productions, boasting the strictest attention to the preservation of The Master's Original Intentions).[18] On the other hand, we have the innovators who have steered Wagner's works into uncharted territory in the hopes of exploring the works' unanticipated and often unconscious historical, ideological, sociopolitical, or aesthetic resonances. In the process, this camp usually dispenses with the aesthetics of Wagnerian naturalism that have characterized conventional Wagner productions. The Kroll Opera *Holländer* is an obvious example. This group is generally traced back to the radical scenic innovations proposed by Adolphe Appia and famously rejected out of hand by Wagner's widow, Cosima.[19]

Both camps seek justification for their positions—and to discredit the other side—by invoking the Master's example: on the one hand, his famous

16. Goehr, *Quest for Voice,* 3, 37.

17. I date the origins of the split to 1903, when Gustav Mahler hired Alfred Roller to design *Tristan* at the Vienna Hofoper. On this production, see Marc Roth, "Staging 'The Master's' Works: Wagner, Appia, and Theatrical Abuse," *Theatre Research International* 5 (1980): 138–57, esp. 149–50; Ashman, "Producing Wagner," 35; Carnegy, "Designing Wagner," 57–58. A translation of Roller's 1909 essay "Bühnenreform" appears in Sutcliffe, *Believing in Opera,* 427–31.

18. On the history of stagings at Bayreuth, see Dietrich Mack, *Der Bayreuther Inszenierungsstil, 1876–1976* (Munich: Prestel, 1976); Oswald Georg Bauer, *Richard Wagner: The Stage Designs and Productions from the Premières to the Present* (New York: Rizzoli, 1983).

19. In addition to the well-known translations of Appia's *La musique et la mise en scène* and *L'oeuvre d'art vivant* published by the University of Miami Press in the early 1960s, there is also a lesser-known, excellent English translation of Appia's 1895 pamphlet "La mise en scène du drame wagnérien": see Appia, *Staging Wagnerian Drama,* trans. with an introduction by Peter Loeffler (Basel: Birkhäuser, 1982). Cosima's rejection of Appia's ideas is detailed in a letter to Count Hermann Keyserling of 11 April 1903. See Dietrich Mack, ed., *Cosima Wagner: Das zweite Leben; Briefe und Aufzeichnungen, 1883–1930* (Munich: Piper, 1980), 629–32. For an account of Appia's relationship to Wagner, see Roth, "Staging 'The Master's' Works"; Geoffrey Skelton, *Wagner at Bayreuth: Experiment and Tradition* (London: Gollancz, 1971), esp. 129–36; Walther R. Volbach, *Adolphe Appia: Prophet of the Modern Theatre* (Middletown, Conn.: Wesleyan University Press, 1968), esp. 70–72; Collier, *From Wagner to Murnau,* 59–76.

if famously ambiguous sound-bite of aesthetic revolution, "Kinder, schafft Neues!" (Folks, create something new!), or, on the other, his many and explicit instructions for a program of absolute fidelity to his intentions.[20] Each side is characterized by a particular mode of reading.[21] The conservative tradition bears the markings of a literalist camp, one where meaning and reference are largely seen as fixed and determined.[22] The more innovative tradition, consisting of those who are committed to reading Wagner against the grain, is represented by a figuralist camp, one that is not just attentive to the malleability of language and reference, but is also intent upon exploring and ultimately staging that malleability.

The differences between the two camps are not as clear-cut as it might initially appear. Conservative productions can be inventive in their literalism, and figuralist productions can be merely willful or inscrutable in their determination to read against the grain. Here, then, we encounter the contingency of unsettledness, the multiplicity of Goehr's "'imperfect practice."[23] Our analysis of the aesthetics of reading that impel a production needs to be inflected by an assessment of the quality of that reading as either strong or weak. For the purposes of this argument, a strong reading is one that accounts for the most meaning of a given opera text. Of course, our sense of a production's success is a matter of interpretation: we have to decide—and can argue about—whether it displays intelligence, coherence, and imagination. A strong reading is surprising, illuminating previously invisible points in the text and thus asserting some distance from prevailing and predictable accounts. A weak reading fails to do so, tending instead to embrace the prevailing understanding of the work's meaning, seeking to reproduce the work's

20. As Lydia Goehr has shown, Wagner was fiercely skeptical of aesthetic exemplarity—but expected his followers to share his own exemplary skepticism. Goehr, *Quest for Voice*, 40.

21. See Klaus Zehelein, "Text und Institution: Rede in Graz," in Votteler, *Musiktheater heute,* 57–67, at 61. Zehelein distinguishes between those who read Wagner's stage directions as directives (*Anweisungen*) and those who read them as text.

22. The literalist position is most prominently articulated by Hans Pfitzner, the conservative nationalist German composer who spelled out the case for a programmatic literalism in his infamous tract *Werk und Wiedergabe,* first published in 1929, the very year of Klemperer's and Fehling's controversial production. See Pfitzner, *Gesammelte Schriften,* vol. 3, *Werk und Wiedergabe* (Augsburg: Benno Filser, 1929). See also Pfitzner, "Der Schutz des künstlerischen Schaffens" (1927), in *Reden, Schriften, Briefe* (Berlin: Luchterhand, 1955), 120–27. For a brief and enthusiastic account of Pfitzner's position as it relates to the staging of operas, see Wolfgang Osthoff, "Werk und Wiedergabe als aktuelles Problem," in *Werk und Wiedergabe: Musiktheater Exemplarisch Interpretiert,* ed. Sigrid Wiesmann (Bayreuth: Mühl'scher Universitätsverlag, 1981), 13–44. I consider the relationship between Pfitzner's aesthetic politics and the dramaturgy of his most famous work, *Palestrina,* in Levin, "Father Knows Best? Paternity and *Mise-en-Scène* in Pfitzner's *Palestrina*," *Musical Quarterly* 85, no. 1 (Spring 2001): 167–82.

23. On this point, see chapter 1, p. 12.

prevailing aesthetic identity, and often presenting itself as a nonreading, one that does not consciously venture an interpretation but instead merely seeks to present the work in its most familiar form. But there are other types of weak readings. They veer between two interpretative poles, offering either what would appear to be no interpretation or one that makes no sense. The latter can be unfamiliar and overtly provocative without being intelligent or offering any particular illumination of the opera text. (It is important to bear in mind that the opera text is not restricted to the score or the libretto, but encompasses multiple signifying systems.) Of course, there are variations to be found within and between these categories: there are weak figuralist readings and strong literalist readings. In the first case, the disruptive effect of the production might be irrelevant to the work; in the latter, the absence of immediately recognizable innovation—such as in costumes, setting, or topical reference—might be juxtaposed to an innovative interpretation on the level of character or conception. Productions that look new are not necessarily strong (in this regard, it makes sense to be wary of what Hans-Thies Lehmann aptly terms "avant-garde conformism");[24] conversely, a traditional-looking production is not necessarily reactionary. These categories apply within and outside of Wagner's work: we can describe the diegetic scene of reading with reference to them and, at the same time, fruitfully apply them to productions of the scene.[25]

The figuralist camp tends to figure Wagnerian form, while the literalist camp tends to be—is of necessity—complicit in its suppression. The reasons for this should be clear. Wagner's conception of the *Gesamtkunstwerk* involves the subordination (or, depending upon your perspective, the suppression) of the differences between signifying systems in the service of an overarching totality. Naturalism emerged as the privileged form for the expression of this consolidation onstage because it was particularly consistent with Wagner's aspiration to expressive economy, but also because it left few traces of the subordination or suppression that underlay it. A new, "natural" mode of expression tended to naturalize Wagner's intervention in operatic

24. See Hans-Thies Lehmann, *Postdramatisches Theater* (Frankfurt am Main: Verlag der Autoren, 1999), 35. Oddly, the section titled "Mainstream und Experiment" in Lehmann's book is left out of the English translation.

25. See, in this regard, Anne Ubersfeld's observation that "To 'read' a production is to perceive how the different codes have been constituted, how the producer has constructed the *tabular* system of the performance. It is the comparison of the ways in which the codes are handled that makes it possible to understand the producer's work in regard to the continuity or rupture of codes—continuity and rupture which are naturally not total: the analyst investigates the *points of rupture* which s/he has managed to pick out in his/her preceding analyses." Anne Ubersfeld, "Pedagogics of Theatre," in *Approaching Theatre*, ed. André Helbo, J. Dines Johansen, Patrice Pavis, and Anne Ubersfeld (Bloomington: Indiana University Press, 1991), 135–64, at 162.

form over and against the preponderance of artifice. In Wagnerian terms, what was natural and cogent (and German) took the place on the operatic stage of what was artificial and senseless (and French or Italian).[26] A figuralist production, on the other hand, might well attempt to *render* this taking-place, or the subordination of divergent signifying systems that it entails.[27] To use Bakhtinian terminology, we might say that a figuralist staging is produced by—and would seek to render—a sense of operatic heteroglossia (or a plurivocity of codes), while a literalist account is more conventionally monologic.[28] Put in terms employed by Goehr in her writing on the *Meistersinger,* a figuralist staging is more likely to be impelled by—and interested in exploring—the doubleness or gap that characterizes the Wagnerian project, while a literalist account would tend instead to be impelled by—and would seek to register—the singularity of the work. Thus, a figuralist production may well be marked by the determination to render the politics of Wagnerian form (this was certainly the case for the centennial *Ring* at Bayreuth that we considered in chapter 1), while a literalist production aims to reproduce the aspirations motivating that form.[29]

At this point, I want to offer a more detailed consideration of the aesthetics of reading that inform these two camps. I will then examine some of the traces of this debate in *Die Meistersinger von Nürnberg* before concluding with a brief examination of three stagings of *Die Meistersinger* that will

26. The same is true, of course, in the auditorium: in the Festspielhaus at Bayreuth, a (German) bench with unimpeded sightlines would induce absorption in the artwork of the future, replacing that absurdly comfy *Fauteuil* in the opera house that inevitably put its occupant to sleep.

27. See Samuel Weber, "Taking Place: Towards a Theater of Dislocation," in David J. Levin, *Opera through Other Eyes* (Stanford, Calif.: Stanford University Press, 1994), 107–46, esp. 110–14.

28. See Ubersfeld's argument that "the principal difficulty in analysing the sign in theatre lies in its polysemy. . . . However, perhaps we do not have to restrict ourselves to the concept of connotation when dealing with theatrical signs, because instead of the denotation-connotation opposition, we can substitute the concept of a plurality of codes that underlie a whole host of performed textual networks. This will account for the possibility of giving privileged status to a secondary network at the level of the performance, the principal network being the one implicated in the principal storyline. There remains the task of identifying the principal storyline—the task of the playwright-reader and the director. *What is interesting in and specific to theatre is precisely the possibility to grant special status to a given sign system, to play various networks off against each other and thereby cause the same text-score to produce interplays of meanings with different resolutions.*" Anne Ubersfeld, *Reading Theatre,* trans. Frank Collins, ed. and with a foreword by Paul Perron and Patrick Debbèche (Toronto: University of Toronto Press, 1999), 16, emphasis added.

29. See Erika Fischer-Lichte's observation that "the avant-garde directed its antitextual gesture not against texts in general but against a very specific conception of the text: against the idea that in texts fixed meanings are established once and for all, meanings that steer, control, and indeed legitimate further cultural productions, for example, those of performance." See Fischer-Lichte, "The Avant-Garde and the Semiotics of the Antitextual Gesture," in *Contours of the Theatrical Avant-Garde: Performance and Textuality,* ed. James Harding (Ann Arbor: University of Michigan Press, 2000), 79–95, at 90.

help to crystallize some of the distinctions between a strong and a weak reading.

In 1885, a few years after Wagner's death, the Viennese critic and music professor Eduard Hanslick described Wagner as "the world's first *Regisseur*."[30] The claim represented a rather backhanded compliment, since in the mid-1880s the term designated an office whose standing was only marginally higher than that of a used car salesman today. A *Regisseur* was somewhere between a stage director and an impresario, but also a kind of market crier, public-relations person, and agent rolled into one. And yet, history has borne out the technical component of Hanslick's claim, for Wagner, beyond his status as composer and impresario extraordinaire, let alone poet, architect, aesthetic theorist, and political agitator, was very much a stage director.[31]

Wagner's music-dramas and writings led to significant innovations in operatic stagecraft. Historically, his emergence as a theorist of innovation on the operatic stage coincides with the emergence of the modern stage director in the mid-nineteenth century.[32] A number of works on the history of directing—and especially works on operatic production practice—locate Wagner and the *Gesamtkunstwerk* at the very origins of a modern, even radical conception of operatic staging.[33] And although Wagner's works undoubtedly gave rise to innovations in staging practice, his relationship to those innovations remains unclear.

30. The quote appears in Eduard Hanslick, *Die moderne Oper*, vol. 3, *Aus dem Opernleben der Gegenwart* (Berlin: Allgemeiner Verein für deutsche Literatur, 1885), 324. For a detailed study of Wagner as stage director, see Martina Srocke, *Richard Wagner als Regisseur*, Berliner Musikwissenschaftliche Arbeiten 35 (Munich: Emil Katzbichler, 1988); for a contemporary account of Wagner's work as a stage director, see Heinrich Porges, *Die Bühnenproben zu den Bayreuther Festspielen des Jahres 1876* (Chemnitz: E. S. Schmeitzner, 1881–96), as well as the somewhat more sober account of Wagner in rehearsals offered in the diary of Richard Fricke, *1876: Richard Wagner auf der Probe* (Stuttgart: Heinz, 1983), published in English as "Bayreuth in 1876," *Wagner* 11 (1990): 93–109, 134–50; *Wagner* 12 (1991): 25–44.

31. Hanslick's claim has been reiterated by a variety of thinkers. Later on I will discuss a very similar argument proposed by Wieland Wagner in an interview that followed upon his 1963 production of the *Meistersinger* in Berlin. In his cultural history of modernity, Egon Friedell claims that "Wagner is always first and foremost a stage director." Friedell, *Kulturgeschichte der Neuzeit* (Munich: C. H. Beck, 1931), 3:370; published in English as *A Cultural History of the Modern Age: The Crisis of the European Soul From the Black Death to the World War*, trans. Charles Francis Atkinson (1933; reprint, New York: A. A. Knopf, 1954), 3:309, translation modified; citations are to the Knopf edition.

32. For a brief account of the rise of the modern theatre director, see David Bradby and David Williams, *Directors' Theatre* (London: Macmillan, 1988), 1–23. For a detailed expansion and revision of Bradby and Williams, see Ehren Fordyce, "When Directing Became a Profession: The Emergence of the Régisseur, Mise en Scène, and Metteur en Scène in Early Nineteenth-Century Paris" (Ph.D. diss., Columbia University, 2001).

33. See, e.g., Amy S. Green, *The Revisionist Stage: American Directors Reinvent the Classics* (Cambridge: Cambridge University Press, 1994), 146; Bradby and Williams, *Directors' Theatre*, 224; Spotts, *Bayreuth*, 55, 62; Peusch, *Opernregie/Regieoper*, 22.

Which brings us to questions of reading: How are we to read Wagner's innovations? What is their status? Are they best seen as fundamentally radical in spirit or ultimately conservative in execution? Are we to emulate the impetus away from an entrenched stagecraft or reproduce the precise terms of its achievements? Put somewhat differently, should we do to standard productions—including standard productions of Wagner's works—what Wagner claimed he did to them, namely, disrupt them, shake them out of dramatic and dramaturgical complacency? Or would it be preferable to do—in a more literal sense—precisely what Wagner did onstage, to fulfill to the best of our abilities the literal terms of the composer's minutely detailed dramatic will? Characteristically, Wagner left plenty of evidence to bolster both sides in this debate: on the one hand, he repeatedly stated and (arguably) enacted his determination to change standard staging practice, on the other, he erected an elaborate apparatus to codify and (arguably) enshrine the precise terms of his staging instructions.

The notion that each new production necessarily undertakes a reading is relatively recent—and controversial. Not until the last quarter of the twentieth century did a consensus emerge (first in Germany, the Netherlands, Belgium, Austria, and Switzerland, then in France and the United Kingdom, and more recently in Italy, Australia, and North America) that a work needs or deserves to be interpreted in a dramaturgical sense such that its meaning, action, and setting would be the product of—and would in turn stimulate—creative or critical engagement.[34] Characteristically, Wagner played an important role in both consolidating and challenging this position.

For most of the twentieth century, the predominant stage aesthetics of Wagner production in the United States derived from (and in turn reflected) a thoroughgoing conviction that critical reading had no place in the opera house. This attitude distinguished opera from other performing arts. Certainly, it is not unusual to conceive of a new production of a Shakespeare play

---

34. To date there has been very little systematic work done on the history of innovations on the operatic stage. Sutcliffe, *Believing in Opera*, offers an important if selective survey of innovative productions. In an essay on Verdi's influence on mise-en-scène, Wolfgang Willaschek argues that the practice of directorial interpretation first arrived on the operatic stage in Italy on 28 May 1955, the date of the premiere at La Scala of Luchino Visconti's production of *La Traviata* starring Maria Callas. See Willaschek, "Regietheater und Film: Zur Wirkungsgeschichte von Verdis Opern," in *Verdi Handbuch,* ed. Anselm Gerhard and Uwe Schweikert (Stuttgart: Metzler, 2001), 550–70, at 557. For a more comprehensive account of the history of operatic stage direction in Italy, see Gerardo Guccini, "Directing Opera," in *The History of Italian Opera*, vol. 5, *Opera on Stage*, trans. Kate Singleton (Chicago: University of Chicago Press, 2002). On the situation on the German operatic stage, see Langer *Der Regisseur.* For early developments in France, see Fordyce, "When Directing Became a Profession." For the situation in the United States, see John Dizikes, *Opera in America: A Cultural History* (New Haven, Conn.: Yale University Press, 1993), 542–44.

as an occasion for a new reading. Even in chamber music and orchestral per-formances, it is common enough to conceive of and describe the perfor-mance as a reading of a work.

According to Wieland Wagner, the resistance to innovative readings is particularly acute when it comes to his grandfather:

> Wagner's stage directions were written for the court theater of his time, for the *proscenium stage,* for the norms of acting in the late Biedermeier period and late romanticism. It's strange: when it comes to Wagner, any and all scenic innova-tions have to be constantly defended and yet, when it comes to Shakespeare, Mozart, or *Fidelio,* that is to say, when it comes to the great, canonical works of the world, the notion of innovation has long since become old hat. This is pri-marily due to the fact that Wagner wrote so many more instructions than other composers, who were much savvier in this regard or simply not so obsessed with stage production. As a composer, Wagner was always a stage director. For him, nothing mattered except the production. I am convinced that even today Wagner would write completely different stage directions.[35]

Wieland's argument is straightforward but not uncontroversial: the com-poser's account of a character, scene, or scenic action needs to be understood as radically contextual, in terms of its meaning and resonance at the time. But that meaning was unstable even then, let alone now, for reasons that are his-torical, philological, and hermeneutic. Beyond these, there are pragmatic and aesthetic grounds for asking whether Wagner's works are best served by re-producing ad infinitum the scenic solutions adduced by the composer in at-tempting to stage his own works. Wieland sensed the need for a new, critical reading of his grandfather's works, and his postwar productions (as well as the scandal that surrounded them) largely document the fruits of that labor.

Why, then, have so many opera houses been so dead set against critical reading? To a certain extent, no doubt, because reading is thought to distract from the music, or rather, from a sense of musical meaning as transcendent and antagonistic to textual meaning.[36] It is part of an age-old debate between

35. Wieland Wagner is clearly arguing from a European perspective. Opera houses in the United States have been as reluctant to accept the notion of innovation when it comes to Mozart or Beethoven as they have when it comes to Wagner; see the vehement attacks on Peter Sellars's pro-duction of the Mozart/da Ponte operas, including, e.g., Donal Henahan, "A Tale of Two Operas, or When Not to Interfere," *New York Times,* 25 October 1987, 27; David Littlejohn, "What Peter Sel-lars Did to Mozart," in *The Ultimate Art: Essays Around and About Opera* (Berkeley: University of Cal-ifornia Press, 1992), 130–55. The Wieland Wagner interview is from *Berliner Abend* (February 1963), reprinted in Bauer, *Wieland Wagner,* 133–34, at 133.

36. Here, I am echoing arguments presented at greater length in my introduction to Levin, *Opera through Other Eyes* (Stanford, Calif.: Stanford University Press, 1994), 1–18, at 2–3.

the mind and the heart, between thinking and feeling. And opera, of course, has long been thought the special province of feeling. In many opera houses, the age-old debate of *prima la musica, dopo le parole* has long since been settled in favor of the primacy of music. And it is not just music that has traditionally won out, but along with it a dramatic and representational vocabulary that is programmatically subservient to the music. The form that subservience takes has for the most part been illustrative in the most predictable—the most literal—sense: setting and acting are made to correspond to and derive from a consensus about musical meaning.

In the United States, the press has long been complicit in the process (as have been many academics), for unlike the journalistic culture in much of the rest of the world, new productions in the United States are generally reviewed by music critics who have little training in evaluating the creative possibilities of dramatic interpretation and thus tend to have little patience for dramatic experimentation.[37] It would be one thing if these critics were evaluating new compact disc releases; but insofar as a new production is staged, we would be better served by critics capable of accounting for its dramatic and dramaturgical achievements as well as its musical accomplishments. This need is most often addressed, for example, in the Western European press, where the arts pages are more extensive and the discussions of stagings typically far more nuanced than in the United States.[38] It is common for, say, the Hamburg or Amsterdam or English National Opera to present a new reading of a piece and for a host of critics to read the production's reading.

And yet there is cause for optimism. A relatively recent development has demonstrably improved the prospects for innovation on the operatic stage: the widespread introduction of supertitles in the opera house. Their use has already had a noticeable effect on the operatic experience in the United States: the terms of understanding have shifted markedly. Before the advent of supertitles, the operatic audience was separated into two camps—the haves and have-nots of plot and meaning, with the privileged few "haves" bearing some knowledge (often an intimate knowledge) of the work, while a substantial number of "have-nots" were left in the dark as to just what was

37. There are, of course, some important exceptions. In recent years, Mark Swed in the *Los Angeles Times;* Anne Midgette, Paul Griffiths, and John Rockwell in the *New York Times;* Tom Sutcliffe in the *Evening Standard;* John Allison in *Opera;* Andrew Clark in the *Financial Times;* Hugh Canning in *The Sunday Times;* and Hilary Finch in *The Times* have been among the relatively modest number of critics writing in English who have tended to offer detailed, nuanced analyses of dramatic as well as musical achievements on the operatic stage.

38. Indeed, discussions of opera stagings in the Canadian press are frequently far more detailed and nuanced than those in U.S. newspapers.

going on. For this latter group, the sense of opera as a forum for vague but nonetheless hyperbolized emotion was reinforced by the evacuation of dramatic specificity. Under such conditions, the recourse to song hardly signified except in the most obvious, formal sense of representing generalized affect. Thanks to the introduction of supertitles in the 1980s—which amounted to a forced redistribution of aesthetic wealth—audiences were faced with a democratization of the means of dramaturgical production. In the mid-1990s a major holdout, New York's Metropolitan Opera, succumbed. Now, it would seem, everybody is reading—or at least has the opportunity to read.

Initially, the results were noticeable in the auditorium; more recently, they have become noticeable onstage as well, especially in houses that had steadfastly resisted this kind of innovation. The details of the text—and thus the work—are starting to make sense; the audience, in vast numbers, is getting it. Almost every major house in North America has had to adjust its dramatic standards—or indeed, has had to *introduce* dramatic standards. Given the newfound and ready accessibility of textual meaning, the text is finally being staged; histrionics front and center, empty posturing, and formulaic gestures no longer suffice. At the very least, people have a more precise sense of the fullness of meaning behind the empty gestures. The result has been more attentive and inventive stagings, stagings that engage the audience's understanding instead of its happy ignorance. What we have, with the introduction of supertitles, is a burgeoning culture of operatic literacy.

We could put this in more explicitly Wagnerian terms. After all, the communitarian sense of understanding produced by supertitles arguably aids in producing precisely the sort of absorption that Wagner imagined—albeit with other means. How does Wagner relate to this newfound literacy? Is there a place for the literate audience in his works?

There is and there isn't. Wagner's famous zeal in disseminating his works (and his works about his works) suggests the extent of his determination to have them read and understood. But if the audience is to be literate, how would Wagner have them read? This is a more troubling question, especially given the divergent models of Wagner production outlined above. For although Wagner's works have attracted radical rereadings, the composer was profoundly wary when it came to critical readings of his own works. Indeed, his zealous commitment to documenting the precise terms of his own stagings suggests not only his well-known determination to preserve his own reading for posterity (if not for eternity), it also suggests a defensiveness surrounding the threat of alternative readings. It is a defensiveness that pervades *Die Meistersinger*.

In Wagner, a critical reading is invariably and necessarily suspicious; not just unnecessary to the work of art, it detracts from it. It seems clear that if others are going to read his works (and here we can include the audience that is now able to read those works via supertitles), Wagner would want them to read *as he reads,* because from his point of view any other form of reading is illegitimate. The act of reading is to be celebrated if and only if it serves the cause of absorption in the work of art: a communitarian reading, then, is acceptable, while an atomized reading—one that fragments the community of the audience—is not. (The trick, of course, for any critical rendering of Wagner's works is to account for this fact in the course of such a reading.) Although this hostility to critical reading recurs in Wagner's writings, it seems particularly interesting for our purposes that it is not restricted to his prose. Indeed, Wagner builds a pet peeve about reading into the culminating scene of *Die Meistersinger:* the notion that a critical reading (which is also to say, a hapless and hostile critic's attempt to read) is detrimental to the work of art, since true art and the true artist have no need of reading.

Wagner's seemingly boundless resentment of his critics is repeatedly associated with a scene of reading. For example, in "A Communication to My Friends," he draws a sharp distinction between those "true" friends to whom he addresses his essay and the no-good critics, who are not invited:

> Obviously, those [who understand the creative artist] can only be the artist's actual loving friends, unlike the critic who intentionally distances himself from [the creative artist]. When the absolute critic gazes upon the artist from his standpoint, he immediately sees absolutely nothing; for even the sole thing that he is capable of seeing—his own image in the mirror of his vanity—is, considered reasonably, nothing. . . . In fact, [the critic] has already so thoroughly practiced himself in this procedure [of mistaking his own shortcomings for those of the artwork and the artist] that he is no longer even willing to let himself be influenced by the sensual appearance [*sinnliche Erscheinung*] of the artwork, but fancies that, with his acquired professional competence, he may make do with the written or printed pages on which the poet or musician—to the extent that his technical powers permitted—had set down his aim as such. The critic projects onto the artist's aim as much of his own discontent—formed unconsciously beforehand—as he needs to find justified there. Though this position is the most untenable of all when it comes to understanding any work of art, particularly in the present, yet it is the only one which enables contemporary art-criticism to maintain its eternal paper life.[39]

39. Wagner, *GSD* 4:291; *PW* 1:273, translation modified.

Whereas Wagner's friends supposedly have a visceral, sensual experience of the work of art, the critic merely reads it.[40] In Wagner's mind, this critical-literal mode of engagement is as ridiculous as it is prevalent. In reading, the critic necessarily misreads, projecting his own inadequacies onto the work and, worse, onto the artist himself. This act of misreading is not simply an unhappy and rare occurrence in a critic's life, it is the epitome, the very foundation of that life.

We do not know whether Wagner had a specific critic in mind when he wrote these lines, and there are many candidates who might have qualified. One who readily comes to mind is Eduard Hanslick. If Wagner is, in Hanslick's eyes, the prototypical *Regisseur,* then Hanslick is, in Wagner's eyes, the prototypical critic. And Wagner's disdain for Hanslick famously took dramatic form in *Die Meistersinger.* The fact that Wagner dubbed his opera's on-stage bureaucrat Hanslich in the first two drafts of *Die Meistersinger* (he later switched the name to Beckmesser) has led a number of writers to examine the details of Wagner's biographical antipathy toward the Viennese critic.[41] But although the biographical terms seem important, one should also note the precise dramatic terms of the attack, for Hanslich/Beckmesser is depicted as attempting—and failing—to perform a reading of a truly radical, organic, and new work of art. Indeed, the opera suggests that recourse to reading is ultimately a sign of weakness and incapacity in the face of radical aesthetic innovation. Wagner dramatizes and celebrates a stark alternative to Hanslich/Beckmesser's mode of reading, namely, no reading at all.

At the conclusion of the *Meistersinger,* Beckmesser famously fails to win the song contest and, in the process, fails to win the lovely maiden Eva.[42] His heavily overdetermined failure is not just a failure of artistry and inborn talent; it is explicitly presented as a failure of reading. But why does he fail? After all, Beckmesser is not illiterate. On the contrary, he is the town clerk and as such is repeatedly referred to as "Herr Schreiber"—Mr. Writer. His sudden and selective illiteracy at the conclusion of the work suggests two things: an incapacity to read what is "new" and a profound corruption in the old literacy. If the old reading and writing (embodied by Beckmesser) involve isolation and

40. There is an interesting analogy between the two positions outlined in Wagner's account here—the critic and the friend—and Wagner's sense of the identity of the virtuoso, who shares some qualities of each. For a suggestive discussion of Wagner's conception of the virtuoso, see Susan Bernstein, "In Formel: Wagner und Liszt," *New German Critique* 69 (1996): 85–97.

41. See, e.g., Peter Gay, "For Beckmesser: Eduard Hanslick, Victim and Prophet," in *Freud, Jews and Other Germans: Masters and Victims in Modernist Culture* (New York: Oxford University Press, 1978).

42. The following discussion resumes arguments developed in greater detail in David J. Levin, "Reading Beckmesser Reading: Antisemitism and Aesthetic Practice in *Die Meistersinger von Nürnberg,*" *New German Critique* 69 (1996): 127–46.

atomization, the new reading and writing (embodied by Walther) will be none at all. It will involve instead the supplanting of both reading and writing by a kind of miraculous dramatic enactment, or *Darstellung*. *Die Meistersinger* provides us with two visions: the ascendant artist of the future as performer (Walther) and the discredited non-artist of the past as paradoxically illiterate man of culture (Beckmesser). This polarization becomes clear on the festival meadow near the conclusion of act 3.

Wagner's stage directions inform us that Beckmesser does not participate in the mass greeting of Hans Sachs—community cobbler and, more important, community hero—at the outset of act 3, scene 5, for the scribe is otherwise occupied, desperately attempting to memorize the prize song he intends to perform. Part of the problem, of course, is that Beckmesser did not compose the song himself, but snitched it from Sachs's workshop. And the song is neither Beckmesser's nor Sachs's, but rather, Sachs's transcription of Walther's luminous and visionary song, which the cobbler coaxed out of his reluctant protégé earlier that very morning. Thus, Beckmesser is trying (but will fail) to learn what Goehr aptly dubs Walther's learning song.[43] This scene of reading crystallizes his atomization in the face of the consolidation of group identity. Thus, as the elements of the newly emerging community are beginning to coalesce, Beckmesser is shown to be very much alone, which—in the aesthetic register—means he is reading with increasing desperation.[44] Beckmesser cannot read the sheet properly because he has not mastered the language or art inscribed upon it. The *proper* art and language will involve the simultaneous culmination and supplanting of reading insofar as it involves, in Sachs's words, the reconciliation of old and new, or, in Wagner's terms, the reconciliation of art and nature. To the extent that Walther's song embodies an art of pure presentation, its proper performance will result in the abandonment of reading, since the new art, like the new artist, has no place for the mediation of writing, seeking instead a presentation of nature more immediate than writing can ever capture.

43. Goehr, *Quest for Voice*, 78.
44. Here is how Wagner describes Beckmesser's actions: "Beckmesser . . . hat schon während des Einzuges, und dann fortwährend, eifrig das Blatt mit dem Gedicht herausgezogen, memoriert, genau zu lesen versucht und oft verzweiflungsvoll sich den Schweiß getrocknet" (Beckmesser . . . has already during the entrance and then continuously afterward been zealously pulling out the paper with the poem, memorizing, attempting to read it exactly, and often desperately drying his perspiration). Richard Wagner, *Die Meistersinger von Nürnberg: Texte, Materialien, Kommentare*, ed. Attila Csampai and Dietmar Holland (Reinbek: Rowohlt, 1981), 131; hereafter cited as MS Ger. Wagner, *Die Meistersinger von Nürnberg*, trans. Susan Webb (New York: Metropolitan Opera Guild, 1992), 237, translation modified; hereafter cited as MS Eng. The German text is from the full score, rather than the published version of 1862; the English version I cite is a modern, literal, facing-page translation.

The transition from reading and writing to *Darstellung* is carefully outlined in the stage directions. When Beckmesser botches the text and is hooted off the little green hill where the performance takes place (it is hard to overlook the anachronous analogy to the "grüner Hügel" that will be the Bayreuth festival house), he storms off and "loses himself among the people."[45] In the wake of his abrupt disappearing act, Sachs goes over and "calmly picks up the sheet that Beckmesser had thrown at him."[46] The text, we might say, serves as the textual remainder of Beckmesser's failure. When Walther steps forward to render the song properly, Sachs hands the text to Kothner with the words "Herr Walther von Stolzing, singt das Lied!—Ihr Meister, lest, ob's ihm geriet!" (Mister Walther von Stolzing, sing the song! You Masters, read, to see whether he has succeeded!).[47] Kothner and the Mastersingers "eagerly read along" as Walther begins his recital. Soon, Walther abandons the printed text. But rather than designating this deviation as an *Entstellung,* or distortion—which is, after all, how Beckmesser's deviation is conceived and described[48]—Wagner terms Walther's departure from the prepared text an *Entrückung,* or enrapturing (according to the score, Walther proceeds "wie entrückt" (as if enraptured). Walther is not the only one: at the very moment of his transfiguration, "läßt Kothner das Blatt, in welchem er mit andren Meistern eifrig nachzulesen begonnen, vor Ergriffenheit unwillkürlich fallen: er und die übrigen hören nur noch teilnahmsvoll zu" (Kothner is so moved that he unconsciously allows the sheet

45. *MS* Ger., 130; *MS* Eng., 233.

46. *MS* Eng., 245.

47. *MS* Ger., 135; *MS* Eng., 247.

48. See Sachs's pronouncement upon Beckmesser's failed performance: "Ich sag' euch Herrn, das Lied ist schön; nur ist's auf den ersten Blick zu ersehn, daß Freund Beckmesser es *entstellt*" [I tell you gentlemen, the song is beautiful: it's only to be gathered from the first impression, that friend Beckmesser *distorted* it]. *MS* Ger. 134, emphasis added; *MS* Eng. 245, translation modified, emphasis added. Here is how Wagner describes the performance by the Beckmesser figure (still named Hanslich) in the second prose draft (1861): "Er trägt nun die zarten und feurigen Verse Konrads *in einer durchaus entstellenden* und lächerlich wirkenden *Weise* vor, sodaß, als die Meister zuerst über *das Unzusammenhängende des Vortrags* den Kopf schütteln, das Volk, anfangs verwundert, dann aber, als Hanslich mit immer mehr Affekt singt, in zunehmende Heiterkeit übergeht, und endlich mit lautem Unwillen und schallendem Gelächter den Sänger unterbricht" (He performs Konrad's tender, passionate verses *in a ridiculously distorted style.* The Mastersingers shake their heads at *the incoherence of the performance;* the people are at first astonished, then, as Hanslich warms to his theme, their astonishment gives way to amusement, until finally they interrupt the performance, torn between pronounced indignation and shattering laughter). The three prose drafts appear in Richard Wagner, *Sämtliche Schriften und Dichtungen,* ed. H. von Wolzogen and R. Sternfeld, (Leipzig: Breitkopf & Härtel, 1911–16) 11:344–55 (draft no. 1); 11:356–78 (draft no. 2); 11:379–94 (draft no. 3), at 370, emphasis added, 390. Published in English as "The Prose Drafts of *Die Meistersinger von Nürnberg* (1)," trans. Jane Ennis, *Wagner* 8, no. 1 (January 1987): 13–22; "The Prose Drafts of *Die Meistersinger von Nürnberg* (2)," trans. Jane Ennis, *Wagner* 9, no. 3 (July 1988): 106–15, at 115, emphasis added, translation slightly modified.

to drop from his hand; he and the Mastersingers are now fully absorbed by listening).[49]

Beckmesser needed the text but could not read it; Walther can read it but does not need it: his performance (and the Mastersingers' listening) supplants reading in the transfigurative sublation of natural, inspirational enactment. Rather than simply rendering the poetry—let alone imitating it, as Beckmesser does—Walther overcomes the text by dropping it. The Mastersingers, properly entranced, do the same, if more literally, at the very moment of that overcoming, and join Walther in abandoning the text, abandoning reading. That moment marks the advent of song in league with word and gesture—a hallmark of the artwork of the future.

Why would the moment be inflected in this way? It seems that Wagner is working out a determination to disavow the dramaturgical means of production in *Die Meistersinger*. The work relies on a dramaturgy of Walther's—and more generally, the True Artist's—spontaneous inspiration (much as it is envisioned in the excerpt from *A Communication to My Friends* quoted above), and yet the song that would attest to that inspiration is fully composed, fully written out. The performed scene of inspiration is in no way the abandonment of reading (because the performer has to perform the printed notes), and yet it needs to appear as such. Carl Dahlhaus defines the problem with characteristic insight and precision:

> Wagner's fundamental aesthetic conviction, which he shared with Kant, was that art, in order to be art, must conceal itself and appear in the guise of nature. The means and expedients must not be allowed to be visible, reflection must be transformed into spontaneity, immediacy must be recreated and still be immediacy, and every trace of effort must be expunged. The paradox is that it takes technique to deny technique. But in Walther the contradictions are resolved in a utopian image: artistry is his natural lot, he improvises what can only be achieved by reflection. The recreated, second immediacy, for which Wagner worked so hard, comes to Walther first time round.[50]

49. *MS* Ger., 135; *MS* Eng., 247.

50. Carl Dahlhaus, *Richard Wagner's Music Dramas*, trans. Mary Whittall (Cambridge: Cambridge University Press, 1979), 69–70. See also Klaus Zehelein, "Über Richard Wagner," in Votteler, *Musiktheater heute*, 108–17, at 112–13. In the course of his remarks, Zehelein makes the exceedingly interesting suggestion that Wagner's programmatic determination to erase the traces of labor from his works is a law of form that Adorno could never quite grasp. This is because, in Zehelein's view, the impulse of form in Wagner is fundamentally oriented toward destruction, "wrecking everything whose particulars promised the emergence of form." For a contrary view, with particular reference to *Die Meistersinger*, see James Treadwell's claim that "Sachs is in fact the only successful plotter in all Wagner's operas. The plans he conceives (in stark contrast to Wotan, a figure to whom he's often compared) actually work out just as they were intended to. It's entirely appropriate that the

If Walther is Wagner's utopian image of the suppression of the means of production, then Beckmesser embodies its dystopic effects, namely the disavowed traces of labor that have to be eradicated. Those traces are musical as well as textual: Beckmesser reads the text of Walther's song and has to make up a tune to fit the words, then has to accompany it on his lute. All the while, the orchestra derides his effort. Walther, on the other hand, has no need of text or tune, since both were born spontaneously in the course of his act 3, scene 2 exchange with Sachs. The work does not just stage the process of utopian dissolution, it also stages a ghettoization that enables it. According to the logic of that ghettoization, the work inflects the problem of atomized, egotistical artistic production as a problem of reading, if only to fob off the practice of reading onto the bad object—as "critic" (and, arguably, as "Jew")—thus ghettoizing him as its agent.[51] The work figures its own aesthetic problematic but disavows it as foreign in—and to—the work.

Reading is a privileged medium for this polemic: the good guy/aristo-crat/artist/hero, after a crash course in composition from his mentor, has no need of reading; he simply creates. The bad guy/critic/pedant, on the other hand, is so foolish that he cannot even rely on his formal training and carefully noted composition. The botched reading spells his demise, but the fact that he would need to read in the first place marks him as a critic and thus antici-pates his undoing. In Wagner the maxim seems clear: live by the written word, die—or, at least, disappear—by the written word. Put less colloqui-ally: true art and reading are thoroughly incompatible. And yet, as Dahlhaus observes, this position is problematic: the artwork—including the artwork that would transmit the claim that reading has no place in artistic creation—must be read. In the case of Die Meistersinger, that reading can render the message—which is, as I have been suggesting, a message about reading—literally or figuratively, but it has to be read to be rendered.

Before turning to the stagings available on DVD or video, I want to issue a brief proviso. Die Meistersinger is a work that has received enor-mous amounts of critical attention, both in performance and in print.

---

opera's plot should centre on a competition and a prize. *Meistersinger* sets up the opposing camps, matches them against each other, and then makes sure the right side wins. This is precisely equiva-lent to the idea of *Erlösung*, redemption: everything turns out for the best, endings are interpreted as triumphs." Treadwell, *Interpreting Wagner*, 166.

51. There is an extensive literature devoted to the question of whether and how Beckmesser can be understood as a "Jew." See, e.g., Barry Millington, "Nuremberg Trial: Is There Anti-Semitism in *Die Meistersinger*?" *Cambridge Opera Journal* 3, no. 3 (1991): 247–60; for a heated retort, see Hans-Rudolf Viaget, "Sixtus Beckmesser: A 'Jew in the Brambles'?" *Opera Quarterly* 12, no. 1 (1995): 35–45.

There is no lack of provocative productions of the work—except, at the moment, on the commercial DVD and video market. I will focus here on two conventional-literalist productions, Wolfgang Wagner's Bayreuth Festival production of 1981, conducted by Horst Stein, and a production by the Australian Opera released in 1990, conducted by Sir Charles Mackerras and directed by Michael Hampe. (More recently, Götz Friedrich's 1993 production from the Deutsche Oper Berlin has also been released in the United States and the United Kingdom.)[52] Given the richness of the piece, it is a shame that more adventurous productions—say, Hans Neuenfels's wildly allegorical Stuttgart staging or Christof Nel's controversial Frankfurt staging—have not been taped for commercial release. There are actually a number of productions that would readily enable us to visualize the distinction between a figuralist and a literalist account, but they are not at present available on the commercial market. The productions I will consider in this chapter do, however, provide us with an important opportunity to refine those categories. For although both of them belong to the literalist camp, they enable us to distinguish between a strong and a weak literalist reading. Following my discussion of the Bayreuth and Australian productions, I will offer a brief consideration of Hans Neuenfels's controversial—and, more to the point, figuralist—Stuttgart production. (In chapters 3 and 4 we will have a chance to examine two figuralist productions in greater detail.)

Let us begin with the Australian production. Although Hampe's version of the festival meadow scene in act 3 is not particularly critical or ironic, it is inventive and amusing, offering a clear and imaginative sense of character and motivation.[53] The set and costumes are conventional: this is clearly a straight *Meistersinger*. But contained within the appearance of conventionality is a recurring and appealing streak of imagination and wit. Hampe and the baritone John Pringle take Beckmesser's performance of the prize song extremely seriously. Pringle's Beckmesser is somber and pompous, but the singer does not condescend to the character. This rather delicate ambiguity is encapsulated in the exaggerated enunciation of the end consonants in the second verse of his prize song ("Frucht," "Bleisaft," and "Wucht") and the intensity and

52. *Die Meistersinger von Nürnberg*, DVD, directed for television and video by Brian Large, produced by Kinowelt Home Entertainment GMBH, ArtHaus Musik no. 100153 (brilliant media, et al., 1995). Wolfgang Brendel (Sachs), Gösta Winbergh (Walther), Eike Wilm Schulte (Beckmesser), and Eva Johansson (Eva); Rafael Frühbeck de Burgos, conductor; orchestra and chorus of the Deutsche Oper Berlin; Peter Sykora, set design; Peter Sykora and Kirsten Dephoff, costume design.

53. *Die Meistersinger von Nürnberg*, DVD, distributed and produced by Home Vision, licensed by Reiner Moritz Associates (Australian Opera, 1990). Donald McIntyre (Sachs), John Pringle (Beckmesser), and Helena Doese (Eva); Sir Charles Mackerras, conductor.

fervor of his performance on the lute. In both cases, the will to artistry is in stark contrast to the actual effect, suggesting that Beckmesser thinks quite highly of his song at the outset.[54] This rift between intended and actual effect crystallizes Beckmesser's relationship to the text: before his song, he enjoys a final moment of cramming behind the backs of the assembled apprentices who seek to silence the crowd; from then on, he no longer needs the song text except when it becomes clear that something has gone seriously wrong. It is only after the first full verse and the crowd's (and the orchestra's) initial rumblings of derision that his demeanor shifts markedly from solemnity to acute concern, which in turn leads him to seek recourse in the text again. At that point he pins the text precariously between the lute and his chest, seeking to read it and perform it simultaneously.

Hampe's account of the scene is characterized by a noteworthy economy in which seemingly unrelated and even irrelevant actions are tied together. For example, the aggression of Beckmesser's demand that the performance stage be stabilized, at the outset of the sequence, comes back to haunt him later, during the course of his prize song, when he inadvertently drops the sheet from which he is furtively attempting to read. At that moment, the crew foreman, whom Beckmesser had abused earlier, prevents any of his charges from coming to Beckmesser's aid. Here, then, we have a restrained but playful account of the scene of reading. The scene of reading is itself a reading, for Hampe needs to make sense of the stage direction, otherwise unexplained in Wagner's text, according to which, before the third verse of his song, Beckmesser seeks to read the page but cannot. Wagner's stage directions state: "Er wackelt wieder sehr: sucht im Blatt zu lesen, vermag es nicht; ihm schwindelt, Angstschweiß bricht aus" (Beckmesser wobbles a great deal again; seeks to read the page, isn't able to; feels faint; anxious perspiration breaks out).[55] In this case, Hampe has read "wobbles a great deal again" in conjunction with "breaks out in sweat" to mean "reaches for his hanky"—which causes him to drop the page. This, in turn, explains why Beckmesser cannot read the text (see figure 9).

Wolfgang Wagner's Bayreuth production is at once more and less faithful to Wagner's stage directions, for although it follows them with dogged regularity (despite some gross exceptions), it does so with little apparent intelligence or imagination.[56]

54. Beckmesser's vain and deluded scene of musical performance recalls Mime's vain and deluded determination to control language in his exchange with Siegfried in act 2, scene 3 of *Siegfried*.

55. *MS Ger.*, 133; *MS Eng.*, 241.

56. *Die Meistersinger von Nürnberg*, DVD, video directed by Brian Large, marketed by Polygram Video, 070 513-3 (Munich: Unitel, 1984). Bernd Weikl (Sachs), Hermann Prey (Beckmesser), and Mari Anne Häggander (Eva); Horst Stein, conductor.

Figure 9 Staging no. 1: Beckmesser studies the text, Australia. In Michael Hampe's 1990 production of *Die Meistersinger von Nürnberg* at the Australian Opera, Beckmesser (John Pringle) desperately consults the text of the prize song in the course of his failed performance.

Here, then, we have less a reading than a weak enactment. Part of the reason for this is undoubtedly historical. There is a kind of manic aura of apolitical lightheartedness that suffuses the Bayreuth production, a kind of will to fun. This is perhaps best understood as a form of sustained abreaction. In Bayreuth in the late 1980s, Sachs's final harangue about the threat of foreign forces arrayed against German art comes to represent an instance of personal but not political ferocity. Some sixty years earlier, that harangue would have—and in some famous instances, did—come off as more transparently applicable to contemporary political sentiments.[57] Hampe in Australia enjoys the privilege of an historical and geographic remove that Wolfgang Wagner—given the place and the family name—cannot claim. But Wolfgang Wagner's depoliticization of the work, his impulse toward grand resolution, is not what is most wrong.[58] Most problematic is that the production goes through the motions of adhering to the directions, but without any evident direction. Although characters largely do what the text prescribes, there

57. See Saul Friedlander, "Hitler und Wagner," in Friedländer and Jörn Rüsen, *Richard Wagner im Dritten Reich* (Munich: C. H. Beck, 2000), 165–178, at 166; Jens Malter Fischer, "Wagner-Interpretation im Dritten Reich: Musik und Szene zwischen Politisierung und Kunstanspruch," in Friedländer and Rüsen, *Wagner im Dritten Reich*, 142–164, at 145.

58. The grand resolution occurs at the conclusion of the work, when the production notoriously deviates from the stage directions, allowing for a reconciliation between Beckmesser and Sachs.

is little dramatic sense or sanction to their actions. Kothner, for instance, receives the text of Walther's song from Sachs and proceeds to read it. But instead of then dropping it "unconsciously" as a result of being "swept away," as the score indicates, he places the text under his seat—quite consciously, or so it appears. There is nothing necessarily wrong with his doing so. Wolfgang Wagner does not err by deviating from the letter of his grandfather's stage directions; he errs by doing so without evident cause or consequence. In Wagner's stage directions, the gesture is a product of a specific and elucidated dramatic moment: Kothner is moved and so he drops the page. In Wolfgang Wagner's production, Kothner's function is less dramatic than bureaucratic: he stows the page, presumably so that the properties department can easily reclaim it for the next performance. But that recourse to bureaucracy is incidental rather than intentional. It would be eminently plausible to render Kothner as a bureaucrat. That, however, is not the case here.

This moment suggests a lumbering, witless quality to the production, one that substitutes broad strokes for nuance or any evident conception of the piece. Gestures are typically melodramatic—grandiloquent and general, with singers breaking erratically into character and actions or hovering in a kind of nebulous dramatic gray zone. This kind of melodramatic acting is the very stuff of parodies in which opera is inane because it is preposterously unmotivated. More to the point, this sort of acting is the very stuff of Richard Wagner's critique of the culture of opera. And therein lies the irony: in Wolfgang Wagner's hands, *Die Meistersinger* emerges as a perfect representation of the very culture of routinized performance practice that the work is so pointedly designed to contest. This production aligns itself more with the bureaucratic relationship to art embodied by the Meistersingers than with the youthful creative impetuousness of Walther or the mature aesthetic integrity of Sachs (see figure 10).

In Wolfgang Wagner's account, onstage actions not only are predictable (and, as such, unsurprising), but appear to be largely unmotivated. We need to note that they are not—or do not appear to be—*intentionally* unmotivated, as in, say, a Robert Wilson production, where the lack of motivation is confounding and programmatic. Rather, the unthinking reproduction here of melodramatic convention leaves intact the trappings and thus the expectation of psychological realism. For example, although Beckmesser demonstratively wobbles when the stage directions suggest he wobbles and takes out the text to read when the score directs him to do so, there is no dramatic context to establish these events as necessary or logical (let alone surprising or interesting). They simply transpire. Rather than a cogent argument for character or situation (which is, after all, what one would expect from a

Figure 10 Staging no. 2: Walther (Siegfried Jerusalem) sings from the heart, enrapturing the Mastersingers and the Folk in Wolfgang Wagner's 1981 production at Bayreuth. Photo © Siegfried Lauterwasser, courtesy of UNITEL.

Figure 11 Staging no. 3: Walther mounts the Quadriga, Stuttgart. In Hans Neuenfels's 1994 production at Stuttgart, Walther (Jörn Wilsing) steps into the position of national hero. Photo © A. T. Schaefer.

literalist mise-en-scène), the production strings together more or less bombastic moments in an entirely rote fashion.

While Michael Hampe and Wolfgang Wagner offer literalist (albeit qualitatively and conceptually distinct) readings of the work, Hans Neuenfels prepared a wildly allegorical account of the work in Stuttgart in the mid-1990s. Neuenfels read the work in light of its historical and ideological sedimentation, staging the aspiration that underlies it. In the scene of Beckmesser's botched reading, Beckmesser is not reading at all. Instead, his performance is rendered as a failure on the level of reception rather than production. Beckmesser doesn't play the lute poorly or attempt to read the song foolishly, and so the force of his failure is displaced onto the onstage audience that rejects it. But the *aspiration* is different here as well (see figure 11).

As Beckmesser undertakes to perform his prize song, a small cart is unexpectedly flown down onto the stage from the flats above the proscenium. This is not just any cart, but the Quadriga that sits atop the Brandenburg Gate in Berlin. (In that sense, the cart is a replica of a replica, insofar as Gottfried Schadow's famous late-eighteenth-century Quadriga sculpture replicates a familiar classical Greek image of the horse-drawn chariot of the gods.) Originally built between 1789 and 1791, the Quadriga is an infamous and contested icon gracing one of the most historically overdetermined points in the city. As is well known, the gates have served as an architecturo-political fetish en-compassing an extraordinary range of German national aspirations from the reign of Friedrich Wilhelm II through the Weimar Republic, to the Nazis and the division of Germany following World War II, to the scenes of mass jubilation acted out upon the gates—and within that cart—during the heady days of German reunification in late 1989. In lieu of stepping onto the small "green hill," Neuenfels has Beckmesser step into the little chariot in order to perform his song. In doing so, Beckmesser could be said to step into history, into a cart that might (but won't) carry him and his love away, but also a cart that materializes the attempt to invent a German national tradition.[59] In Wagner's conception, Beckmesser has no place in that invented tradition—and thus, in the Stuttgart production, he is unmasked as an impostor and expelled.

Neuenfels stages Beckmesser's song as an occasion, a laughable attempt to assume the position normally held by the figure of Victory drawing the horses. We might describe that empty position as a placeholder for the national hero—a role that has historically accrued to the figure of Walther in the reception of Wagner's work. And of course, in the following scene, Walther will step out of the crowd and into the cart and be properly crowned victorious. In this way, Neuenfels reads the subsequent ideological and historical trajectory of the work into its diegesis. And of course Beckmesser fails: his song, like the cart, barely gets off the ground. The allegorical read-ing of the work displaces the scene of reading within it: Beckmesser's crisis is not one of reading, but of being read—he is not what the people had in mind.

In order for Neuenfels to stage the work thus, he apparently disregards the scene of reading. (In doing so, he arguably "does a Walther"—allowing inspi-ration to guide his creative abandonment of the text. More likely, he staged the scene in light of its dramaturgical function.) But I need to reiterate: the mere fact of disregarding the explicit terms of the text does not, in and of itself, either qualify or disqualify the reading. Nor, of course, does it consti-tute a strong or weak reading per se. As I have suggested, Neuenfels reads a different text: rather than submitting to the explicit terms of the work's in-tended appearance, he expands the horizon of textuality to incorporate the work's dramaturgical aspirations as well as its historical appropriation and dissemination. In doing so, he does not merely stage the work's historical

59. See Goehr, *Quest for Voice*, 52, who is extending an argument famously introduced by Eric Hobsbawm in the introduction to *The Invention of Tradition*, ed. Hobsbawm and T. Ranger (Cam-bridge: Cambridge University Press, 1983), 1–14.

fate, but rather accounts for its overdetermined aspirations, aspirations that undoubtedly contributed to that fate.

Hampe's job is much easier (at least conceptually) and involves much less risk. He stages the work in a familiar fashion—and with a modicum of invention. There is undoubtedly something worthwhile in the project of preparing an imaginative rendering of the work as it was presumably conceived: it provides us with a functional reproduction. But given the preponderance of productions that would thus reproduce the work and the resolute lack of imagination that characterizes so many of them, it seems important to ask: just how many literalist accounts of Wagner's work do we really need? It seems to me that the canon retains its vitality through attentive and imaginative readings: it is not served particularly well by either rote repetition or, for that matter, knee-jerk updating. A careful reading need neither fetishize the text nor abandon it. But we must maintain an acute sense of textual complexity and a nimble sense of textual parameters in order to maintain the vibrancy of the texts that we would cultivate.

✳   ✳   ✳

The three productions of *Die Meistersinger* discussed here present us with an appealing conjunction of the theory and practice of reading. As I have suggested, Wagner clearly inflects Walther's (final) performance as a strong reading. And indeed, it bears the hallmarks of one: as we have seen, Walther first disregards the established rules of artistic production, then acquires them, then sets them aside in order to forge ahead (musically, dramatically) on his own terms.[60] At the same time, Beckmesser's reading is explicitly presented as weak: it is clearly not the product of an individual aesthetic identity, but rather attests to the spectacular absence of such an identity; put somewhat differently, his song testifies to the parasitic nature and aesthetic failings of its (non-)creator. But this constellation in turn needs to be read.

What I am asking of a production is not that it stage the work in one way or the other, but that it arrive at an interpretation through a process of creative dramaturgical engagement. In the scene we have been considering, that would mean reading the failure of staging a reading (in Beckmesser's case) or reading the renunciation of staging a reading (in Walther's case) and accounting for the terms of that failure and renunciation. It is not enough simply to check off Wagner's stage directions as if they were a shopping list. To do so would produce a failed reading (which would amount to a failed reading of a failed reading). Such a failure (for example, in the Bayreuth production) is

60. See Goehr, *Quest for Voice*, 78.

attributable less to the character or the singer than to the mise-en-scène. And until we develop a vocabulary with which to evaluate the interpretive achievements of a mise-en-scène, we risk an ongoing critical dysfunction, the terms of which extend beyond interpretive literacy. What is at stake is our capacity to recognize and account for the creative and interpretive achievements of opera in performance.

3

FIDELITY IN TRANSLATION

Mozart and Da Ponte's *Le nozze di Figaro*

At the outset of an amusing essay entitled "Taking Fidelity Philosophically," Barbara Johnson suggests that

> while the value of the notion of fidelity is at an all-time high in the audiovisual media, its stocks are considerably lower in the domains of marital mores and theories of translation. It almost seems as though the stereo, the Betamax, and the xerox have taken over the duty of faithfulness in reproduction, leaving the texts and the sexes with nothing to do but disseminate.[1]

If reference to the Betamax does not date Johnson's claim, the suggestion that texts have been left to disseminate freely surely does. Far from being outmoded, the imperative of fidelity remains very much a thing of the present. And yet, the ongoing vitality of a discourse of fidelity should not be mistaken for a consensus regarding its terms. The fidelity debate—what fidelity is, what it entails, how we recognize it, and how we sanction its violation— erupted with particular fervor, and at times fury, in the American academy in the mid-1980s. It also emerged—at about the same time, with much the same intensity and many of the same terms—on the stages of a number of North American opera houses. In this chapter, I would like to examine a production that lent focus and vitriol to that debate in the United States: Peter Sellars's 1988 staging of Mozart's *opera buffa* of 1786, *Le nozze di Figaro*.

During the 1980s Sellars set out to explore the contemporary resonances of a number of canonical eighteenth-century operas that he and his

---

1. See Barbara Johnson, "Taking Fidelity Philosophically," in *Difference in Translation,* ed. Joseph F. Graham (Ithaca, N.Y.: Cornell University Press, 1985), 142–48.

Figures 12–14 Sellars stages Mozart. During the 1980s, Peter Sellars and designer Adrianne Lobel set each of the Mozart–Da Ponte operas in contemporary New York: *Così fan tutte* in a diner (*top*), *Don Giovanni* in a South Bronx slum (*bottom*), and *Le nozze di Figaro* in the Trump Tower (next page *top*).

Figures 12–14 (*continued*)

collaborators (including an ensemble of youthful, energetic, and largely undiscovered singers) inflected as resolutely, flamboyantly topical.[2] Sellars's longtime designer Adrianne Lobel set each of the three operas that Mozart composed to libretti by Lorenzo Da Ponte in quintessentially American sites: *Così fan tutte* was set at a New York diner, *Don Giovanni* in the South Bronx, and *Figaro* in Trump Towers (see figures 12–14). The Mozart productions elicited a great deal of attention and controversy: they represented one of the earliest and most visible statements of postmodern operatic production in the United States. According to Tom Sutcliffe,

> in Sellars' theory, opera unites Stanislavsky's notion of psychological realism and Meyerhold's concept of abstract design—the latter described by Sellars as a "choreographic bio-mechanical approach to art through action." With emotional truth and freedom of expressive gesture as the twin poles of 20th-century art, Sellars holds it as crucial that opera should combine Brechtian alienation with a deeply emotional (and music-induced) identification with the characters' human feelings.[3]

2. For detailed discussions of Sellars's work in opera, see Marcia J. Citron, "A Matter of Time and Place: Peter Sellars and Media Culture," in *Opera on Screen* (New Haven: Yale University Press, 2000); Sutcliffe, *Believing in Opera*, 195–226.

3. Sutcliffe, *Believing in Opera*, 200.

Not surprisingly, Sellars's work in opera—but certainly not just in opera—
has produced a cottage-industry of criticism: Andrew Porter (writing in the
New Yorker) loved the Mozart, David Littlejohn (writing in the *Guardian*)
loathed it, and Edward Said (writing in the *Nation*) wasn't exactly sure.[4] In this
case, the revolution was televised: all three of the Mozart–Da Ponte productions were taped by the Austrian television network ORF and broadcast
repeatedly on European and American television in the early 1990s.[5]

The three Mozart–Da Ponte productions intersect in interesting ways
with textual theory that was circulating in the academy at the same time. And
although I do not want to claim that all things ultimately return to or spring
from the academy, it is noteworthy that in the mid-1980s, when Sellars was
preparing the Mozart productions, a host of literary scholars—including
Paul de Man, Jacques Derrida, and Barbara Johnson—were ruminating about
the possibilities and limitations of fidelity in translation, about what it might
mean for one text to be true to another.[6] But what would it mean to bring
translation theory to America's operatic stage, let alone broadcast it to living
rooms throughout much of the Western world?

If the translation studies of the 1980s taught us anything, it is that the
traffic in discourses is not an orderly or predictable process—indeed, it is not
restricted to the commerce *between* texts, but bears the marks of difference
within texts. Translation, then, is not merely a matter of functional expression (transporting meaning from A to B), but could alert us to the very conditions (which is also to say, the limits) of expression. As Philip Lewis puts it:

> The real possibility of translation—the translatability that emerges in the
> movement of difference as a fundamental property of languages—points to
> a risk to be assumed: that of the strong, forceful translation that values
> experimentation, tampers with usage, seeks to match the polyvalencies or
> plurivocities or expressive stresses of the original by producing its own.[7]

4. On Sellars's production, see esp. Richard Trousdell, "Peter Sellars Rehearses *Figaro*," *TDR* 35,
no. 1, issue 129 (Spring 1991): 66–89. Trousdell's essay includes excerpts of reviews by Andrew
Porter, Will Crutchfield, Mark Swed, and Edward Said, among others (see Trousdell, *Sellars*,
68–69). For a sustained denunciation of the Mozart productions, see Littlejohn, "What Peter Sellars Did to Mozart." For a more recent critical consideration of Sellars's production of *Don Giovanni*,
see Wye Jamison Allanbrook, "Zerlina's 'Batti, Batti': A Case Study?" in Smart, *Siren Songs*, 62–66.

5. For a detailed account of the production history, see Citron, *Opera on Screen*, 209–10.

6. One of the nodal points for the academic discussion of textual and referential fidelity has been
Walter Benjamin, "Die Aufgabe des Übersetzers" (The Task of the Translator). See, e.g., Paul de
Man, "'Conclusions': Walter Benjamin's 'The Task of the Translator,'" in *Resistance to Theory* (Min-
neapolis: University of Minnesota Press, 1986); Jacques Derrida, "Des tours de Babel," trans. Joseph
Graham, in Graham, *Difference in Translation*, 165–207, 209–48.

7. Philip Lewis, "The Measure of Translation Effects," in Graham, *Difference in Translation*,
31–62, at 41.

Perhaps we can translate this polemical and idiosyncratic conception of fidelity in translation from the realm of poetics to that of performance? Indeed, I propose to read the Sellars production of *Figaro* as just such an experiment in translation.

*   *   *

As a number of theorists—including Loren Kruger, Patrice Pavis, and Romy Heylen—have pointed out, theater is an undertheorized arena for translation studies.[8] When translation theorists consider works onstage, they tend to focus upon the translation of texts from one language and culture into another: Schiller in English, Shakespeare in German. And indeed, there is an extensive literature on the many translations of Mozart and Da Ponte's opera.[9] But when Kruger, Pavis, and Heylen consider theater in translation, they have something less immediately obvious in mind, namely mise-en-scène as translation. Here is how Pavis puts it, in a seminal essay entitled "Toward Specifying Theatre Translation":

> In order to conceptualize the act of theatre translation, we must consult the literary translator as well as the director and actor; we must incorporate their contribution and integrate the act of translation into the much broader "translation" that is the mise-en-scène of a dramatic text. In order to outline some problems peculiar to translation for the stage and the mise-en-scène, we need to take account of two factors: (1) in theater, the translation reaches the audience by way of the actors' bodies; [and] (2) we cannot simply translate a linguistic text into another; rather we confront and communicate

8. See Patrice Pavis, "Toward Specifying Theatre Translation," trans. Loren Kruger, in *Theatre at the Crossroads of Culture* (London: Routledge, 1992), 136–59; Loren Kruger, "Translating (for) the Theatre: The Appropriation, Mise en Scène and Reception of Theatre Texts" (Ph.D. diss., Cornell University, 1986); Romy Heylen, "Theatre as Translation/Translation as Theatre: Shakespeare's *Hamlet* by the *Théâtre du Miroir*," in *Translation, Poetics, and the Stage: Six French Hamlets* (New York: Routledge, 1993); Horst Turk, "Soziale und theatralische Konventionen als Problem des Dramas und der Übersetzung," in *Soziale und theatralische Konventionen als Problem der Dramenübersetzung*, ed. Erika Fischer-Lichte, Fritz Paul, Brigitte Schultze, and Horst Turk (Tübingen: Gunter Narr, 1988), 9–53.

9. See, e.g., R. St. Hoffmann, "Glossen zur Frage der *Figaro*-Übersetzung," *Die Musik* 18 (1926): 355–61; Siegfried Anheißer, "Die Frage der Figaro-Übersetzung," *Die Musik* 24 (1932): 30–35; Sherwood Dudley, "Les premières versions françaises du *Marriage de Figaro* de Mozart," *Revue de musicologie* 69, no. 1 (1983): 55–63; Adolf von Knigge, "Dramaturgisches blatt zum *Figaro*," *Acta Mozartiana* 35, no. 3 (1988): 49–52; Harald Goertz, "Zum Text-Dilemma: Original—Übersetzung—Obertitel [sic] für Da Ponte?," in *Das Phänomen Mozart im 20. Jahrhundert: Wirkung, Verarbeitung und Vermarktung in Literatur, bildender Kunst und den Medien*, ed. Peter Csobadi, Wort und Musik: Salzburger Akademische Beiträge 20 (Salzburg: Ursula Müller-Speiser, 1991), 223–39. Jürgen von Stackelberg has asked whether Da Ponte's libretto would not be best understood as a translation of Beaumarchais's play. See von Stackelberg, "Cherubino d'amore: Von Beaumarchais zu Da Ponte," *Arcadia* 25, no. 2 (1990): 137–43, at 137.

heterogeneous cultures and situations of enunciation that are separated in space and time.[10]

The Sellars production of *Figaro* renders this confrontation of "heterogeneous cultures" in a straightforward—and surprising—way: out of a radical (and carefully cultivated) sense of temporal and aesthetic separation, the production proposes a fundamental similarity. The performance text suggests a political and social equivalence between the culture of the eighteenth-century feudal court depicted in Mozart and Da Ponte's opera text and the culture of late-1980s New York City. It is, I suspect, an equivalence borne of a sense of the contemporaneity of the opera text (and Beaumarchais's play text before it). As Marcia Citron puts it: "Sellars has explained the rationale for his modernized productions numerous times. The basic idea is that because we cannot recoup the reactions of eighteenth-century audiences to the shock value and avant-garde aspects of these works, we have to recast them in the 'image language' of today." [11] At the same time, the performance text reinflects this sociopolitical equivalence as *aesthetically* heterogeneous: while the singers' costumes are pronouncedly "up to date," their voices nonetheless intone Mozart and Da Ponte's eighteenth-century words and music. This is by no means self-evident. There have been numerous examples of "updatings"—Elton John and Tim Rice's *Aida* is one familiar example—where the contemporaneity is located in the music, and by extension in the voices, and not in the costumes. In the Sellars production, the opera text is—which is to say, the words and music are—assiduously anachronistic: the music director, Craig Smith, famously chose to perform an uncut version of the score. The heterogeneity of the production text is a product of its twin, conflicting projects—juxtaposing as it aligns eighteenth-century opera and contemporary social relations.

From the very outset of *Le nozze di Figaro*, fidelity is in question: for the opera text, on a thematic level; for the performance text, on a formal level. In terms of the opera text, our introduction to the piece's dramatic world is also an introduction to the count's extramarital ambitions. And recalling that the production was first staged in the 1980s, I assume that we can, without too much effort, imagine the extent to which the performance text immediately presented itself as a radically unconventional—even transgressive—account of that dramatic world. In the Sellars production, dramaturgical fidelity is clearly distinct from—even at odds with—a fidelity to conventional representational forms. Translation theory can help us to draw the distinction.

10. Pavis, "Theater Translation," 136.
11. Citron, *Opera on Screen*, 215.

As I have already suggested, the affinity between mise-en-scène and translation has been inflected in a variety of ways. The French director Antoine Vitez sees the link in a shared impossibility or necessary contingency. According to Vitez, "One can stage plays without end, just as one can translate without end. And it is exactly because it is impossible to translate that I maintain: the production of a play is a translation. One cannot, but one has to try." [12] But wherein lies this impossibility? For Vitez, it derives from an inevitable insufficiency. From his standpoint, a stage production, like a translation, is never conclusive; it always invites—and even deserves—improvement.

Of course, there are other models. According to Jacques Lassalle, both translation and performance "fill in the gaps in the source text: in every text of the past there are points of obscurity that refer to a lost reality. Sometimes only the activity of theater can help fill the gaps." [13] Lassalle's point alerts us to one of the most pressing questions raised by the Sellars production: not just *how* temporal and conceptual gaps are filled in the process of translation, but *whether* they ought to be filled in the first place. What, we need to ask, does the Sellars production do? Does it produce a chasm or a bridge between contemporary conditions and Mozart and Da Ponte's eighteenth-century work? [14] Does it underscore difference or erase it?

Translation is an especially productive metaphor with which to address these questions. After all, translation is a tool with which to negotiate difference, be it linguistic, cultural, or indeed, historical. But that negotiation takes different and at times contradictory forms. According to one school of thought, translation generally aims to *erase* difference by transporting a text from a source language to a target language. From this point of view, the most successful translation is one in which the temporal and referential gaps—the fact of a translation following upon an original—are rendered invisible. To cite but one familiar example: the publication in the 1990s of *The Iliad* in a new translation by Robert Fagles was celebrated by a number of critics for having rendered the epic in unusually transparent, compelling, and "natural" language. [15] By contrast, another philosophy of translation

---

12. See Antoine Vitez, "The Duty to Translate: An Interview with Antoine Vitez," in *The Intercultural Performance Reader,* ed. Patrice Pavis (New York: Routledge, 1996), 121–30, at 126–27. A bit earlier on, Vitez makes a similar point: "It is just this which characterizes translation: the fact that it must be perpetually redone. I feel it to be an image of Art itself, of theatrical Art, which is the art of infinite variety. Everything must be played again and again, everything must be taken up and retranslated" (124).

13. Pavis, "Theater Translation," 146.

14. See Wye Jamison Allanbrook, Mary Hunter, and Gretchen Wheelock, "Staging Mozart's Women," in Smart, *Siren Songs,* 47–66, at 49.

15. Homer, *The Iliad,* trans. Robert Fagles (New York: Penguin, 1990).

seeks to *reaffirm* difference, in order to clarify, rather than repress, the distinction between source and target. Thus, to return to our example, Richmond Lattimore's translation of *The Iliad,* first published by the University of Chicago Press in the 1960s, was greeted as an attempt to render—rather than to smooth over—the thoroughgoing strangeness of Homer's epic.[16] As we will see, the Sellars production does both: in its topicality, it erases difference; in its philological rigor and its representational heterogeneity, it underscores it. But to what end? And in what sense is this contradictory impulse best understood in terms of translation? Here the German philosopher Brigitte Scheer's conception of mise-en-scène as translation is of some help:

> To the extent that it is a poietic translation, the mise-en-scène of a dramatic text can be understood as the attempt, through embodiment and articulated sensory processes [*sinnliche Prozesse*], not only to lend form to the realization of the work for the stage, but beyond that, to expand the field of that which can be meaningfully experienced [*des sinnvoll Erfahrbaren*].[17]

Poietic translation? The term designates the attempt to render an interpretive impetus—to render *underlying* rather than manifest meaning. Scheer's proposition echoes Lewis's aesthetics of translation. As a strong poietic translation, the Sellars production is arguably one that, to quote Lewis's formulation, "values experimentation, tampers with usage, seeks to match the polyvalencies or plurivocities or expressive stresses of the original by producing its own."[18]

✳   ✳   ✳

Before turning to the production, I want to offer a brief overview of Sellars's career prior to his work on Mozart and Da Ponte's piece. Born in 1957, Sellars was already directing at the American Repertory Theater (ART) in Cambridge, Massachusetts, in 1980. His first opera production came at ART in 1981–82, when he directed Handel's *Orlando* (derived from Ariosto's *Orlando furioso*), setting it at Cape Canaveral. (Get it? Orlando/Cape Canaveral?) In 1983 Sellars was appointed director of the Boston Shakespeare Company; a year later, he was named director of the newly created and short-lived American National Theater Company at the Kennedy Center in Washington, D.C.

---

16. Homer, *The Iliad,* trans. Richmond Lattimore (Chicago: University of Chicago Press, 1961).

17. Brigitte Scheer, "Inszenierung als Problem der Übersetzung und Aneignung," in *Ästhetik der Inszenierung,* ed. Josef Früchtl and Jörg Zimmermann (Frankfurt am Main: Suhrkamp, 2001), 91–102, at 102; my translation.

18. See also Nattiez, "'Fidelity' to Wagner," 77–80.

Following the success of his 1985 production of Handel's *Giulio Cesare* at the Summerfare Festival at Purchase, New York (the production was set at the Cairo Hilton and featured overt references to contemporary American foreign policy),[19] Sellars was invited back to the festival to produce the three Mozart–Da Ponte operas in subsequent summers: *Così fan tutte* premiered in 1986, *Don Giovanni* in 1987, and *Le nozze di Figaro* in 1988. The Sellars productions were unusual in part because their frame of reference was not just insistently pop cultural but also unabashedly American. Here, then, was a young American director staging works from the European operatic canon with frequent and transparent reference to recent American history and familiar American icons.

Not surprisingly, a number of the reviews of Sellars's productions of the three Mozart–Da Ponte operas focused on questions of fidelity, on how and whether a given production had been true to Mozart and Da Ponte in translating eighteenth-century references into contemporary terms. As we saw in the preceding chapter, this is a problem that is especially familiar in opera circles when it comes to Wagner. Essentially, we might paraphrase Nattiez and say that Sellars's production poses the question for Mozart that Chéreau's centenary *Ring* posed for Wagner, namely: in order to be faithful to Mozart, does one have to de-Mozartize him?[20] To address that question—or indeed, to dispense with it—we need to gain a clearer sense of what is at stake in the piece and in this production.

Le nozze di Figaro and the Economy of Desire

It is clear enough that *Le nozze di Figaro* celebrates the expiration of a law— the *jus primae noctis* or *droit du seigneur*—while staging the ambivalence attending its passing.[21] But if the master's (in this case, the count's) right is in the process of expiring, what takes its place? The immediate answer is: an individuated order of desire, one where sex is the product of love and not power. As Michael P. Steinberg puts it, "The opera's political and dramatic focus is the emancipation of modern subjects and the resulting equilibration of desire and stability. The modern subject is thus defined as a subject of

19. For a detailed discussion, see Sutcliffe, *Believing in Opera*, 207–11.

20. In Nattiez's formulation: "It is difficult to resist the conclusion that, in order to be faithful to Wagner, one has to de-Wagnerize him." Nattiez, "'Fidelity' to Wagner," 91.

21. On the spurious history of the *droit du seigneur*, see Alain Boureau, *The Lord's First Night: The Myth of the Droit de Cuissage*, trans. L. Cochrane (Chicago: University of Chicago Press, 1998). See also Michael P. Steinberg's discussion of Boureau's claim; Steinberg, "Staging Subjectivity," in *Listening to Reason: Culture, Subjectivity, and Nineteenth-Century Music* (Princeton, N.J.: Princeton University Press, 2004), 40.

desire."[22] At the end of the opera, it would seem that order has been reestablished: the couples have been re-formed and reformed—that is, the cast appears to have been paired off to everyone's satisfaction. Scholars—and audiences—have long debated the ambivalence of this resolution. Michael Steinberg's account is worth quoting at length:

> Count Almaviva, in the finale of *Le nozze di Figaro,* abandons baroque postures and politics, including sexual politics. In his final solo utterance, to which Mozart gives the opera's final musical idea for solo voice, he seems to generate an authentic voice for the first time. Mozart gives his sincerity the benefit of the doubt, rewarding him with fermatas and with the invitation to linger on the half-step, chromatic passage from A sharp to B natural between the second and third syllables of *"perdono."* The arduous half-step passage combines a certain pained eroticism with a purposive political ardor. The moment expresses at least a flash of hope that the Count and the social system he exemplifies have made a similar "small step for man" onto new emotional and political ground. The Count's tone supplies the Countess with the unimpeachable sincerity of her forgiving response, "Più docile sono e dico di sì," as well as the vocal ensemble's brief development of her remark. Alternatively, ardent sincerity can amount to a deceptive artifice.[23]

Cultural theory has alerted us to the toll that such a resolution exacts: the order here, we might observe in tandem with Judith Butler, looks like the compulsory order of heterosexual coherence.[24] The price of order, then— not surprisingly—is repression.

But what, precisely, is repressed? We can look to the work's conclusion for some clues. It presents a flurry of domestication: Figaro and Susanna are rejoined, as are the count and the countess, as well as Bartolo and Marcellina. And what about Cherubino and Barbarina? The piece figures them among those uniting or united at the work's conclusion. And yet, right to the end of the work, Cherubino embodies a certain libidinal surplus. Thus, while the *other* characters are set to be married or reconciled in marriage— their various infidelities demonstratively (which is to say, ambivalently) forgiven or forgotten—Cherubino and Barbarina's marriage remains unscheduled when the opera comes to a close.

22. Steinberg, "Staging Subjectivity," 20.

23. Ibid., 49.

24. See Judith Butler, *Gender Trouble: Feminism and the Subversion of Identity* (New York: Routledge, 1990).

Although I agree with Christopher Heppner's observation that "there is no conclusion to the stories of Cherubino and Barbarina," I am less convinced by his explanation for this lack of conclusiveness:

> Barbarina and Cherubino are too young to be fixed into stable postures; they remain unsettled energies that join the other disturbing eddies around the Count and Countess to make this long crazy day but a magical moment in the continuing flux of human desires wise and foolish, constructive and destructive. The silence of Da Ponte/Mozart about the final disposition of the two youngest lovers reflects the continuing power of desire to destabilize and reshape relationships.[25]

Heppner's essay focuses on the myriad instances where characters (e.g., the count, Marcellina, Cherubino, Barbarina) do things in exchange for sexual or sexualized favors. Thus, for example, he suggests that Barbarina "is living her love life as if it were a trading enterprise, assuming that the accomplishment of her desires depends on her willingness to satisfy the desires of others, as she hopes her gifts will bring their appropriate reward."[26] My interest here is in a different, more abstract economy. Beyond tracking the precise exchanges of sexual favors in the work, I want to assess the *conceptual* economy that would structure and enable such exchanges. And in order to do so, I would have us attend to the figure of Cherubino. To the extent that Cherubino embodies something that would resist being tied down, we might describe that "something" as the fact or problem of the figure's peculiar embodiment itself, a kind of erratic traffic in and between gender.

The practice of performative transvestitism—of trouser roles—was, of course, common enough in late-eighteenth-century opera.[27] According to Margaret Reynolds,

> the eighteenth-century audience was one skilled in the suspension of disbelief, but quick also to perceive the wit that might lie in a disjuncture between the real and the apparent, and willing to play the game of cross-dressing

25. Christopher Heppner, "'*L'ho perduta*': Barbarina, Cherubino, and the Economics of Love in *Le nozze di Figaro*," *Opera Quarterly* 15, no. 4 (Autumn 1999): 636–59, at 657.

26. Heppner, "'*L'ho perduta*,'" 654.

27. Indeed, as Heather Hadlock points out, the convention—also known as breeches part, pants part, *Hosenrolle*, or *travesti*—lasts well into the nineteenth century. See Hadlock, "The Career of Cherubino, or the Trouser Role Grows Up," in Smart, *Siren Songs*, 67–92, at 67, 68, and 262 n. 4. For an exceedingly suggestive discussion of the cultural sedimentation that has accrued to the famous eighteenth-century castrato Farinelli (including the 1994 film *Farinelli, il castrato*), see Katherine Bergeron, "The Castrato as History," *Cambridge Opera Journal* 18, no. 2 (July 1996): 167–84.

trompe l'oeil. In Handel's day there was sexual anarchy on stage. Men (or ex-men) played the parts of heroes in high voices. Women, dressed up as men, sang heroes in high voices. Men, dressed up as women, played their consorts with high or low voices. And if you couldn't hire the singer of the sex re-quired, you settled for the voice and didn't worry.[28]

So if cross-dressing was relatively common, what makes it interesting here? Why should we care that this libidinally overcharged young man is played by a woman? According to Reynolds, Cherubino was different: "Cherubino was not one of the old-fashioned, haphazard, largely innocent travesti roles where the voice was what mattered and the body beneath was irrelevant. Far from it. This time, perhaps for the first time, this young woman dress-ing as a man dressing as a woman was explicitly about sex." [29]

And, I would add, about gender. Indeed, Cherubino's position as a liminal figure bears implications for the opera's political status.[30] The performance text alerts us to the terms of this threat—not by reminding us of opera's im-plication in a (prerevolutionary) culture of aristocracy seen to be lacking in virility, but by translating Cherubino's character into the urban and gender politics of late-twentieth-century America. And although the production does not inflect the page's unruliness as explicitly political (Cherubino is not an agitator), the combination of Cherubino's agitated libido and liminal gen-der identity is immediately recognizable as an irritant to the sexual and social order. The production lends a distinct social profile to the otherwise general-ized sense that Cherubino is forever out of line and in the way.[31] In order to see how this is so, we need to consider the conclusion of the opera—what Da Ponte and Mozart write and what Sellars stages.

28. Margaret Reynolds, "Ruggiero's Deceptions, Cherubino's Distractions," in *En Travesti: Women, Gender Subversion, Opera,* ed. P. J. Smith and Corinne E. Blackmer (New York: Columbia University Press, 1995), 132–51, at 138.

29. Reynolds, "Ruggiero's Deceptions," 140.

30. On the page *en travesti* as a liminal figure, see Hadlock, "Career of Cherubino," 68–69. Al-though such speculation takes us too far afield, I wonder whether Cherubino contributes to a dis-course of anxiety that arose in a number of urban metropolises in the course of the eighteenth cen-tury about the impact of opera on the integrity of gender identities. In the course of a detailed and extremely suggestive discussion of the situation in Britain, Suzanne Aspden points out that the pre-ponderance of transvestitism constituted one of the principal reasons eighteenth-century Italian opera was repeatedly denounced for its ostensibly nefarious effects on the social order, including es-pecially the order of gender. See Aspden, "'An Infinity of Factions': Opera in Eighteenth-Century Britain and the Undoing of Society," *Cambridge Opera Journal* 9, no. 1 (March 1997): 1–19, at 7.

31. As Reynolds puts it: "Cherubino's role . . . is an anarchic one. He crosses gender and ques-tions sex difference. He crosses class, being both aristocratic and yet at home with servants. . . . He is always appearing in the wrong places, much to the Count's discomfiture; thus he unsettles every social order." Reynolds, "Ruggiero's Deceptions," 141.

Let us begin at a transitional point in act 4, between the meditative andante echoing the countess's forgiveness and the celebratory ferocity of the finale.

At this point, the music downshifts noticeably, melodic material is suspended, the forte voices disappear, and the full orchestra is replaced by pianissimo strings. The moment does not call attention to itself as especially important: this is not, say, the commendatore's appearance in the waning moments of *Don Giovanni*, a far more drastic and dramatically significant turn announced with tremendous force and accompanied by duly ominous shifts in key and coloration. Despite its relative dramaturgical inconsequence, this transitional moment in *Figaro* allows us to pose a familiar question: how does a given mise-en-scène relate the music and relate to it?

Such a query is usually posed in the service of a by-now predictable polemic about the resolute unmusicality of contemporary stage productions and the prevailing will to violate musical dicta. Stage productions are generally expected to present the moment in a familiar form, to reproduce its reproduction. In this case, "fidelity to the work" (or what the Germans refer to as *Werktreue*) translates into fidelity to the conventions of its presentation. As the reader will have inferred by now, I am skeptical of such claims. For in the end, there is no absolute musical mimesis, no basis for the dictation presumed by such critics. What critics take to be dramatic mimesis is instead merely a consensus about presumed correspondences between musical expression and stage representation, between what and how music unfolds and how that unfolding, in turn, ought to take shape onstage.[32] The same can be said for the work's linguistic component—the spoken and sung words. Writing in the mid-1920s, the British dramatist, scholar, and stage director Harley Granville-Barker argued that the words of a play need to be understood as a system of signification, akin to a score: "To begin with, the written text is not the play's final and complete manifestation. . . . If we nowadays forget to think of the text as something in the nature of an orchestral score, it is only because the notation is so familiar."[33] Because they are embedded in an opera text, it is easier, but no less important, for us to

<hr/>

32. See, on this point, Tim Carter, "Re-Reading 'Poppea': Some Thoughts on Music and Meaning in Monteverdi's Last Opera," *Journal of the Royal Music Association* 122, no. 2 (1997): 173–204, esp. 174.

33. Harley Granville-Barker, "On Translating Plays," *Transactions of the Royal Society of Literature*, n.s. (Essays by Diverse Hands) 5 (1925): 19. As Loren Kruger puts it, commenting on Granville-Barker's claim: "This notion of the dramatic text as score, as schematic signifying structure that guides but does not completely determine the play's meaning in performance allows us to conceive of the *mise-en-scène* or *performance text* as one concretization of that structure." Kruger, "Translating (for) the Theatre," 16.

Musical Example 2 A momentary stasis before the finale. The penultimate andante ends in a conclusive cadence, but the key change that will introduce the finale is still three measures away. In the intervening three bars, all voices remain silent, and the full orchestra is replaced by lilting pianissimo strings.

Musical Example 2 (continued)

recognize the words and music as "scored." In the case of canonical works, both systems (the musical score and the words) have been subject to a consensus of meaning and form, which has in turn expressed itself in a consensus about how these works are to be presented and understood. (In chapter 6, I will consider a noncanonical work, one for which no such consensus exists: Alexander Zemlinsky's *Der König Kandaules*.) For much of the past century, modernist stage practices have been contesting that consensus. Despite the mixed results, some of which I sought to examine in the preceding chapter, modernist stagings have alerted us to the necessary contingency of the relationship between music and mise-en-scène and have pointed to a multiplicity of possible relations between musical and dramatic discourse—from conventional correspondence to dialectical difference to (un-)conventional defiance. In the wake of the scenic innovations of the past century, I can see no grounds for an imperative to match music to conventional gestures beyond our interest in the historicity of that consensus. We may well have an interest in reconstructing the performance practices of a particular era, such as the French seventeenth-century court opera, in order to observe the historically particular codification of such a consensus. But beyond its historical particularity, and despite the historical record (where it has often absolutely controlling), such a consensus does not compel reproduction, nor should it constrict modes of mise-en-scène.[34]

In the absence of such a mimetic imperative, how can we think through the relationship between musical and dramatic expression in mise-en-scène? More specifically, if the transitional music in *Figaro* does not necessarily signify anything concrete, if there is no necessary dramatic gesture to signify it, how can we judge? To begin with, we might shift the terms of analysis, from a language of presumed correspondences to one of proposed relations. Thus, rather than asking whether the stage action corresponds to the music, we might ask what kind of relation it poses to the music.

But in order to address that question, we need to have a clearer sense of what the music does. According to Wye Jamison Allanbrook,

---

34. The French group Les Arts Florissants is of particular interest in this regard, since it has undertaken both historical reconstructions and distinctly modern reinterpretations, often by the same director. Its production of Marc-Antoine Charpentier and Thomas Corneille's *Médée*, staged by Jean-Marie Villégier in 1993–94, offered a vision of the way the work might have been produced in 1693 at the court of Louis XIV. Villégier was also responsible for preparing a wildly imaginative and keenly modern staging of Pellegrin and Rameau's *Hippolyte et Aricie*. Both productions were conducted by William Christie. For a brief introduction to the collaboration between Villégier and Christie, see Geoffrey Burgess, "(Re)presenting Rameau's *Hippolyte et Aricie*," *Cambridge Opera Journal* 10, no. 3 (November 1998): 223–24.

The spring of tension is coiled to its tightest by the three-measure lead-in to the final *Allegro assai*—a fall to the dominant of D major which is necessitated by the plagal relation of G and D (if an artificial dominant were not introduced, D major would sound too much like the dominant of G major). Whereas the broad key-area plan of the second-act finale required 244 measures of E-flat cadence to round off its long harmonic period, the last finale, because of its segmental nature, localizes tension: the coiled spring of the *alla breve* explodes into a brief, quick-tempoed march. After a dominant pedal and a touch of the tonic minor to drive the wedge deeper (and to catch the tone of the line "Questo giorno di tormenti, / Di capricci e di follia" [This day of torments, of caprice and folly], mm. 449–56), the tonic bursts triumphantly forth on the words "in contenti e in allegria / Solo amor può terminar" [only love can end in happiness and gaiety].[35]

In the Sellars production, the shift between the andantino and the allegro of the finale is registered onstage: the characters are temporarily suspended in mid-action in a moment of musical self-reflexiveness, as fleeting as the musical material that it engages.[36] Teetering on the brink of a musical and scenic resolution whose forcefulness attests to its ambivalence, the characters amassed at the front edge of the stage take a sudden, unexplained, and otherwise uncharacteristic turn toward the introspective, turning slowly, quizzically, as if asking: Where are we? What is going on?

Here, music is allowed to enter into the space of scenic articulation (usually reserved for drama) and, momentarily at least, to dominate it—but not for reasons that we would normally associate with such an intrusion. This is not a moment of musical commentary, a moment of what, in the course of the nineteenth century, audiences came to understand as the orchestra's autonomy from the expressive capacities of the voice.[37] Instead, the music

35. Wye Jamison Allanbrook, *Rhythmic Gesture in Mozart:* Le Nozze di Figaro *and* Don Giovanni (Chicago: University of Chicago Press, 1983), 193.

36. Carolyn Abbate examines a cross-section of such self-reflexivity in *Unsung Voices,* charting the shifting dramaturgical status of music in nineteenth-century opera, but not just there. In her chapter 3, "Cherubino Uncovered: Reflexivity in Operatic Narration," Abbate focuses upon the count's extraordinary act 1 narrative of having found Cherubino in hiding. As he recounts and dramatizes the tale (which took place in Barbarina's room the day before), the count once again finds Cherubino hiding (in Susanna's room, where he is telling the tale). Abbate, *Unsung Voices: Opera and Musical Narrative in the Nineteenth Century* (Princeton, N.J.: Princeton University Press, 1991), 61–118.

37. On this development, see Gary Tomlinson, *Metaphysical Song: An Essay on Opera* (Princeton, N.J.: Princeton University Press, 1999), 59. In chapter 4 of his book, Tomlinson charts the implications of this development for nineteenth-century opera and beyond.

Figure 15 The momentary stasis, staged. Sellars's staging of this pre-finale moment mirrors the momentary stasis in the music.

merely effects a harmonic and functional state of transition. Let me repeat: the passage does not draw attention to itself as noteworthy; it hardly demands to be staged. As the Sellars production suggests, it is entirely unclear what the mimetic referent here would be. Usually the moment goes unnoticed onstage, and in the Sellars production it is staged as a moment of involution, of absent reference. Indeed, one could argue that this particular passage *needs* to pass without any noticeable effect onstage, for otherwise it risks rupturing the fabric of dramatic verisimilitude. This is because, in the dramaturgy of late-eighteenth-century comic opera, a functional transition is allowed to transpire in the music, but only as long as it stays there. To stage that transition is to place before the audience the mechanics rather than the effects of operatic discourse — akin to showing rather than merely effecting a change of scene.

The Sellars production is noteworthy for rendering the moment. Here we have a demonstration of what happens when a mise-en-scène attends to and stages its component parts. But that is not the only reason I propose to attend to this scene. Although I have been insisting that the moment in *Figaro* is of no special dramatic consequence, it is certainly a signature gesture of Mozart's operatic dramaturgy to allow for moments of purely musical transition and to allow those moments to resonate within the space normally reserved for dramatic enactment. In chapter 4 we will consider a similar moment in *Die Entführung aus dem Serail*, in the course of the extended quartet, no. 16, that concludes act 2.[38] Both conclusions, of act 2 in *Die Ent-führung* and act 4 in *Figaro,* remind us that the transition from dramatic tension and complication to resolution is often astonishingly abrupt in Mozart's operas, and these productions alert us to that abruptness.[39]

But how so? As is well known, the conclusion of *Le nozze di Figaro* is a study in comic—and ironic—misrecognition. First, the count mistakes his wife for Susanna, and seeks to seduce her; then, when he happens upon Figaro seducing a woman (who turns out to be Susanna), the count mistakes her for the countess and denounces Figaro for compromising his, the count's, honor. The count's steadfast refusal to pardon anyone wilts when the countess appears on the scene: it is he, now, who must beg her forgiveness. As Dolar observes, "The count, being the one who has the power of granting mercy, must now plead for that mercy he just refused the others. A moment ago the community knelt before him; now he must fall to his knees before the countess—and also before the community that is on her side. Now the power to grant mercy lies with the countess and, consequently, also the power to heal the community, to establish its continuity."[40] The andante of the count's supplication is echoed by the remaining principals, whose professed determination to be content thus assumes a somber—and arguably ironic—musical expression.[41] As Wye Jamison Allanbrook observes,

> the Count's "Perdono" seems heartfelt and is moving, but it is hard to forget that *alle breve* caught the rhythm of his hypocrisy earlier in the opera. Furthermore, the mere fact that it must be public forces a contrast between this controlled pageant and the thorough intimacy of the B-flat pastoral

38. Wolfgang Amadeus Mozart, *Die Entführung aus dem Serail (The Abduction from the Seraglio),* singspiel in three acts, K. 384, to a libretto by Christoph Friedrich Bretzner (*Belmont und Constanze, oder Die Entführung aus dem Serail*), adapted and expanded by Gottlieb Stephanie the Younger. Premiere: Vienna, Burgtheater, July 16, 1782.

39. See Bernard Williams, "Mozart's Comedies and the Sense of an Ending," *Musical Times* 122 (July 1981): 451–54.

40. Mladen Dolar, "If Music Be the Food of Love: *Figaro,*" in Žižek and Dolar, *Opera's Second Death,* 39.

41. A number of critics would disagree with the claim that the conclusion is ironic. See, e.g., Joseph Kerman, who argues with passion and precision that "the dramatic strength of *Figaro* stems directly out of Mozart's realization of values latent in the Italian comic-opera style. This fact is clearest of all from the opera's resolution, the reconciliation between the Count and Countess before the final curtain." Kerman, *Opera as Drama* (New York: Vintage, 1956), 103. For a detailed and polemical analysis of the ironies of the act 4 conclusion, see Dietmar Holland, "'Il resto nol dico': Zur 'Sprache' der Musik und Ihrem (verdeckten) 'politischen' Gehalt in Mozarts *Nozze di Figaro,*" in *Mozart: Die Da Ponte-Opern,* ed. Heinz-Klaus Metzger and Rainer Riehn, *Musik-Konzepte* Sonderband (Munich: Edition Text + Kritik, 1991), 112–28, at 126–28.

reconciliation of Susanna and Figaro. There is little reason given to hope that Almaviva's public apology will affect his actions in private. The mad day has brought the servant couple through a crisis to establish a firmer foundation for their marriage, but the noble couple is repeating, not for the first or last time, a ritual act of apology and forgiveness.[42]

The somber mood is quickly replaced by the more raucous—but no less overdetermined—allegro assai in D major, discussed above, in which the principals announce their imminent departure for "the ball, the game," and "the party."[43] The Sellars production, however, enacts the scene's drastic shift in register and tone, presenting it as a capitulation to the imperatives of the stage (see figure 16). The principals arrange themselves in the form of a Broadway chorus line, replete with group whirls, coordinated claps, and a lean-in. The Sellars production does not just arrive at the insight that the finale has less to do with dramatic than with formal resolution, it stages that insight. In this sense, the performance text appears to contradict Jessica Waldoff and James Webster's claim that "owing both to the deep-seated nature of these conflicts [of class and sex] and to the very complexity of the action, the moments of reconciliation in *Figaro* are profoundly satisfying as dramatic resolutions." Surely the satisfaction of a dramatic resolution must be judged on the merits of its own achievement as dramatic resolution. The Sellars production arguably offers a dramatization of dramatic *irresolution*, of the jarring and unprepared nature of the resolution in *Figaro*.[44]

Like the music, the mise-en-scène of the final chorus abruptly shifts registers, lifting its characters from the realm of dramatic verisimilitude that they had been inhabiting and landing them instead in a province of pronounced theatricality. Although the mode of representation has shifted drastically—we might describe it as a shift from scene to shtick—the dramatic stakes of the scene remain intact. Thus the production clarifies that the move to shtick (even if it is understood as a utopian moment) involves

---

42. Allanbrook, *Rhythmic Gesture in Mozart,* 193. Along similar lines, Christopher Heppner observes that "a wistfulness underlies these final moments [of the work]. We intuit, after our initial delight at seeing the Count on his knees, that the Countess's victory may be over her own despair and potential bitterness rather than over the Count's selfish philandering." Heppner, *"L'ho perduta,"* 657. See also Williams, "Mozart's Comedies" 453–54; Kerman, *Opera as Drama,* 103–8.

43. As Tim Carter puts it, "The final D major chorus runs the danger of sounding trite: Mozart has gone too far to pull back." Tim Carter, *W. A. Mozart: Le nozze di Figaro,* Cambridge Opera Handbooks (New York: Cambridge University Press, 1987), 121.

44. Needless to say, the extent to which the dramatization is "satisfying" or indeed "profoundly satisfying" is ultimately a matter of taste. See Jessica Waldoff and James Webster, "Operatic Plotting in *Le nozze di Figaro,*" in *Wolfgang Amadè Mozart: Essays on His Life and His Music,* ed. Stanley Sadie (Oxford: Clarendon, 1996), 250–95, at 263.

Figure 16 Finale: a chorus line. Just as suddenly as everyone onstage stopped moving in the moment before the finale, so as the finale starts do they form a chorus line and perform coordinated Broadway-style gestures—here, a lean-in with faces out to the audience.

not a suspension of drama, but rather a shift in its representational terms. In the final moments, amid the raucousness, the principals pair off and exit the stage. And as the final accord resounds, we are afforded a fleeting glimpse of a single figure, Cherubino, left behind. What are we to make of this?

Insofar as Mozart and Da Ponte's piece makes a spectacle of the need to discipline desire, Cherubino fits in by, essentially, sticking out. If the count is the privileged object for the lesson being taught in the piece—a lesson, we should note, about fidelity—then Cherubino is its delinquent pupil, the id to the piece's superego. But how can we trace the simultaneity of this embodiment? How can we track both of its registers—as libido and as superego? I think we can do so by examining the terms of illicit desire within the piece. Thus, while *Le nozze di Figaro* itself distinguishes between sanctioned and illicit desire—Figaro's desire for Susanna finds sanction, but the count's desire for her is deemed illicit—it also poses the same distinction within the category of illicit desire itself. Cherubino serves as an overdetermined agent of this illicit desire in both its sanctioned and illicit forms.

We can identify two forms of libidinal transgression within the piece, one of which is familiar and sanctioned, the other, repressed. The sanctioned form involves the two principal couples in the piece: the servant couple of Figaro and Susanna, who are about to be wed; and the noble couple, the count and countess, whose marriage is on the rocks. To the extent that both couples are at risk, the count is at fault: he wants Susanna, who does not want him, and the countess wants him, although he no longer wants her. The count's transgressive (because extramarital) desire for Susanna is inflected as reactionary (insofar as it harks back to the now-discredited *droit du seigneur*) and irresponsible (insofar as he thus puts his own marriage at risk). The count's secret promiscuity is no secret at all in the piece: almost everyone seems to know about it. The resulting transgressions—the count's attempts to seduce Susanna and Barbarina—are sanctioned insofar as they form the core of what we might term the overtly covert expression of desire, the stuff of the comedy played out here: his actions are recognizable and recognizably transgressive. There is, of course, a series of subsidiary transgressions related to this principal one, for the count seems to be sleeping around all over town, or at least all around the court.

Cherubino is the surplus figure in this illicit economy of desire, the figure whose desire seems to circulate freely among women, from Susanna to the countess to Barbarina. But although the diegesis insistently displays the heady freedom of Cherubino's desire, the force of convention has sharply restricted our ability to interpret the nature of that freedom. That is, while Cherubino is "free" to love women, we have hardly been free in our reading of that freedom. Cherubino's "illicit" desire has tended to operate according to a strict system of authorization, what we might describe as the authorization of sexuality itself. Insofar as Cherubino is conceived of as a man, "his" illicit (because roving) desire is authorized. This young man loves all women. How risqué, and yet, how *comfortably* risqué![45] Things get somewhat less predictable if we attend to the performative nature of Cherubino's masculinity and heterosexuality. As long as the rift between Cherubino's anatomical sex and performative gender is seen as meaningless, the work's edginess comes off smoothly. But if we apply some pressure to that rift, we gain access to what we might describe as Cherubino's illicit, if also explicit, desire—a desire, that is, for women, which is, after all, what Cherubino announces in the page's famous arietta of act 1, scene 5, "Non so più":

Non so più cosa son, cosa faccio.	I no longer know what I am, or what I'm doing.
Or di foco, ora sono di ghiaccio.	First I'm like fire, then I'm like ice.
Ogni donna cangiar di colore.	Every woman makes me blush and
Ogni donna mi fa palpitar.	Every woman makes me tremble.

45. It is this reading of Cherubino that leads Søren Kierkegaard, in *Either/Or*, to describe the page as a nascent Don Giovanni. Kierkegaard, *Either/Or: A Fragment of Life*, 2 vols., trans. David F. Swenson and Lillian Marvin Swenson (Princeton, N.J.: Princeton University Press, 1944), 1:81.

Figure 17 Cherubino on defense. Cherubino (Susan Larson), clad as a modern-day sports-obsessed adolescent, re-buffs Susanna's attempts to take back the countess's ribbon. The ribbon remains suggestively wrapped around the stick, in Cherubino's zealous grasp.

Solo ai nomi d'amore di diletto,	At the very mention of love
Mi si turba, mi s'altera il petto,	My breast is troubled and excited
E a parlare mi sforza d'amore,	and when I hear of the power of love,
Un desio ch'io non posso spiegar.	I feel a desire I can't explain.[46]

The Sellars production's account of act 1, scene 5, is especially instructive. Cherubino (Susan Larson) enters noisily, wearing jeans, sneakers, a red baseball cap, and a Marcel Dionne New York Rangers jersey. After dumping an equipment bag and hockey gear near the doorway to Susanna and Figaro's room, the page heads to the fridge for a long swig of milk straight from the carton.

From the outset, then, this production inflects Cherubino with an adolescent swagger—at once insistent and oblivious. When Susanna (Jeanne Ommerlé) reaches over to retrieve the countess's ribbon from Cherubino (who has just grabbed it out of her hand), the page wields a hockey stick in self-defense (see figure 17). The most memorable, even notorious, instance

46. I have slightly modified the English translation in *Le nozze di Figaro* (libretto) in *Mozart's Librettos,* trans. Robert Pack and Marjorie Lelash (Cleveland, Ohio: World, 1961), 89–211, at 110–11; for another English version, see *Le nozze di Figaro* (libretto), in *The Metropolitan Opera Book of Mozart Operas,* exec. ed. Paul Gruber, trans. Judyth Schaubhut Smith (New York: Metropolitan Opera Guild, 1991), 159–285, at 183.

of this adolescent oblivion is when Cherubino's groin joins the cellos in enacting the musical pulse during the course of "Non so più." With this gesture, Sellars physicalizes the hyperbolized confusion and oblivion registered in the page's aria: this is libido on autopilot.

Traditionally, Cherubino's bald exposition of desire in "Non so più" has been understood (or, rather, it has been made understandable) as a marvelous evocation of male heterosexual desire. The corporeal signifier is thus overlooked in deference to a linguistic signified. And yet, the corporeal is very much at the center of Cherubino's character, just as the interplay between the corporeal and the textual is very much at the center of Da Ponte and Mozart's opera text. Thus, in act 2, scene 3, and again in act 3, scene 7, Cherubino is dressed in women's clothing. Conventionally, Cherubino has been made to bear the truth of anatomical femininity on "her" sleeve, but only in order to disavow that truth as mere fiction: since the character is thus presented as a "she" in drag, she must be a "he." But as Heather Hadlock points out, neither Beaumarchais's play nor Mozart's opera, "replete with scenes of veiling, revelation, and disguise, ever allows us to relax our scrutiny of Cherubino's body; indeed, both works invite us to look at that body whenever it is present, and to imagine it when it is temporarily removed from sight."[47] The Sellars production brings the body to our attention in interesting—and, for the time, distinct and unusual—ways. In focusing on Cherubino, we not only gain insight into the stakes of fidelity in the opera text (because the page famously functions as an avatar of desire in its roving, anti-institutional forms), we also gain insight into the logic of translation that animates the production text as well (because the page's appearance and disposition encapsulate the production's theory of translation).

Reading the Sellars Production

If ever a director relied upon a dramaturgy of forceful, even programmatic translation, it is Peter Sellars. The profusion of critical invective that has frequently greeted his productions has made it difficult to determine what the productions actually do. More recent writing is more balanced and thus more productive. Wye Jamison Allanbrook published a cogent account of Sellars's staging of Zerlina's "Batti, batti" in *Don Giovanni*. Allanbrook counterbalances her critique of "Sellars' misguided attempt at social realism" with the observation that "there are many moments in Sellars' three Mozart productions that I admire—some extravagantly; it is just that his cultural

47. Hadlock, "Career of Cherubino," 70.

opportunism makes him wildly erratic, causing him in [Zerlina's] aria to go completely wrong." [48]

Presumably, the "social realism" and "cultural opportunism" that Allanbrook has in mind encompass Sellars's penchant for immediate, transparent topicality. In Allanbrook's view, what gets lost in Sellars's translation is a sense of the irony that informs and undercuts Mozart and Da Ponte's claims. Allanbrook's observation directs our attention to the compositional and representational logic of Sellars's performance texts. Could it be that the determination to translate eighteenth-century court culture into twentieth-century terms leaves absolutely no room for noncongruity, difference, or distance? Sellars, it would appear, is wildly erratic because his reach is so vast, his insistence on correspondence so totalizing. What, if anything, can resist the will to contemporaneity expressed in this production?

Given the production's reputation for scandal and campy shtick, we should be careful not to overlook its intelligence. Indeed, although few critics have seemed to notice, the production's ostentatious irreverence is implicitly juxtaposed to an equally high degree of seriousness. The countess is most obviously pathos laden, but that is not necessarily what I have in mind. My sense is that even—perhaps especially—Barbarina is serious here: she bears a kind of erratic emotional charge that surges unpredictably but not uncontrollably. This, then, is a fraught *Figaro*. The production's emotional terms are situated in a recognizable social and historical—even a technological—context: from images of Trump Towers and a surfeit of Macy's shopping bags in the overture, to a CD, a boom box, a (massive!) cell phone, and Barbarina's Batman earrings in the final act. But despite the up-to-date trappings (many of which are, by now, comically dated), there is a pathos that pervades or at least recurs, one that is, if not timeless, then at least not time bound: there is a sense that the cruelty, for example, between the count and countess is recognizable *despite* the trappings that would render it au courant. The production is emotionally fraught: the personages are erratic personalities, and the production expends a good deal of energy drawing our attention to a schizoid, at times hystericized vulnerability of character and situation in the opera text. [49] In order to clarify the terms of this vulnerability, I propose to return to the production's inflection of Cherubino, for the page's confusion is rendered in unusual and interesting ways.

48. Allanbrook, "Zerlina," 64–65.

49. There are exceptions: Antonio the gardener is simply and monotonously enraged, whereas the rest of the characters convince out of some complexity. But Antonio's emotional monochromaticism makes good sense, given the comparatively narrow range of musical expression that Mozart affords him.

If the count's desire is excessive, it is so in predictable, familiar, and, as I have argued, dramaturgically sanctioned ways. When it comes to the count's libido, Sellars evokes not merely Trump Towers, but Donald Trump. And those around the count seem to translate easily into equally familiar, if less specifically referential figures: the young and comparatively impoverished lovers; the jilted trophy wife; the sly, slick, nefarious gossip. Cherubino, however, isn't as easily placed, despite the geographic and cultural specificity of the hockey-player jersey. The kind of irresolute singularity Cherubino offers at the conclusion of this production is, I think, in part attributable to the necessary irresolution of gender that the figure embodies. Cherubino stands—or staggers—alone at the work's conclusion (and the page staggers alone *as* the work's conclusion), an embodiment of a gender that is not one.[50] As such, the work will conclude on a fitting note of irresolution, with Cherubino's ongoing circulation as a figuration and condensation of the surplus of gender and, at the same time, as a surplus in Sellars's peculiar and characteristic insistence on a dramaturgy of translation.

But how are we to make sense of this? Let us proceed with the first part of the claim—that Cherubino circulates, at the conclusion of the work, as a figuration and condensation of the surplus of gender. Traditionally, of course, Cherubino has represented a kind of kitschified, prettified, unthreatening desire, an oversexed if sexually neutral figure, an embodiment of a thoroughly packaged confusion. In the Sellars production, the packaging (in the form of that New York Ranger's jersey) is initially unfamiliar, but, more important, so are its contents. Cherubino emerges as something like a hermaphroditic figure. More to the point, he is a figure isolated in a self-contained and self-perpetuating mode of hyperbolized desire. This desire is doubly confusing in its multiplication of objects and subjects. The performance text inflects Cherubino's object choices much like the page's subject position: both are particularized *and* ungrounded, fixed *and* roving. Cherubino's desire is not necessarily or simply a cross-dressed desire, but an undecidable one—one that is arguably, oddly both male and female. Cherubino is not presented in fixed form, but appears—and works—as a boy, as a girl, as a girl playing a boy, as a boy playing a girl, and finally, but also most confoundingly, as a girl playing a girl. Each of these roles has its diegetic sanction, of course; but in this production, that sanction is in a kind of haphazard dialogue with—and certainly does not correspond to—that role playing. Cherubino is thus made to embody a fundamental instability, a kind of polyvalent sex and gender, unsteadily encompassing male and female positions of identity and desire.

50. See Luce Irigaray, "This Sex Which Is Not One," in *This Sex Which Is Not One*, trans. Catherine Porter with Carolyn Burke (Ithaca, N.Y.: Cornell University Press, 1985).

These days, the protocol by which gender identity is assumed has attained the status of a critical truism: the subject comes to bear the signifiers of masculinity or femininity via various unconscious acts of semiotic appropriation. That appropriation has been understood as a cultural performance of sorts. Having discriminated properly, the subject emerges—which is also to say, disappears—within the designated boundaries of quotidian gender performativity.[51] Bearing the proper trappings, he or she can blend into the gendered crowd. Sellars's production clearly does not bind Cherubino to this protocol. The page is a liminal figure who circulates between camps rather than heading toward or emerging from within them. Despite appearances, then, Cherubino is not engaged in a masquerade, for the logic of masquerade presupposes a fixity of reference that is temporarily suspended. Rather, the figure embodies a permanent state of semiotic suspension, one where the signifiers have lost their grounding in the body.

It is not that I cannot tell that this character is played by Susan Larson; rather, it is that I can not tell what Susan Larson is playing——which is unusual for the figure and disorienting for the viewer. Normally the terms of masquerade are perfectly clear, even if—indeed, especially when—they are not convincing: what is suspended is disbelief. When we see, say, Brigitte Fassbaender as Octavian in Strauss and Hofmannsthal's *Rosenkavalier* playing at being a boy and, eventually, playing at being a boy playing a girl, the masquerade is perfectly transparent. (Terry Castle has pointed out that this mode of masquerade produces a different modality of performative meaning and interpretive anxiety).[52] Heather Hadlock describes the problem:

> Opera is unique, perhaps, in how little visual verisimilitude it demands: we expect to look through or disregard a singer's body and instead "see" the voice. Yet trouser roles require a more elaborate scaffolding from which to suspend our disbelief, for in order to accept the character *en travesti* as *male,* we must rationalize away the evidence of both our eyes and ears. In contrast, with male travesty practice, which expects the audience to see, hear, and laugh at the discrepancy between performer and role, one can never be certain just what degree of double vision the audience is meant to bring to its scrutiny of the woman-as-pageboy. Such characters, particularly when they speak of love, often appear in shadow: the cross-dressed female body and its desires, though repeatedly characterized as harmless, are just as frequently veiled from sight.

51. See, e.g., Butler, *Gender Trouble;* Andrew Parker and Eve Kosofsky Sedgwick, eds., *Performativity and Performance* (New York: Routledge, 1995).
52. See Terry Castle, "In Praise of Brigitte Fassbaender (A Musical Emanation)," in *The Apparitional Lesbian* (New York: Columbia University Press, 1993).

The pageboy casts the audience into a figurative darkness, a clouding of the mind's eye that results from the never-explained clash between the page's visual and vocal incarnations; in some sense, the trousered soprano who plays the page is also doomed perpetually to obstruct our view of him.[53]

In a sense, of course, the Sellars production challenges this obstruction by foregrounding the terms of sartorial counterfeit. But the confounding effect of this thematization is, strangely enough, not transparency but an underlying—if nonetheless entirely visible—undecidability. The performance text translates a conventional obstruction into a visible confusion. Thus, in this production, the "play" of gender confusion is different, insofar as the undecidability, rather than being a shared conceit (where the mechanics of suspension are familiar, its operations and implications predictable) itself becomes the stuff of performance. Watching this performance text, I am no longer sure what disbelief I am suspending and what it means to suspend it. Here, then, we begin to trace out a figure who can be understood to embody not just an excess of sexual energy, but an indeterminacy of gender, a figure who circulates as a remainder, an excess that is not properly domesticated at the work's conclusion. To domesticate Cherubino would mean not just having the page coupled up—say, with Barbarina; it would also mean deciding one way or the other, and in this production, the figure remains undecidable to the very end.

If Cherubino is properly understood as embodying this excess and undecidability, how would that inform our understanding of the work or, for that matter, its performative dramaturgy in the Sellars production? Any number of critics have pointed to Cherubino's antics in the piece and, more recently, to Cherubino's sexual indeterminacy in the production.[54] But in each of these essays, the dramaturgical coherence of those antics remains rather hazy. In order to venture an alternative explanation, I would like to return, as promised, to the second part of my claim: that Cherubino's ongoing circulation at the conclusion of the work figures a surplus of translation. Cherubino's mad dash at the conclusion of the production, like the figure's tantalizing suspension in a liminal gender identity in act 3, is legible not just as an instance of Sellars's kooky inspiration or his determination to surprise and perplex, but as an implicit thematization of the process of translation that characterizes his work.

---

53. Hadlock, "Career of Cherubino," 69.

54. See Richard Dellamora, "Mozart and the Politics of Intimacy: *The Marriage of Figaro* in Toronto, Paris, and New York," in *The Work of Opera: Genre, Nationhood, and Sexual Difference*, ed. Dellamora and Daniel Fischlin (New York: Columbia University Press, 1997), 255–75, esp. 259.

Let us return briefly to the question of translation, and in particular to the intersection of translation theory with performance practice. When it comes to matters of directorial initiative, "fidelity to the composer's intention" is a familiar mantra for those who would preserve conventional staging practices. And yet, that intention is exceedingly difficult to secure.[55] For the original—at least in the eyes of many translators, like many stage directors—is not necessarily stable, its meaning not necessarily fixed. Thus, to the extent that there is an imperative of fidelity, it could be recast as a fidelity to a fundamental and underlying tension—we might call it an underlying infidelity of referentiality—that characterizes any work.

As Barbara Johnson puts it: "If the original text is already a translatory battle in which what is being translated is ultimately the very impossibility of translation, then peacemaking gestures such as scrupulous adherence to the signifier are just as unfaithful to the energy of the conflict as the tyranny of the swell-footed signified."[56] Far from accepting the notion that the letter and spirit of a text can be transplanted safely from one language to another, Johnson perceives the letter and spirit of a text to be fundamentally and originally at odds. A translator, she argues, would need to be faithful to that conflict. "It is necessary," she writes, "to be faithful to the violent love-hate relation *between* letter and spirit, which is already a problem of translation within the *original* text."[57] So what is a stage director to do?

If language is already in the process of producing an excess of signification, an unruliness that is normally repressed, recourse to translation could enable that surplus to emerge more clearly. That, I suspect, is what is going on in this performance text. In the course of a programmatic commitment to translating *Le nozze di Figaro* into the discourse of contemporary popular culture, this production ends up rendering a set of conflicts that is otherwise left merely implicit or more commonly repressed. In the case of this particular opera text, the production is on particularly solid—which is to say, unstable—ground. The dramaturgical and directorial program of rendering explicit the terms of expression and repression—a program that informs many of the productions Sellars produced during the course of the 1980s—is driving the dramaturgical and thematic concerns within the opera text. In the case of *Le nozze di Figaro,* the process of de-repression, the

55. See Nattiez, "'Fidelity' to Wagner," 80. "To say 'what Wagner [in this case: Mozart Da Ponte, Sellars . . .] meant' is never to read his intentions directly but to construct hypotheses about his intentions and his poietic universe based on traces which we can read and contextual types of information—historical, sociological, philosophical, ideological, aesthetic, musical, and so on—which we have at our disposal."

56. Johnson, "Taking Fidelity Philosophically," 147.

57. Ibid.

way that the work is made to bear the traces of its own repression, is un-usually explicit. While other operas might obliquely raise questions of the circulation of desire and the imperative of repression, here those otherwise subliminal concerns are the very stuff of the work. The Sellars production focuses upon those concerns with unprecedented vigor. We might say that the production consists, in large part, of their re-production.

The production of excess or surplus in the course of domestication—the riot amid the programmatic imposition of order—takes place in *Le nozze di Figaro* on three levels: on the level of the opera text, where the imposition of marital order does not quite encompass all of its intended subjects; on the level of the performance text, where the process of translation yields a kind of errant signification, one in which the trappings of contemporaneity have no apparent bearing upon the production and circulation of meaning; and on the level of gender, where the generalized imperative of performative coherence is suspended, circulating instead in a kind of queer state.

Although this production renders the concerns of the eighteenth-century aristocratic court in twentieth-century terms, it hardly suppresses the re-sulting disjunctions. The project of updating is narrowly drawn and, as such, overtly anachronistic. Meaning arises out of the tension between discursive registers: in the textual register, Da Ponte's colloquial eighteenth-century operatic Italian and Beaumarchais's drama are implicitly juxtaposed to the American vernacular of the subtitles;[58] in the performative register, the growing sense of irony that was accruing to the tradition of trouser roles in Mozart's day contrasts with the wholesale suppression of that irony in con-ventional operatic performance in the 1980s.[59] If, at the conclusion of the text, there is a sense of ambivalence and loss that tinges the triumphant re-turn of fidelity, there is, in this production, a scrupulous attentiveness to that ambivalence and the contradiction that it suggests. Here, then: an unsettling fidelity to the politics and aesthetics underlying the eternal return of fidelity. What better translation could we hope for?

58. The subtitles were prepared by Brooks Riley. For a review that takes particular umbrage at the tone and content of the subtitles, see Andrew Clements, "Peter Sellars as Seen on TV," *Opera* 42, no. 6 (June 1991): 641–44. See also Citron, *Opera on Screen,* 217–18, for a detailed consideration of the titles.

59. On Cherubino and translation, see von Stackelberg, "Cherubino."

DECONSTRUCTING SINGSPIEL
Mozart's *Die Entführung aus dem Serail*

In the last chapter, we considered how Peter Sellars stages the transition in act 4 of Mozart and Da Ponte's *Nozze di Figaro* from the meditative andante echoing the Countess's forgiveness to the celebratory ferocity of the finale. As promised in the course of that discussion, we will consider a similar moment in *Die Entführung aus dem Serail,* in this case a transition that occurs in the course of the extended quartet (no. 16) that concludes act 2. In the swirl of indignation and accusations between the two sets of lovers—the noble Konstanze and Belmonte, and the servants Blonde and Pedrillo—Mozart inserts a brief twelve-measure andantino in 6/8, framed by fermatas and with a four-measure musical introduction.

Unlike the transitional passage in *Le nozze di Figaro,* which follows the announced resolution, the andantino section comes at a moment of palpable tension. In the wake of Belmonte's reunion with Konstanze, Belmonte and Pedrillo have questioned Konstanze and Blonde's fidelity, and while the men are reassured by their partners' heated retorts to the accusation, the women remain outraged.[1] Here Mozart drops in the four-measure orchestral introduction of the andantino, which mollifies the rhythmic restatement of the impasse in the preceding adagio section while introducing melodic material that anticipates the impending resolution. Thomas Bauman offers a precise and cogent characterization of the entire andantino section:

> In itself a beautiful homophonic rumination in siciliano tempo, its transcendent effect derives from the place it occupies in the finale's music-dramatic

---

1. Ruth Bernard Yeazell's account of the scene is particularly apt: "No sooner do the women deny their guilt—Blonde characteristically follows up with a slap—than the lovers retract their

Musical Example 3 Another momentary stasis. Like its cousin preceding the finale to *Le nozze di Figaro*, this andantino passage from *Die Entführung aus dem Serail* constitutes a momentary stasis. Both musically and dramatically, however, here the break is more pronounced—musically, it is longer (twelve bars plus a four-bar introduction) and contains a change in meter; dramatically, it occurs not following a resolution, but rather at the height of the scene's tension.

Musical Example 3 (continued)

Musical Example 3 (*continued*)

curve. The workings of Belmonte's and Pedrillo's jealousy have brought the protagonists to a moment akin in its own modest way to the sublime crux of *Le nozze di Figaro,* when the Count kneels to beg the Countess's forgiveness. The reflections of the four in [Gottlieb] Stephanie's verses do not in themselves merit Mozart's expansive, quasi-choral vestments, but the turning point in the lovers' falling out does.[2]

While I agree with the general comparison Bauman makes here, I would modify its address. In my view, the best analog for the andantino passage in the *Entführung* is not the count's kneeling in *Figaro,* but the equivalent four-measure transitional section for unaccompanied orchestra following the countess's assent and the choral *sotto voce* acclamation that greets it. (See musical example 2.) In both of these instances, the space of drama is temporarily but palpably occupied by music: the fact of musical transition suspends the

---

suspicions with a bit of reasoning that can at best be termed perfunctory. . . . The anxieties provoked by the harem, in other words, are not so much settled as sung away." Yeazell, "Harems for Mozart and Rossini," *Raritan* 16, no. 4 (Spring 1997):86–105, at 96–97.

2. Thomas Bauman, *W.A. Mozart: Die Entführung aus dem Serail,* Cambridge Opera Handbooks (New York: Cambridge University Press, 1987), 52.

Figure 18 Another momentary stasis, staged and filmed. Neuenfels's staging of this stasis reflects the total rupture in the music: the singers stop acting and suddenly begin to dance. In the filming of this production, as evidenced by this frame, the cinematography undergoes a similar break: instead of providing a conventional frontal image, the camera pans across the actors' feet and shadows on the floor, a reflection of their dance.

drama. And although in *Figaro* Peter Sellars is unconventional in registering the (purely musical) transition within the space of drama, that moment is obviously fleeting, like the music that accompanies it.[3] Sellars suddenly shifts his—and our—focus, from an inventive account of the drama to a brief (and equally inventive) account of the incursion of music into the drama. Figure 18 presents, for the sake of comparison, an account of the andantino section of the quartet at the conclusion of act 2 of *Die Entführung aus dem Serail* as staged by Hans Neuenfels at the Stuttgart Opera in 1998.

As in the Sellars account, the segment suggests a break in dramatic continuity, but the terms of that break are more jarring: Sellars stages the suspension of drama within the terms of verisimilitude (thus, his characters seem temporarily confused), but Neuenfels stages the moment as a break in the very mode of representation. Thus, his singers suddenly, momentarily, become dancers. This is but one of the ways in which Neuenfels could be said to radicalize Sellars. And this scene in the Stuttgart production is symptomatic not merely as a local instantiation of how one might stage the incursion of music onto the stage, but of a larger project that will occupy us in this chapter.

3. In the Sellars production, we arguably—and improbably—encounter a literalization of Wagner's famous aspiration for *sichtbar gewordene Taten der Musik* (deeds of music made visible).

The Stuttgart production of *Die Entführung aus dem Serail* proposes a thoroughgoing—and thoroughly provocative—dramatization of operatic form. This sounds less promising—and less amusing—than it is. Neuenfels interrogates the constitutive elements of Mozart's singspiel and renders the interplay of those elements—singing, acting, speaking, orchestral music—as the subject, rather than merely the object, of mise-en-scène. With Neuenfels's staging, the interplay of means forms the stuff of drama. In the following, I want to examine how this is so and consider some of the implications.

The Birth of Singspiel out of the Spirit of Formal Analysis: Mozart's *Entführung* in Stuttgart

In 1998 the Stuttgart State Opera, one of Germany's most influential and daring houses, engaged Hans Neuenfels, a by now middle-aged enfant terrible of Germany's theatrical establishment, to prepare a new production of Mozart's *Entführung* (1782). The Stuttgart *Entführung,* voted Production of the Year in the annual *Opernwelt* awards, is at once astonishing and dizzying, even for a spectator familiar with Mozart's singspiel and accustomed to Neuenfels's penchant for subjecting works to relentless interpretive pressure. Some of the grounds for the spectator's disorientation are obvious: Neuenfels radically cuts much of Gottlieb Stephanie the Younger's original dialogue and adds a great deal of his own,[4] and, even more surprisingly, he doubles each of the principal roles (with the exception of Pasha Selim), splitting them into distinct roles played by a singer and an actor. Here, then, the production realizes in surplus form what the opera text otherwise constitutes as a lack: if the pasha is normally understood (and cast) as an actor lacking a singer's voice, here each of the other principals in the opera—each one, of course, a singer—is supplemented by an actor. The actors don't do all of the talking. Indeed, they only speak roughly half of the spoken text (and the distribution varies markedly from scene to scene and from role to role); the singers, on the other hand, do all of the singing. I will have more to say about these large-scale interventions in the work a bit later in this chapter. For now, I want to focus on the overall impression made by this production. What is ultimately most striking about the Stuttgart *Entführung* is not the doubling of the major roles or the surgery effected upon the libretto, but the breathtaking theatrical invention that Neuenfels educes from the work. Some of this invention can be readily traced to (what's left of) the text of the work and its dramaturgy, although it is no less surprising and exciting as a result: for example, when we first encounter Osmin in act 1, scene 2, singing the lied "Wer ein Liebchen hat

---

4. Neuenfels is accorded a credit in the playbill for adapting the text.

Figure 19 Osmin finds a sweetheart. Osmin (Roland Bracht) sings a verse of "Wer ein Liebchen hat gefunden" to a decapitated head.

gefunden" (He who has found a sweetheart), he is carefully removing and nuzzling the body parts of a woman, recently slaughtered, from an Ottoman chest (see figure 19).

This puts a gruesome twist on the literal terms of Osmin's lied, with its suggestion that "he who finds a sweetheart" should "reward her with a thousand kisses." (Indeed, Osmin's status as a kind of ill-will ambassador from what Barthes called "The World of Wrestling" is borne out by his recurring and generalized fantasy—expressed in aria form—of decapitation, hanging, skewering, burning, binding, drowning, and skinning.)[5] From the

5. See Osmin's aria: "Erst geköpft, dann gehangen / dann gespießt auf heiße Stangen, / dann verbrannt, dann gebunden / und getaucht, zuletzt geschunden" (First beheaded, then hanged, then spitted on hot skewers, then burned, then bound, and drowned, and finally skinned). The text is taken from *Wolfgang Amadeus Mozart: Die Entführung aus dem Serail; Texte, Materialien, Kommentare,* ed. Attila Csampai and Dietmar Holland, Rororo Opernbücher (Reinbek bei Hamburg: Rowohlt, 1983), 32; hereafter cited as *Entführung,* libretto (Ger.). The English translation is from *The Metropolitan Opera Book of Mozart Operas,* trans. Susan Webb, 73–157, at 94; hereafter cited as *Entführung,* libretto (Eng.). The Metropolitan Opera translation includes changes to the libretto attributed to Christoph Friedrich Bretzner. See the appendix to *Entführung,* libretto (Eng.), 154–57. On these

outset, then, Neuenfels recasts the terms of fantasy in the work, from the pervasive will to diversion (and its correlative, a will to literalist interpretation) that characterizes most productions to a more complicated exploration of the terms that underlie and enable that diversion.

Even so, what Neuenfels comes up with is unusual. The Stuttgart production does not focus upon the most obvious topical intersection of Mozart's late-eighteenth-century work and contemporary Germany, namely, the place and function of Turkey in the imagination of the German-speaking world. Twenty-five years after the publication of Edward Said's *Orientalism* (and Neuenfels's notorious Frankfurt production of *Aida,* which could be said to have introduced Said's argument into opera production), the ideological stakes of colonial fantasy have become clear enough for anyone interested in noticing.[6] The egregiousness of abduction operas is by now familiar—even if it is often overlooked or repressed.[7] Though any number of traditional productions simply ignore the political stakes of the representation of "Turks" in the work, productions that are only slightly adventurous tend to frame that modest adventure in political terms.

Take, for example, August Everding's otherwise conventional 1980 production at the Bavarian State Opera in Munich, conducted by Karl Böhm and featuring Edita Gruberova as Konstanze. In this production, Thomas Holtzmann as Pasha Selim was costumed as an Iranian mullah.[8] The will to contemporaneity did not extend beyond the pasha: the rest of the characters were costumed—and otherwise inflected—in thoroughly conventional ways: for example, Osmin was outfitted with a big belly, long pointy slippers, and a circuitous "Ottoman" mustache; Pedrillo was decked out in

revisions, see Bauman, *Entführung,* 106–8. For the Barthes essay, see Roland Barthes, "The World of Wrestling," in *Mythologies,* ed. and trans. Annette Lavers (New York: Hill & Wang, 1972), 15–25.

6. Edward Said, *Orientalism* (New York: Pantheon Books, 1978). On Neuenfels's *Aida,* see Samuel Weber, "Taking Place: Toward a Theater of Dislocation," in *Opera through Other Eyes,* ed. David J. Levin (Stanford, Calif.: Stanford University Press, 1994), 107–26. Clemens Risi begins a discussion of the practice of foregrounding the relationship between the stage and the audience with a brief consideraton of Neuenfels's *Aida.* See Risi, "Shedding Light on the Audience: Hans Neuenfels and Peter Konwitschny Stage Verdi (and Verdians)," *Primal Scenes: Proceedings of a Conference Held at the University of California, Berkeley, 30 November–2 December, 2001,* special issue, *Cambridge Opera Journal* 14, nos. 1–2 (March 2002): 201–10.

7. See, e.g., Ruth Bernard Yeazell, "Harems for Mozart and Rossini," *Raritan* 16, no. 4 (Spring 1997): 86–105. Daniel Wilson's account of the history of the form is less theoretically engaging but more historically comprehensive than Yeazell's essay. Wilson, "Turks on the Eighteenth-Century Operatic Stage and European Political, Military, and Cultural History," *Eighteenth Century Life* 9, no. 2 (January 1985): 79–92.

8. The production, released by DGG on DVD, featured Edita Gruberova as Konstanze. For a production still of Holtzmann confronting Gruberova, see Attila Csampai and Dietmar Holland, eds., *Wolfgang Amadeus Mozart: Die Entführung aus dem Serail,* Rororo Opernbücher (Reinbek bei Hamburg: Rowohlt, 1983), 198.

rustic, colorful German finery; and so on. Holtzmann's pasha-*cum*-mullah hardly forms any kind of dramaturgical crux: his status as mullah has no noticeable effect on the rest of the production. It certainly could have, since a pasha in the imagination of late-eighteenth-century Vienna is arguably analogous to a mullah in the imagination of late-twentieth-century Munich. But having rendered the pasha visibly relevant, the rest of the figures in the Munich production were left to roam freely in the kitschified landscape of a fantasized late-eighteenth-century Ottomania.

We can see how the form of updating (which I discussed in greater detail in chapter 3) would be thus constructed and constricted. It boils down to dramaturgical tokenism: the pasha-mullah serves as an Orientalist Maguffin, an attractor for all that renders the piece awkward. As a result, the production ends up oddly distended, anticipating the structure (but not the humor) of *Space Jam*, the 1996 Michael Jordan–Bugs Bunny film in which the real-life hero is surrounded by cartoon characters. In Munich, as in the Warner Brothers film, the mullah figure who organizes the fantasy of the work is rendered materially contemporary, while the rest of the characters who enable the fantasy are rendered in cartoon form.[9] The significant difference, of course, is that the film celebrated this conceit while the Munich production suppressed it. That is, the Munich production in no way signaled an awareness of the irony of its uninflected, conventional depiction of the Turks (or, for that matter, the Europeans). This is Orientalism on automatic pilot, outfitted with the flimsiest of postmodern licenses.

Neuenfels's Stuttgart production explores less familiar terrain, expanding its focus beyond the politics of Orientalism (e.g., what it means for Osmin and Selim to be inflected as "Turks") to consider what we might term the politics of Orientalist form (e.g., what it means for Selim to be a speaking role).[10] The production redirects our attention to the work's formal conditions, to what we might term, in the wake of Said's critique, the apartheid of form—namely, the manner in which acting and singing relate to one another. The

9. The film, produced by Warner Brothers and directed by Ivan Reitman, featured the voices of Theresa Randle, Wayne Knight, Bill Murray, Billy West, and Danny DeVito.

10. It is not the only production to offer a novel and formal account of the piece. In the mid-1980s Ruth Berghaus produced a tendentiously structural account of the piece in Frankfurt. Her extraordinarily spare production focused on the work's interpersonal psychology, setting the work in a large box that was variously opened up or shut in, and that tilted rather mysteriously from side to side. The more constricted the sides of the box were, the more open were the characters within it: thus, for example, when the box was opened up entirely (say, for the appearance of the Janissaries), the characters within it were entirely "public" and emotionally shut in; when the box was shut in on all sides (say, for Selim's confrontations with Konstanze), the characters within it were much more emotionally open. For an extended account of Berghaus's production, see Sutcliffe, *Believing in Opera*, 133–38; a number of Mara Eggert's photographs of the production (albeit in black and white) can be found in Sigrid Neef, *Das Theater der Ruth Berghaus* (Frankfurt am Main: S. Fischer, 1989), 123–32.

Stuttgart production situates *Die Entführung aus dem Serail*, which so often has an air of fluff about it, right in the conceptual (and at times, even the thematic) thicket of much more obviously thorny pieces—such as Schoenberg's *Moses und Aron*, to name an unlikely analog.[11] In *Moses und Aron*, Schoenberg frames the distinction between Moses's sacred, transcendent aspirations and Aron's profane and quotidian aspirations in terms of a split between discourses, such that Moses *speaks* his sacred message in a highly mannered, more or less incomprehensible, oracular, and unpopular (read: Schoenbergian) form, while Aron, ever the populist, *sings* to the masses—readily, fluently, and comprehensibly (which is to say, in aesthetically compromised but politically efficacious form).[12] Although the overt stakes of Mozart's work could not be more different (it is much less programmatically concerned with aesthetics and wholly unconcerned with Schoenberg's modernist program), Neuenfels's production suggests that the piece's concerns dovetail into those of Schoenberg's work.

From Singspiel to Sing/*Spiel*

In the Stuttgart production, Mozart's work emerges not as fragmented, but as split. This sense of splitness is derived from the logic of the work in general, and the figure of Pasha Selim in particular. As a speaking part, Selim embodies the splitting off of the spoken word from music. He doesn't merely embody the voice of (apparent) alterity in power; beyond that, he embodies the power, such as it is, of an alterity of voice—the power, that is, of the speaking voice on the operatic stage. But what are the terms of this split? We can say— or to the extent that this merely rehearses a critical truism, we can repeat— that the Enlightenment speaks in this piece, insofar as Selim will famously assume the role of its spokesperson.[13] But what does it mean for the Enlight-

11. The problem of Mozart's work (or of Mozart's work in the Stuttgart production) is not that of a sacred fragment per se (which is how Adorno characterized the crisis of Schoenberg's uncompleted work), but it raises some of the same questions. For a detailed discussion of those questions in Schoenberg's work, see Adorno, "Sacred Fragment: Schoenberg's *Moses und Aron*," in *Quasi una fantasia: Essays on Modern Music*, trans. Rodney Livingstone (London: Verso, 1994); Philippe Lacoue-Labarthe, "Adorno," in *Musica Ficta (Figures of Wagner)*, trans. Felicia McCarren (Stanford, Calif.: Stanford University Press, 1994), 117–45; Tomlinson, *Metaphysical Song*, 149–54.

12. Mladen Dolar points to Hildegard von Bingen's *Ordo virtutum*, another analogous work organized around similar questions, if in reverse form. In this work, the virtues, personified, sing, while the only speaking role is assigned to the devil—who is the devil, as Dolar points out, "because he cannot sing." See Mladen Dolar, "The Object Voice," in *Gaze and Voice as Love Objects*, ed. Renata Salecl and Slavoj Žižek (Durham, N.C.: Duke University Press, 1996), 7–31, at 23.

13. Ivan Nagel formulates the point with characteristic elegance: "Among opera's almighty rulers, [Pasha Selim] is the first, possibly the last, sensible man." Nagel, *Autonomy and Mercy: Reflections on Mozart's Operas*, trans. Marion Faber and Ivan Nagel (Cambridge, Mass.: Harvard University Press,

enment to be characterized by—or indeed, relegated to—speech in an opera? And if Selim ends up speaking for the Enlightenment, what, then, is the function (or, indeed, what are the functions) accorded singing in the piece?

These questions gesture toward a long history of fretting over the cultural modalities of the voice—with the singing voice's penchant for transcendence and intoxication (what Gary Tomlinson has termed the "noumenal temptation")[14] arrayed against the spoken voice's more abstract and rational offices, including its presumed affinity with phenomenality and analysis. In his recent work, for example, Hans Ulrich Gumbrecht proposes a binary typologization of modes of self-definition in Western culture, distinguishing between representation and re-presentation; between a hermeneutic culture (or "subject culture," derived from a Cartesian inheritance) and a presence culture, understood as intrinsic to cosmology, where knowledge emerges through revelation rather than analysis, and meaning through embodiment rather than signification.[15] In Gumbrecht's polemical and amusing account, the singing voice in opera imparts presence, despite the determination of a hermeneutic culture to lasso it into the service of meaning:

> Not by coincidence did Modernity begin with the protestant redefinition of the Eucharist from a device that produces "God's real presence" into a "representation" of Christ's Last Supper with his disciples. Ever since (and more or less unofficially), the Eucharist and transubstantiation as its core event have been an embarrassment for those Catholic theologians who desperately wanted to be modern and, in principle, this has been true for virtually all phenomena of re-presentation within the self-image of modern western culture. Such phenomena of re-presentation exist either in niches of our culture

---

1991), 17. See also Brigid Brophy's observation that "[Mozart] has built his Pasha Selim to the precise specification of Voltaire's ideal: the noble, pagan, philosophic, exotic, benevolent despot who is amenable to education." Brophy, *Mozart the Dramatist: The Value of his Operas to Him, to His Age, and to Us* (New York: Da Capo, 1988), 223. In his Cambridge Companion to *Entführung*, Bauman suggests that the allusion in Bretzner's text to Selim's status as "renegade" (an allusion replicated in Stephanie's adaptation) alerts us to Selim's Western origins. In Bretzner's version, where Belmonte emerges as the pasha's son, this lineage is indisputable. This no doubt helps to explain Selim's sudden shift to Enlightenment beneficence as the product of his early upbringing. In Mozart and Stephanie's adaptation, the pasha's precise lineage is cloudier. See Bauman, *Entführung*, 33.

14. Tomlinson, *Metaphysical Song*, 92.

15. Hans Ulrich Gumbrecht, "Ten Brief Reflections on Institutions and Re/Presentation" in *Institutionalität und Symbolisierung: Verstetigungen Kultureller Ordnungsmuster in Vezgangenheit und Gegenwart*, ed. Gert Melville (Cologne: Böhlav. 2001), 69–75. A German version of Gumbrecht's lecture was published as "Produktion von Präsenz, durchsetzt mit Absenz: Über Musik, Libretto und Inszenierung," in *Ästhetik der Inszenierung*, ed. Josef Früchtl and Jörg Zimmermann (Frankfurt am Main: Suhrkamp, 2001), 63–76, at 67. Gumbrecht returned to the argument in "Beyond Meaning: Positions and Concepts in Motion" in *Production of Presence: What Meaning Cannot Convey* (Stanford, Calif: Stanford University Press, 2004), 51–90.

which, despite often being enormously popular, cannot be culturally canonized (this continues to be the case with sports); or they thrive under cover of an official self-reference that subsumes phenomena of re-presentation under a discourse of representation (when we talk about an opera production, much more reference is usually made to the staging of the libretto than to the volume of the voices and to the choreography of the bodies on the stage).[16]

The idiosyncratic alliance Gumbrecht proposes here between the operatic voice onstage and a culture of re-presentation revisits the terms of Jacques Derrida's account of "phonocentrism"—that is, the unconsciously systematic allegiance posited in metaphysics between the voice as a guarantor of presence in contradistinction to the word, figured as secondary, parasitic, an avatar of absence.[17] And yet, as Mladen Dolar points out, there is more to the story that Derrida tells than an unshakable alliance between metaphysics, presence, and the voice.

According to Dolar, "There is a dimension of the voice that runs counter to self-transparency, sense, and presence: the voice against the logos, the voice as the other of logos, its radical alterity."[18] Dolar traces this dimension through a political history of musical aesthetics, as suggestive as it is cursory—from the Chinese emperor Chun through books 3 and 4 of Plato's *Republic*, Augustine's *Confessions*, the Council of Trent, Cromwell, and the creation of an Institut national de la musique on 18 Brumaire of Year 2 of the French Revolution. Over the course of three millennia, then, Dolar repeatedly encounters urgent statements of the same anxiety: "Music, in particular the voice, shouldn't stray away from words, which endow it with sense; as soon as it departs from its textual anchorage, the voice becomes senseless and threatening, all the more so because of its seductive and intoxicating powers."[19] Dolar's ac-

---

16. Gumbrecht, "Ten Brief Reflections," 70–71. Gumbrecht's argument here echoes an earlier polemic in which he pleaded for an institutionalization of the question of the relative value of texts in communicative situations—as Gumbrecht put it, a "Polemik gegen den Hang der Libretto-Spezialisten, um jeden Preis 'Harmonie zwischen Text und Musik' zu finden (oder zu stiften) oder die Ehrenrettung der Libretti zu betreiben, weil sie von den Feuilletonisten und Wissenschaftlern ach so ungerecht behandelt zu werden pflegen. Denn der Fall intendierter Gleichgewichtigkeit zwischen Musik und Text scheint die Ausnahme im Musiktheater zu sein, und nicht einmal auf Komplementarität mit Musik angelegte Texte darf man unter Absehung von dieser Komplementarität lesen." Hans Ulrich Gumbrecht, "Musikpragmatik: Gestrichelte Linie zur Konstitution eines Objektbereichs," in *Oper als Text: Romantische Beiträge zur Libretto-Forschung,* ed. Albert Gier (Heidelberg: Carl Winter, 1986), 15–24, at 18–19.

17. See Jacques Derrida, "The Signifier and Truth," in *Of Grammatology,* corrected ed., trans. Gayatri Chakravorty Spivak (Baltimore, Md.: Johns Hopkins University Press, 1997).

18. Dolar, "The Object Voice," 24.

19. Ibid., 17. For an exceedingly interesting discussion of Dolar's argument, see Abbate, *In Search of Opera,* 70–71. In Gary Tomlinson's account, music in its modern, post-Renaissance conception

count dovetails nicely with Gumbrecht's account of the operatic voice on-stage in the service of re-presentation (a matter, as he puts it, of "volume") distinct from and even antithetical to representation (what Gumbrecht refers to as "the staging of the libretto").

And yet, although this musical voice is consistently arrayed in opposition to the word and the law, Dolar directs our attention to another voice with the same characteristics—a voice beyond logos, a lawless, senseless voice—that serves the opposite function. And how might we describe this other, senseless voice that serves to support the letter and the Law?

> There is also another voice: the "voice of the Father," the voice that inherently sticks to logos itself, the voice that commands and binds, the voice of God . . . The Law itself, in its pure form, before commanding anything specific, is epitomized by the voice, the voice that commands total compliance, although senseless in itself.[20]

Here is the "object voice," which, along with the object gaze, Lacan added to Freud's list of partial objects (breasts, feces, phallus).[21] In Dolar's revised account, the relation of the object voice to the word is not only oppositional—a matter of hostility, surveillance, and confinement:

> If the Law, the word, the logos, had to constantly fight the voice as the other, the senseless bearer of *jouissance,* feminine decadence, it could do so only by implicitly relying on that other voice, the voice of the Father accompanying the Law. Ultimately, we don't have the battle of "logos" against the voice, but *the voice against the voice.*[22]

---

derives from a willed independence from words. According to Tomlinson, with Lully's recitative "the style ceased to be one that revealed a (normally occult) *sameness* and came instead to entail the mitigation of the innate *difference* between the signifying operations of words and tones. The 'problem' of recitative was born, a problem nonexistent in the participatory metaphysics of the late Renaissance from which the style had first emerged. It is not saying too much to add that this problem is an early symptom of the emergence of a new, general category of discursive practice in the West, a category independent of words that would commandeer for its name the age-old term *music*." Tomlinson, *Metaphysical Song,* 42; see also 84ff. on the development of a new, supersemantic musical object in the Wagnerian period.

20. Dolar, "The Object Voice," 25.

21. See Salecl and Žižek, introduction to *Gaze and Voice as Love Objects,* ed. Renata Salecl and Slavoj Žižek (Durham, N.C.: Duke University Press, 1996), 3.

22. Dolar, "The Object Voice," 27. Žižek makes a similar point, warning against "the mistaken impression that we are dealing with a simple opposition between the 'repressive' articulated word and the 'transgressive' consuming voice: on the one hand, the articulated Word that disciplines and regulates the voice as a means of asserting social discipline and authority, and on the other hand, the self-enjoying voice that acts as the medium of liberation, of tearing apart the disciplinary chains of law and order. . . . The excess of the voice is . . . radically undecidable." Žižek, "'I Hear You With My Eyes'; or, The Invisible Master," in Salecl and Žižek, *Gaze and Voice,* 90–126, at 104.

I want to argue that the Stuttgart production engages this notion of the voice against the voice, allowing it—as a dramaturgical motor—to drive the production. It does so in both a very particular sense and a general sense. Beyond querying the place and status of Selim's speaking voice in this singspiel, the production queries the multiple instantiations of voices in the work, including the modes of voice within roles (e.g., Konstanze as actress/Konstanze as singer) as well as the modes of voice within the opera text (e.g., the orchestra's voice in contradistinction to the speaking voice or in concert with it). The Stuttgart *Entführung* queries the compound elements of singspiel, asking what distinguishes *singen* from *spielen,* a seductive and intoxicating singing voice from the father's speaking voice, Gumbrecht's/Abbate's/Jankélévitch's presence culture from hermeneutic culture: the production repeatedly draws our attention to the chasms, tensions, and traffic between them.

How does Neuenfels transform what innumerable critics, beginning with Goethe, have taken to be a lowbrow musical comedy into a thoroughly self-conscious work whose discursive channels have become the object of the mise-en-scène rather than merely serving as its means?[23] By attending to the work's component parts. This strategy is reflected in the production's taping: the production, taped and broadcast in the spring of 1999 by Arte, the European cable arts network, is unusual not simply on account of Neuenfels's unusual production aesthetics, but because the video production sought a filmic correlative to those aesthetics. The camera roves idiosyncratically, focusing at times on seemingly incidental or inconsequential details—Belmonte's shadow, Konstanze's hand—and seldom offering a traditional, centered account of what transpires onstage.[24]

---

23. On *Entführung* as lowbrow musical comedy, see John Stone, "The Grand Diversion: Mozart and *Die Entführung aus dem Serail,*" *Cambridge Quarterly* 21, no. 2 (1992): 107–19. Even when it's not seen as lowbrow in particular, *Die Entführung* is frequently bracketed out of accounts of Mozart's more psychologically sophisticated works. Thus, for example, Gordon Rogoff writes that the three Mozart–Da Ponte operas, *Don Giovanni, Così fan tutte,* and *Le nozze di Figaro* "have in common one theme or subject that imposes on them a specific psychological atmosphere, more severe, intense, ironic, and highlighted in these operas than in *Entführung aus dem Serail* or *Zauberflöte:* an atmosphere of seductive intrigue." The Stuttgart production suggests that the "psychological atmosphere" of the *Entführung* (and any other work, for that matter) is not simply given, but is, in part, a function of staging. See Gordon Rogoff, "That True Phoenix, da Ponte," in *Vanishing Acts: Theater since the Sixties* (New Haven, Conn.: Yale University Press, 2000), 196.

24. All in all, the Südwestfunk-Arte camera crew produces images that are less willful and more artful than those produced by Peter Sellars, who oversaw the television production of his Mozart–Da Ponte productions—and has overseen the video production of his subsequent productions. Although it is a bit of a stretch, I would suggest that the closest model for the production values of the Südwestfunk-Arte *Entführung* broadcast might be Jean-Marie Straub and Danièle Huillet's 1974–75 film of Schoenberg's *Moses und Aron.* On Straub and Huillet's film, see Barton Byg,

The curtain rises in act 1 to reveal a male figure in darkness, offset against a large three-dimensional butterfly bathed in blue light. The butterfly is presumably a materialization of an analogy from Osmin's act 1 lied, "Wer ein Liebchen hat gefunden." In the second stanza, Osmin notes that in order to keep a sweetheart true, "Schließ' er Liebchen sorglich ein: / Denn die losen Dinger haschen / Jeden Schmetterling und naschen / Gar zu gern von fremden Wein (He should carefully lock her up; / For the silly things chase / Every butterfly, and partake / All too gladly of someone else's wine).[25] In Osmin's (surveilling) eyes, Pedrillo and Belmonte, of course, are the "butterflies" whom Blonde and Konstanze will chase. At the same time, the capacity of the caterpillar to metamorphose into a butterfly presumably offers the production an exemplary way to figure some of its principal concerns, from the obvious (e.g., Selim's metamorphosis from terrorist to enlightened regent) to the more obscure (e.g., the splitting of actors and singers into distinct roles). The male figure standing in the darkness onstage in front of the butterfly will turn out to be not just Belmonte, but two Belmontes—the singer (Mathias Klink) and, directly behind him, an actor (Alexander Bogner) who, during the course of the opening aria, mirrors the singer's actions. Although the actors and singers will, at times, mirror each other's gestures in the course of this production, that mirroring will be the exception and not the rule, since the actors and singers are clearly accorded distinct personalities—they interact with one another and act or sing autonomously as well—and thus rarely end up doing the same things or acting in similar ways. The two Belmontes may look the same—they are roughly the same height and build, with the same mustache, dressed in the same black Spanish suit and hat—but they have very different, if interrelated, roles. The two Osmins are of very different build, and one Konstanze is blonde while the other is a brunette. The interactions between the two Pedrillos are the most self-conscious: when they first enter, the two are arguing about who will speak their first line. How are we to make sense of this splitting, and how might we begin to describe its effects?

To begin at a lexical level, the split is anticipated in the compound generic designation of the piece as a singspiel, the hybrid operatic genre, officially fostered in Joseph II's Vienna, that required extensive sections of spoken German dialogue.[26] According to Wolfgang Hildesheimer, the hybridity of the form inevitably split it into its component parts: "The *Singspiel* never was

"Musical Modernism and the Schoenberg Films," in *Landscapes of Resistance: The German Films of Danièle Huillet and Jean-Marie Straub* (Berkeley: University of California Press, 1995).

25. *Entführung,* libretto (Ger.), 29; *Entführung,* libretto (Eng.), 88.

26. For a detailed discussion of the historical origins and generic implications of *Die Entführung aus dem Serail* as singspiel, see Bauman, *Entführung,* chapters 1 and 2.

a satisfactory formal structure. The spoken text, which must further the action, also furthers the collapse of the musical continuity. A number can be no more than a number." [27] The Stuttgart production interrogates this collapse and explores its dramatic implications. Thus, what might initially seem like a Fordist bureaucratization (where singers do the singing and actors the acting) becomes the stuff of reflection and play. By staging a distinction between speaking and singing, the Stuttgart production repeatedly draws our attention to the fact—unsurprising in retrospect, but astonishing in effect—that they serve very different functions in this work.[28] The alternation between speaking and singing is more than a vehicle for play or, indeed, for ostentatious directorial invention. Rather, their alternation serves as an unanticipated *point de capiton* (or quilting point) for understanding the work.[29]

As I have indicated, this quilting point emerges in the wake of extensive alterations to Stephanie's libretto. Neuenfels cuts roughly half of the spoken text (although the text that Mozart set to music, like the music itself, is left entirely intact). In its place, Neuenfels puts condensed versions of information essential to the story and, more frequently and more interestingly, material that engages the distinctions between singing and acting (as well as the singer's role and the actor's role) in the work. Although the effect is initially disorienting, it ends up being less jarring than amusing. Throughout the piece, the actors and singers allude to the condition of and the distinctions between acting and singing. In attending to these distinctions and dramatizing them, the Stuttgart production draws our attention to a set of problems that is otherwise merely implicit in the work and thus usually overlooked. As a result, it becomes clear that the singers and actors in Mozart's work inhabit the same territory, albeit in very different ways. I want to be very clear about the claim here: although the alterations to the spoken text—sometimes quite drastic—are Neuenfels's doing, they alert us to structural and dramatic conditions that are central to Mozart's work. Here, then, we have an instance of what we might term radical fidelity: a program of fidelity whose intentions and interests distinguish it from conventional reproduction. The Stuttgart production models a form of fidelity to deep

27. Wolfgang Hildesheimer, *Mozart*, trans. Marion Faber. (New York: Farrar, Straus, Giroux, 1982), 327.

28. See Otto Michtner, *Das alte Burgtheater als Opernbühne: Von der Einführung des deutschen Singspiels (1778) bis zum Tod Kaiser Leopolds II (1792)*, Theatergeschichte Österreichs, Bd. 3, Hft. 1 (Vienna: Hermann Böhlau, 1970), 37; Robert Haas, ed., "Einleitung," in *Ignaz Umlauf: Die Bergknappen*, Denkmäler der Tonkunst in Österreich, Jahrg. 18, Nr.1, Bd. 36 (Vienna: Österreichischer Bundesverlag, 1911), xxvii.

29. On the "quilting point" see Slavoj Žižek, *The Sublime Object of Ideology* (New York: Verso, 1989), 87–89.

Figure 20 Singers and Spielers. In act 1, scene 9, Belmonte converses with Pedrillo. Or rather, in the Stuttgart production, two Belmontes converse with two Pedrillos—as well as with each other.

structure, such that the interventions on the level of the text (which appear to instantiate a thoroughgoing disregard for the sanctity of the text) function as an attempt to elucidate the logic and condition of textuality in the work, to enable its particular terms to emerge all the more clearly.

An example will help to clarify the point. In act 1, scene 9, Belmonte (the Spanish nobleman who has just arrived in Turkey to rescue his beloved Konstanze along with his servant Pedrillo and Pedrillo's beloved Blonde) speaks briefly with Pedrillo about some of the perils surrounding life at the pasha's court—or rather, Pedrillo talks about life at the court, while Belmonte is in a daze at having finally seen Konstanze. In the Stuttgart production, there are, of course, two Pedrillos and two Belmontes (a singer and an actor), so what might otherwise be a brief and intimate conversation emerges on the Stuttgart stage as a rather involved conversation involving four figures (see figure 20).

In the following, I juxtapose Stephanie's original text (in plain text) with Neuenfels's additions (in italics) and cuts (struck through). The reader will note that I have suffixed "-Actor" or "-Singer" to each character's name in order to distinguish between the actors and the singers playing a role.[30]

---

30. See *Entführung*, libretto (Ger.), 38–39; *Entführung*, libretto (Eng.), 103–4, translation modified. Neuenfels moves the first line of the scene, Pedrillo's "Ha, Triumph, Triumph! Herr, der erste Schritt wär getan," to the conclusion of scene 8.

Belmonte-Singer: ~~Ach, laß mich zu~~
~~mir selbst kommen!~~ Ich habe sie
gesehen, hab das gute, treue,
beste Mädchen gesehen!— O
Konstanze, Konstanze! Was
könnt' ich für dich tun, was für
dich wagen?

Belmonte-Actor [to Belmonte-
Singer]: Bitte, beruhige Dich,
Belmonte! Bitte!

Pedrillo-Actor [to Belmonte-Singer]:
~~Ha, gemach, gemach, bester~~
~~Herr! Stimmen Sie den Ton~~
~~ein bißchen herab; Verstellung~~
~~wird uns weit bessere Dienste~~
~~leisten.~~ *In Ihrer Verfassung ist*
es besser, wenn er [Belmonte-
Actor] Ihre Rolle eine Zeitlang
übernimmt. Wir sind nicht
in unserm Vaterlande. ~~Hier~~
~~fragen sie den Henker danach,~~
~~ob's einen Kopf mehr oder~~
~~weniger in der Welt gibt.~~
Bastonade und Strick um
den Hals sind hier ~~wie~~ ein
Butterbrot ~~Morgenbrot.~~

Belmonte-Actor: Bastonade?

Pedrillo-Actor: Stockschläge auf die
Fußsohlen.

Belmonte-Actor: Um Gottes willen!

Belmonte-Singer: Ach, Pedrillo,
wenn *ihr* die Liebe *kenntet!*—

Pedrillo-Actor: Was wollen Sie damit
sagen? ~~Als wenn's mit unserei-~~
~~nem gar nichts wäre!~~ *Wir haben*
genauso unsere zärtlichen Stun-
den wie Sie! Und denken Sie
denn, das mir's nicht im Bauche
grimmt, wenn ich mein Blondchen von ~~so einem alten Spitz-~~
~~buben, wie der~~ *diesem*

Belmonte-Singer: ~~Ah, let me return~~
~~to my senses!~~ I have seen her, I
have seen the good, true, best
maiden!— Oh Konstanze,
Konstanze! What could I do
for you, dare for you?

Belmonte-Actor [to Belmonte-
Singer]: Please, calm yourself,
Belmonte! Please!

Pedrillo-Actor [to Belmonte-Singer]:
~~Ha, gently, gently, dear~~
~~master! Lower your voice a~~
~~little; pretense will serve us~~
~~far better.~~ *Given your state,*
I think it'd be better if he
[Belmonte-Actor] took over your
role for a while. We are not in
our fatherland. ~~Here they ask~~
~~the executioner whether there~~
~~is one head more or less in the~~
~~world.~~ Here bastinado and a
rope around the neck are as
normal as ~~a morning roll~~
bread and butter.

Belmonte-Actor: Bastinado?

Pedrillo-Actor: Thwacks with a stick
on the soles of the feet.

Belmonte-Actor: Lord have mercy!

Belmonte-Singer: Ah, Pedrillo, if you
[*plural*] had experienced love!—

Pedrillo-Actor: What do you mean?
~~As if with our sort there were no~~
~~such thing!~~ *We have just as many*
tender hours as other people. And
do you think that it doesn't gripe
me in the belly when I have to
see my Blondie shadowed by
~~an old rascal like~~ *that* monster
Osmin?

Ungeheuer Osmin ~~ist,~~ bewacht
sehen muß?

Pedrillo-Singer [zu Pedrillo-Actor]:	*Pedrillo-Singer [to Pedrillo-Actor]:*
Du bist gut in Form, Pedrillo.	You're in fine form, Pedrillo. Keep it
Mach' weiter so. Ich kümmere mich	up. In the meantime, I'll concern
inzwischen um unseren Sänger-	myself with our singer-friend,
Freund, Belmonte. Ruf mich, wenn	Belmonte. Call me when you're in a
Du nicht weiter weißt. [Ab mit	pickle. [Off with Belmonte-Singer]
Belmonte-Singer]	
~~Belmonte: O wenn es möglich wäre,~~	~~Belmonte: Oh if it were possible to~~
~~sie zu sprechen—~~	~~speak to her—~~
~~Pedrillo: Wir wollen sehen, was zu~~	~~Pedrillo: We'll see what's to be done.~~
~~tun ist. Kommen Sie nur mit mir~~	~~Just come with me into the gar-~~
~~in den Garten: aber um alles in~~	~~den; but for heaven's sake: cau-~~
~~der Welt: vorsichtig und fein.~~	~~tiously and quietly. For every-~~
~~Denn hier ist alles Aug' und Ohr.~~	~~thing here has eyes and ears.~~

This fairly representative sample of Neuenfels's interventions in the text
affords us an opportunity to examine the division of characters into distinct
singer and actor parts. How does the division function? Let us begin with the
Belmontes. Here, as at various points in Neuenfels's revised text, Belmonte-
Actor tells his singer double to calm down. The actor, we might say, embodies an imperative of rationalist restraint, while the singer tends instead toward lyrical (which is also to say, emotional) effusiveness.

In fact, Belmonte-Actor's repeated remonstrations are grounded in Gottlieb Stephanie's libretto (and indeed, in Bretzner's text as well),[31] although
they have been rather forcefully redistributed. For example, in the section
of text quoted above, Neuenfels cuts Pedrillo's warnings to Belmonte from
the libretto ("Ha, gemach, gemach, bester Herr! Stimmen Sie den Ton ein
bißchen herab; Verstellung wird uns weit bessere Dienste leisten. . . . Kommen Sie nur mit mir in den Garten: aber um alles in der Welt: vorsichtig und
fein. Denn hier ist alles Aug' und Ohr" [Ha, gently, gently, dear master!
Lower your voice a little; pretense will serve us far better. . . . Just come with
me into the garden; but for heaven's sake: cautiously and quietly. For everything here has eyes and ears]). The terms of those warnings, however, are
anticipated, in much more direct and hyperbolic form, in Belmonte-Actor's
remonstration to his singer double: "Bitte, beruhige Dich, Belmonte! Bitte!"
(Please, calm yourself, Belmonte! Please!). The division between singer and

---

31. For a detailed comparison of the two versions of the work, see chapter 4 of Bauman, *Entführung*, 36–61.

actor alerts us to the dramaturgical fact of Belmonte's hotheadedness, and, beyond that, to its lyrical origins.

The Stuttgart production clarifies what is otherwise merely implicit in the work, namely, that Belmonte's hotheadedness derives in part from a spilling over of his (hotheaded) musical affect into the spoken realm. Indeed, Belmonte-Singer's musical claims (to Konstanze's goodness, to his love for her, and even to his own hotheadedness) are often reiterated—somewhat awkwardly—in spoken form. The claims of his recitative and aria in act 1, scene 5, "O, wie ängstlich, o wie feurig" (Oh, how anxious, oh, how fiery!) find subsequent dramatic reiteration in his proto–Sturm und Drang claims here that "I have seen her, I have seen the good, true, best maiden!—Oh Konstanze, Konstanze! What could I do for you, dare for you?" (It makes sense that Neuenfels assigns these lines to Belmonte-Singer, given their obvious affinities with what we might term Belmonte's lyrical program.) In turn, Belmonte-Actor (standing here for the condition of Belmonte speaking rather than singing) is forever seeking to dampen the tendency toward excess embodied by Belmonte-Singer (standing here for the condition of Belmonte singing rather than speaking). The textual traces of the relationship between singer and actor should lead us to note that the striking and unusual distinctions between singer and actor in the Stuttgart production— effected, as we have seen, by rewriting—are born of the most familiar of critical methodologies: close reading. It seems important to emphasize this point since so many of the most striking and seemingly disparate productions (e.g., those by Neuenfels, Peter Sellars, Philipp Himmelmann, Atom Egoyan, and Christopher Alden) appear to share a commitment to close reading.

A further addition to the Stuttgart libretto suggests a similar point about the origins of Belmonte's character, if in a different way. As I indicated above, Stephanie's libretto tends to reiterate the dramatic substance of Belmonte's musical material in his spoken lines. The Stuttgart production stages this condition: although Belmonte-Singer is repeatedly shown to be—and labeled as—hotheaded, Belmonte-Actor appears to be quite vacant, something suggested by his repeated calls for his counterpart to calm down and his frequent queries—in this case, "[What is] bastinado?" Although this vacancy is unquestionably a product of (unusual) directorial and dramatic interpretation, it also derives from an insight about Belmonte in the absence of his musical material.

In Stephanie's libretto and in Neuenfels's production, the dramatic personae of the other principals are much more fully fledged. Let us consider Pedrillo-Singer's comments to his actor double in the same scene. In Neuenfels's account, the scene shows Pedrillo-Actor to be something of a master of dramatic invention,[32] which renders his musical double temporarily superfluous—as a result of which he leaves, telling Pedrillo-Actor to call when he's "in a pickle." Of course, Pedrillo's musical prowess will be required soon enough. In the final scene of the first act, Belmonte and Pedrillo will attempt to talk their way past Osmin-Singer into the palace. Blocked by and in speaking with Osmin, Pedrillo(-Actor) will call upon his singer counterpart, and in tandem with the Belmonte(-Actor and -Singer), they will act and sing their way past both Osmins and into the palace in the trio with which the act closes.[33] But what exactly is the pickle in which Pedrillo-Actor finds himself during the course of this confrontation with Osmin? The production stages it as the pickle of dramatization itself.

Until the very last moments of the production, that is, until Pasha Selim's concluding gesture of enlightened mercy, the principals are repeatedly shown to be cornered in and by dramatization—not just in the course of their spoken exchanges, but by their very recourse to speaking. Music, on the other hand, is repeatedly shown to offer transcendence, even if, in Mozart's inflection, it is often a melancholy transcendence. As such, music seems to provide the only escape from the intractability that repeatedly results from spoken dramatic exchange. Here, then, is a formal correlative to the overt dramatic concerns of the piece: like the arrival of the Europeans at Selim's palace, music offers a means of escape from what we might loosely term the prisonhouse of language, or, more precisely, an escape from a condition and a realm marked—by its ruler, at least—as spoken and not sung. But escape to where? In the logic of the piece, the liberation afforded by music is a liberation from representation into presence. But the mise-en-scène complicates this rather formulaic insight, first and foremost by topographizing it. In Christian Schmidt's set, music and drama come to occupy distinct spaces. In the following section, I want to examine the logic and effects of this spatial dramaturgy.

The Topography of Discourses

The split between actors and singers is itself doubled in the materiality of the stage, for built about twenty-five feet back from the front of the main stage is another stage, heightened and recessed (see figure 21). Here, then, we encounter not just a stage within (or upon) a stage, but along with it a doubling of the space of articulation and presentation. And while the main stage

32. In fine Hegelian form, Pedrillo the servant's dramatic mastery is juxtaposed to his master's lack of dramatic prowess.

33. Trio, no. 7, Osmin's "Marsch! Marsch! Marsch!" (March, march, march!).

Figure 21 Two stages. All of the actors in this frame are standing on the main stage. Upstage, behind the hunched-over Selim, are the curtain and proscenium arch of the rear stage.

accommodates both singing and speaking and the competition between them, the rear stage serves a different—and surprising—function as a place spatially and conceptually above and beyond that competition.

At times, this above-and-beyond emerges on the most basic level of plot. Characters coming onstage from the pasha's castle at times enter the main stage from the rear stage.[34] In these cases, the rear stage marks the castle as a diegetic border for the work, a place just beyond dramatic events in the opera. This is not to say that the rear stage looks like a castle—it looks like a stage. Rather, it serves as a conduit, a means of access. More frequently, and more interestingly, the rear stage serves as a site of musical spectacle. But not in a traditional sense: that is, what transpires on the rear stage is not a dramatic spectacle accompanied by music, but rather, various instantiations of the spectacle of music itself. Thus, the rear stage serves as a space of para- or extranarrative musicality—in essence, an opera seria stage.[35]

---

34. Thus, for example, when Osmin comes upon the group of Europeans seeking to escape in act 3, scene 5, he enters from the rear stage.

35. A number of the production's critics recognized it as such. See, e.g., Gerhard R. Koch, "Das doppelte Blondchen," *Frankfurter Allgemeine Zeitung*, February 2, 1998, Feuilleton section, 31; Wolfgang Schreiber, "Wer nicht singt, muss böse werden," *Süddeutsche Zeitung*, February 2, 1998, Feuilleton section, 14.

The chorus of Janissaries is relegated to this rear stage for both of its appearances in the work, and, in a very different dramaturgical register, so are Konstanze (for her second-act recitative and aria "Welcher Wechsel herrscht in meiner Seele") and Blonde (for her second-act aria "Welche Wonne, welche Lust"). In each of these instances, the rear stage serves as a space above and beyond the quotidian competition between acting and singing, that is, beyond the particular representational problems that Neuenfels focuses upon and locates on the main stage. The rear stage serves as a privileged and literalized place holder for a separate, distinct space of musicality—an uncontested space of musical (self-) presentation.

The rear stage lends physical (if duly theatricalized) form to the piece's split between discursive modes: here musicality's remove from what Gumbrecht terms "hermeneutic culture" takes on a material form. The *singen* of singspiel is at times duly elevated (and doubly theatricalized by the stage upon the stage), and the *spielen*—the stuff of drama, its narrative telos and transactional terms—takes place down below.[36] Rather than being merely clever or willful, this topographization alerts us to the dramaturgical construction of the work, to the architecture of key moments, and more particularly, to key fissures. By splitting the stage (into a main stage and rear stage) and the players (into singers and actors), the Stuttgart production materializes fissures that it derives from the work's structure, for example, a fissure between singspiel and opera seria or between acting and singing.[37] But beyond that, it also shows that these fissures mark the internal logic of the work. In one sense, this is a familiar insight: in *Die Entführung,* as so often in Mozart operas, chasms suddenly open between or even within characters who have been alienated according to the terms of the plot: Konstanze's intense dismay at Belmonte's doubts about her fidelity in act 2, scene 9 (a rift between the characters) arguably produces a chasm within Konstanze, where she nec-

---

36. We might say that Christian Schmidt's set for the Stuttgart production realizes the condition of the "double stage" that Gilles de Van describes as a recurring feature in the history of opera: "The story is the point of departure, but the music finally creates a gray area between the opera, which proposes a meaning, the singer, who personifies it, and the spectator, who absorbs it. . . . This indistinctness creates a sort of double stage, an inner and an outer stage of the drama, with practical consequences that composers seem to have always been aware of, judging from their concern for dramatic rhythm—in the sense of alternating the phases of introspection and dramatic action. What happens chiefly is that less importance is given to the cohesion of the parts with the whole and of the different situations with the 'chain' linking them, with the result that there is a greater tolerance for fragmentation." Gilles de Van, "Aesthetics," in *Verdi's Theater: Creating Drama through Music,* trans. Gilda Roberts (Chicago: University of Chicago Press, 1998), 24–60, at 50.

37. See Thomas Bauman's claim about "the central aesthetic problem of the opera": "Its stylistic diversity does not really lie between the individual musical numbers but between the competing claims of Mozart's music and Bretzner's dialogue." Bauman, *Entführung,* 93.

essarily calls into question her pronounced and defining devotion to Bel-monte. But the Stuttgart production goes much further, showing that chasms also emerge within and between characters on the level of form. Thus, as I suggested above, Belmonte-Actor is shown to embody a post-seria principle of reasoned (noble, dramatic) restraint, while Belmonte-Singer re-peatedly embodies a thoroughgoing, antirationalist musicality.

These fissures emerge most forcefully in moments of transition. The Stuttgart production makes it clear that in Mozart's singspiel, the infrastruc-ture that would enable traffic between drama and song is quite crude: there are no elaborate on- and off-ramps, indeed, there are hardly any ramps at all. Which is not to say that Mozart's work fails to propose inventive means of ne-gotiating the transition between spoken word and song.[38] Rather, this pro-duction applies a great deal of pressure to those means, exploring a series of aporias that open up—the result of what Thomas Bauman labels "the very palpable aesthetic jolt"—as the piece shifts between modes.[39]

One of the most striking examples of this topographical dramaturgy is Konstanze's second-act recitative and aria "Welcher Wechsel herrscht in meiner Seele" (What change prevails in my soul; no. 10) The shift announced in the opening lines of the recitative echoes a shift in the work's compositional register—not just a shift from E-flat major to G minor, or from word to song, but from the extended series of relatively comical (spoken and sung) ex-changes between Osmin and Blonde to an expansive and solitary instance of musical introspection. Blonde's brief lines at the opening of the scene set the stage for Konstanze's appearance: insofar as they tell us what the subsequent recitative and aria will tell us, they constitute a model of clunky dramatic telegraphing. Not surprisingly, Neuenfels cuts them. Absent Blonde's lines, Konstanze is left to come more or less out of the blue—literally: she emerges slowly from a darkened, barren landscape in the recesses of the rear stage amid a gentle (and utterly improbable) snowfall (see figure 22).

The landscape is radically distinct from anything that has preceded it in the work: as such, it serves as a materialization of the (psychologically, dra-maturgically) uncharted quality of the musical material and of its status as a departure from the dramatic continuity and from inherited compositional constraints.[40] In the larger dramaturgical topography of the work, the aria

38. As Thomas Bauman points out, Mozart "begins some numbers off–centre tonally or syn-tactically, creating the effect of taking up the music already in progress. On other occasions he me-diates with the most traditional form of sung speech—recitative." Bauman, *Entführung*, 72.

39. Ibid., 72.

40. On the compositional status of the aria, see Bauman's argument that the "sublime setting of the first two lines of Constanze's meditation 'Traurigkeit ward mir zum Loose' in Act II" exemplifies the "unprecedented freedom and plasticity" of Mozart's compositional work in *Die Entführung*:

Figure 22 Out of the blue. The curtain of the rear stage has just risen to reveal an empty void filled by gentle snow-fall. Out of this darkness emerges a dark-clad Konstanze (Catherine Naglestad), who sings her aria "Welcher Wechsel herrscht in meiner Seele." The *spielen* on the main stage during the previous scene thus gives way to *singen* on the rear stage.

rehearses the sort of sudden shift that we encountered with the appearance of the andantino section in the quartet that closes act 1: in this case, a shift from the rapid-fire dramatic interplay between Osmin and Blonde to Konstanze's sustained, introspective, lyrical evocation of doubt. To return to language introduced in chapter 1, it strikes me that Clemens Risi's distinction between sense and sensibility (*Sinn/Sinnlichkeit*) in opera can help us to map the topographization of the Stuttgart production.[41] Risi's distinction is drawn from his attempt to account for the play of new interpretive ideas, on the one hand (the *sense* of performance) and the experiences of eventness, on the other (its *sensibility*). Konstanze's gradual emergence from a gentle snowfall during the course of "Welcher Wechsel herrscht in meiner Seele" stages (or materializes) the piece's sudden shift to sensibility, a shift announced in the logic, mood, scoring, and words of the aria itself.

The distinction between the two modes—and its implications for the dramaturgy of the work—emerges most forcefully in Belmonte and

---

"'Accompaniment' is too narrow a term for a complex of phrasing, harmonic rhythm, cadences, motivic structure, and dialogue with the instruments. Mozart used all these elements with unprecedented freedom and plasticity." See Bauman, *Entführung,* 89.

41. See Risi, "Sinn und Sinnlichkeit". The discussion in chapter 1 can be found at pp. 10–11.

Konstanze's ecstatic act 3 recitative and farewell duet (no. 20, in B-flat major), "Welch ein Geschick! O Qual der Seele!" (What a fate! Oh anguish of the soul!). The (singer-) lovers' expressed determination to die together (which they sing from the rear stage) horrifies the assembled crowd left behind on the main stage—a crowd made up not just of Belmonte and Konstanze's actor doubles, but of their companions (both Pedrillos, both Blondes) as well. The production underscores the generic origins and implications of this moment—its grounding in, or, better, its stratospheric flight into a defiant, antirationalist musicality.

By setting these arias on the rear stage, Neuenfels topographizes their distinctness. We experience the production of presence—that is, a lyrical recitation that is spatially and dramaturgically distinct from drama. The production clarifies the singular quality of Konstanze's anguish—or, later, her own and Belmonte's ecstatic will to death—in terms of the architecture of the piece. In doing so, it materializes what we might term a zone of sensibility—a space where the piece's shift from *spielen* to *singen* and from functional drama to pure musicality can take material form. (Implicitly, the production also alerts us to the politics of that zone—to the question of who gains access to it and who is denied that access.) In situating Konstanze-Singer on the rear stage and leaving it to her, the production clarifies that the emergence of *singen* involves the suspension of *spielen*.

The conclusion of act 2 makes a similar point in a different way. The final strophe of the quartet that concludes act 2 is characterized by a typical suspension of drama: the space of the work is given over to an Italianate-finale celebration of love ("Es lebe die Liebe, es lebe die Liebe" [Long live love]).

As the finale gains momentum, the action is suspended, arrested in the course of musical recitation. Here is a choral moment that retraces the generic itinerary of Konstanze's aria—the evacuation of drama in favor of musical recitation, which Neuenfels stages by literalizing its terms. As the voices of the orchestra and the singers merge, the director lends physical form to their sudden union: the orchestra pit rises to the level of the stage, and the singers move out into the orchestra for what constitutes an impromptu (and very brief) concert performance (see figure 23). Much as Neuenfels staged the suspension of dramatic continuity in favor of Konstanze's musical spectacle above and beyond the main stage in act 2, scene 2, here the Stuttgart production stages the evacuation of drama and the concomitant emergence of musical recitation at the end of the act by extending the stage's forward reach, refunctionalizing it as a concert stage, and enacting its shotgun marriage with the pit.

In locating most of the action on the main stage, Neuenfels does not abandon this split between regions—rather, he recasts it. For there is also a

Figure 23 The orchestra rises. To emphasize the sudden dramatic emptiness of the choral finale to the second act, Neuenfels has the orchestra pit literally rise to the level of the stage and has the singers mingle with the orchestra: a staged performance turns into a concert performance.

split *within* the main stage, as I have been suggesting: an internal split, what we might term the split within singspiel. Just as the rear stage (and, momentarily at least, the fore- or concert stage at the end of act 2) serves as a place holder, an impossible materialization of a space beyond or before *fabula*, we might say that the main stage serves as a space where generic problems are worked through. That is, the main stage is not just the place where the singspiel's trials take place, but where its trials *as a singspiel* take place, a forum for the play of sense and sensibility. By contrast, the rear (or, indeed, the secondary) stage, like the suddenly elevated orchestra pit at the end of act 2, is a place of uncontested—often even unmotivated—musical enactment. In the following section, I want to examine how Neuenfels inflects the work's trials as a singspiel.

The Dramaturgy of Enlightenment

As I have been arguing, the Stuttgart production links a series of binary distinctions in Mozart's work—between Europeans and Turks, between enlightenment and barbarism—to the distinction between speaking and singing. Some of this linkage is merely implicit, such as the access to the zone of music above and beyond narrative: thanks to its topographization of discursive modes, the production demonstrates (but hardly trumpets the fact) that the substance of musical reflection—the discursive field where reflection takes place in the work—is reserved for the Europeans. By allocating spaces of introspective lyrical recitation (usually, but not always, at the margins of the stage) and then implicitly reserving those spaces for the Europeans (such as the sudden emergence of a forestage that materializes when the pit rises to the level of the main stage during the finale of act 2), the Stuttgart production suggests that the Europeans alone are accorded the privilege of sustained lyrical expression and its prerequisite, psychological interiority. (When, in the end, Selim reveals himself to be an erstwhile European, he is accorded a modified version of this space where interiority finds musical—or in his case, proto- or paramusical—expression. We will examine this scene below.) But if the rear stage and the forestage, at least in the sense of extradramatic music, emerge only implicitly as a zone of European privilege, the Stuttgart production presents the main stage—the space of drama—as a much more overtly contested space. The terms of contestation repeatedly center on cultural difference, inflected by the Europeans as a matter of access to the trappings of Enlightenment.

Die Entführung aus dem Serail famously offers a lesson in civilization, and the Stuttgart production sharpens the stakes of that lesson, staging the violent effects of the European mantle of civilization, itself a flimsy cover for deep existential doubt. Here, then, we encounter what we might term the production's representational program, its main-stage attraction. By dividing the stage and the players, the Stuttgart production alerts us to the distribution of resources within the work—that is, who gets what and how. The rear stage, we might say, registers the effects of this distribution; the main stage enacts its terms. What transpires on the main stage in Stuttgart will repeatedly suggest that a mastery of forms—be it the forms of Enlightenment civilization or the forms of singspiel—translates into mastery, period.

Before Selim renounces the trappings of barbarism in order to emerge as the consummate Enlightenment rationalist at the end of the work, the Europeans wield the trappings of civilization to outfox and humiliate those ignorant of its precise exigencies. They do so, it turns out, in order to displace onto the "Turks" the doubts repeatedly expressed in their musical material. At the outset of act 2, Blonde's pedagogical aria "Durch Zärtlichkeit und Schmeicheln" would teach Osmin how to treat a "European lady." In the Stuttgart account of the aria, Osmin-Singer is invited to observe as both Pedrillos assist Blonde-Singer with the intricacies of an eighteenth-century lady's *toilette* (see figure 24).

Osmin's introduction to *raffinesse* is thus also—and more obviously—a lesson in his own ignorance. The terms of dramatization come to echo the

Figure 24 Osmin's introduction to *rafinesse*. As Osmin looks on (not visible here), both Pedrillos attend to Blonde, with the intent of showing the barbarian just how to treat a proper lady.

pedagogical terms of the aria: the distinction between the haves and the have-nots (or the civilized and the barbaric, or the European and the Turk) is produced through manners and enacted through music.[42]

An earlier scene operates according to a similar logic. When we left them at the conclusion of act 1, Pedrillo and Belmonte were trying to get past Osmin and into the palace. But even when Pedrillo and Belmonte engage Osmin musically, the latter remains unmoved and, more important, immobile. The impasse is expressed musically: that is, Belmonte and Pedrillo respond to Osmin's musical material, which remains unperturbed by their engagement. Thus, in the course of the confrontation, Osmin, Belmonte, and Pedrillo share essentially equivalent textual and musical material. A brief

42. The dramaturgy of that scene recalls the Victory March in Neuenfels's infamous 1978 Frankfurt production of *Aida,* where the Ethiopians—naked, disoriented, cowering together—are herded into place before a lavish banquet table and ostentatiously presented with European cutlery which they do not know how to use. The massive onstage audience of Egyptians, bedecked in tails and dresses and situated in the boxes of an elite nineteenth-century opera audience, look on appreciatively as some of the Ethiopian "barbarians" jump onto the banquet table, stuffing themselves with handfuls of the roasted meats arrayed on the banquet table while others tear about the stage in fright. The pompous spectacle of the "barbarians'" rampage in *Aida,* like the much more modest scene of the Turk observing the way to dress a European lady here, serves to celebrate the advancement and "civilization" of one culture by contrasting it to the impoverishment and barbarism of another.

consideration of text and music suggests that this is not the most sophisticated of exchanges:

Belmonte and Pedrillo:	Wir gehn hinein!	We're going in!
Osmin:	Sonst schlag' ich drein.	Or else I'll use force!
Belmonte and Pedrillo:	Wir gehn hinein!	We're going in!
Osmin:	Sonst schlag' ich drein.	Or else I'll use force!
Belmonte and Pedrillo:	Wir gehn hinein!	We're going in!
Osmin:	Sonst schlag' ich drein.	Or else I'll use force!

In the Stuttgart production, the musical and textual impasse is not broken by having Belmonte and Pedrillo simply push Osmin aside, as the stage
directions suggest, but by having them introduce the trappings of European
civilization. That is, the Pedrillos and Belmontes are able to distract the two
Osmins by suddenly bringing a telescope and a Warholian image of a buxom
redhead onstage.[43] The Osmins are utterly confounded and, eventually, fas-
cinated by these distractions—most especially by the picture, which Osmin-
Singer lays upon the ground and mounts. By introducing these "civilized"
props, the Europeans literally and figuratively separate themselves from
their more "primitive," "ignorant" Ottoman impediments. In the particular
pickle at the conclusion of act 1 (as throughout the production), the introduction of music shifts the terms of engagement, while the subsequent introduction of cultural artifacts from the "civilized world" resolves the impasse. The scene offers a rare moment of *singspielen*—where dramatic *and*
musical invention are marshaled in the service of the Europeans' cause.

If the Europeans can *sing* and *spiel,* as I have been suggesting, this distinguishes them most decisively from Selim, whose spoken reflections are duly
thoughtful, but stunted by his lack of recourse to music. The inverse is also
true: Osmin's extensive access to musical expression famously distinguishes
him from the tenor, form, and content of "European" music. Osmin has a
great deal of musical material, which is in turn characterized by an extraordinary vocal range, but these ultimately represent matters of quantity, not
quality: in terms of character psychology, Osmin is (and remains) crude and
unsophisticated, the obverse of sensible. An example may help. In the course
of his duet with Blonde, no. 9, "Ich gehe, doch rate ich dir" (I am going, but
I advise you) in act 2, scene 1, Osmin's andante reflection "O, Engländer,
seid ihr nicht Toren" (O Englishmen, aren't you fools) is uncharacteristically

43. The reference to the telescope may allude to Sir William Herschel's invention, in 1782, the
same year as Mozart's composition of *Die Entführung,* of a telescope of unprecedented power, one
which led to Herschel's discovery of Uranus.

Musical Example 4 Osmin's simplicity, musicalized. In this andante section of the opening duet of act 2, Osmin's simplicity is juxtaposed musically with Blonde's sophistication: he is reduced to providing the melodic basis for her embellishments.

gentle, even introspective.[44] But it remains melodically and harmonically elementary, providing a bass line to Blonde's elaborate, characteristically defiant, and comparatively sophisticated melodic embellishment.

Osmin's passage is psychologically (and thus dramaturgically) novel in that it lends voice to a mode of interiority not otherwise borne out by Osmin's music and words. But even that interiority and reflection are in the service of his consternation at Blonde's unwillingness to follow his orders. It's not that Osmin has no interiority, but that the expression of his interiority, like its objectives, is inflected here as unschooled.

44. Wolfgang Amadeus Mozart, *Die Entführung aus dem Serail*, vocal score based on the Urtext of the New Mozart Edition, ed. Gerhard Croll, piano reduction by Jürgen Sommer (Kassel: Bärenreiter, 1982), mm. 56–82, pp. 112–114.

The performance text makes clear that those who wield the logic of enlightenment as a weapon are also tormented by its terms. Although the Turks in the opera text are variously inflected as unmusical or amusical, the Europeans, in their access to music, are shown to be riven by doubt. The Stuttgart production demonstrates that while the Europeans wield culture, they are also wielded by it. More important than the bungled abduction, Belmonte's arrival precipitates a discursive intervention in the seraglio resulting in a cascade of doubts—primarily about fidelity—which in turn produces a cascade of music that gives voice to and works through (*durcharbeiten*) those doubts. Examples of this cascade of doubts include Belmonte's recitative and aria, no. 4, "O wie ängstlich" (Oh, how anxiously) in act 1, scene 5; Konstanze's aria, no. 6, "Ach ich liebte, war so glücklich" (Ah, I loved, was so happy) in act 1, scene 7; and the quartet finale of act 2, no. 16, "Ach, Belmonte, ach mein Leben!" (Ah, Belmonte! Ah, my life!). Selim may speak the Enlightenment, but in not singing, he is kept at some remove from its existential anxieties: thus, his formal situation (as an Other to singing) is arguably a corollary to his political situation (as an Other to European modes of power) and can be seen as a staging of his psychological situation (as an Other to European modes of doubt). In the Stuttgart production, Selim—but not just Selim—comes to wear these distinctions on his sleeve.

The Trappings of Enlightenment Fantasy

As is often the case in comedies (and always the case in Neuenfels's productions), the stakes of character identity are hyperbolized in costume (designed for Stuttgart by Bettina Merz) as well as affect. This is most obviously true with Osmin, the bad-object Ottoman counterpart to the pasha's enlightened nobility. As I suggested at the outset of this chapter, Roland Bracht, who sings Osmin, and Andreas Grötzinger, his actor double, come straight from the bad-guys' dressing room of World Wrestling Entertainment (the Turkish Barbarians?): both Bracht and Grötzinger sport a red Ottoman kilt and beneath it, a skintight beige body suit depicting exotic Ottomaniana. (Despite the shared costumes, the juxtaposition between the two players is quite marked, since Bracht is as hefty as Grötzinger is slender.) The initial appearance of the chorus of Janissaries in act 1, scene 6, is pitched at the same level of lurid fantasy: they carry impaled heads and babies upon the stakes that they rattle, and their costumes inflect them as comic-book renderings of Ottoman barbarians. (They will return, at the conclusion of the work, in tuxes and evening dresses, marking their compliance with a new regime of enlightenment.)

These costumes are not just visually striking, they are also readily legible in terms of the production's dramaturgical logic. Thus, beyond the predictable comic-book appearance of both Blondes as the personification of an English maid (which is spelled out in the text), the costuming inflects the remaining principals as comic-book figures as well, with the arguable exception of Selim and Konstanze. Both Pedrillos appear as eighteenth-century, froufrou-ified Boy Wonders (with lavish blonde hair and pink frills), in contrast to the macho and Zorroesque Spanish appeal of the two Belmontes. Konstanze, on the other hand, is the least obviously inflected of the group: she appears as the naturalized embodiment (which is also to say, in the costume) of loveliness in its contemporary European forms.[45] Like the chorus, Pasha Selim enacts in one body the split otherwise enacted by the doubling of roles: he first appears onstage as a charismatic modern terrorist, à la Abu Nidal or Carlos the Jackal,[46] skulking about amid his band of followers, wearing a black ski mask and trench coat, bearing Konstanze-Actor, passed out, in his arms. For the final scene of absolution, Selim's outfit will bear out his shift in identity: he reappears in tails (see figures 25 and 26). In that sense, we might say that Selim embodies a trajectory from terrorism to the paternal law—appearing first as an outlaw, if only to emerge not just *in* but *as* the name of the father.[47]

A Lyrical Voice of the Father?

Something strange happens in the wake of the production's topographization of discourses, its assignment of spoken and sung text to distinct bodies and realms. Like the reified identities—for example, the Turkish despot or the

45. I employ the plural because, like the Osmin doubles, the actress and singer playing Konstanze look noticeably different: Catherine Naglestad, the soprano, is a slender, relatively placid brunette, while the actress, Emanuela von Frankenberg, is a slender, demonstratively frenetic blonde.

46. Until his reported death in 2002, Abu Nidal, the alias of Sabri al-Banna, served as the reputed leader of the Abu Nidal Group, also known as the Fatah Revolutionary Council and, earlier, Black September. Ilyich Ramírez Sánchez, nicknamed "Carlos the Jackal," was, until his arrest and imprisonment in 1994, one of the most prominent "revolutionary terrorists," thought to be behind the hijacking of an El Al jet at Entebbe, Uganda, and for the attacks on Israeli athletes at the 1972 Olympic games in Munich.

47. See Gilles de Van's suggestive ruminations on the relationship between song and the law: "Musically, as an order governing the individual but at the same time restraining him, the law is for the most part expressed by a declamation very close to *recto tono*, that is, to a minimum amount of song, as, for example, the voice in *Idomeneo*, the Commendatore in the graveyard scene of *Don Giovanni*, Monterone in *Rigoletto*, the priests in *Aida*, and so on. The more the voice embodies the law as supreme authority, the more rigid song becomes, confining itself to a solemn, austere declamation that shuns melisma. In short, the law kills song but at the same time serves as its guiding light." De Van, "Aesthetics," 57.

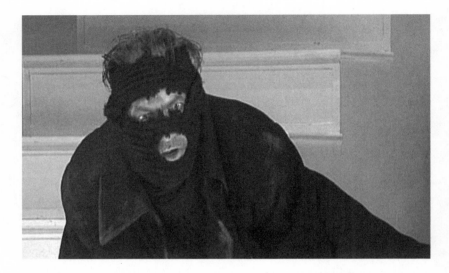

Figures 25 and 26 The civilization of Pasha. Selim's transformation during the opera is encapsulated in his costume: he first appears as a terrorist (*top*); by the end of the opera, he is wearing tails (*bottom*).

European nobleman—which are cultivated in the piece only to be reversed and presumably discarded, the production ends up complicating the very generic identities that it has done so much to fix. Thus, having been clearly distinguished in the course of the production, *singen* (as the means of lyrical transcendence or re-presentation) and *spielen* (as the means of representing action) are reproduced, by the conclusion of the mise-en-scène, as reversible. In this way, we might say, the production goes about deconstructing the piece's claims to singspiel—interrogating its component parts—if only, in the end, to reconstitute them. But how?

In some of the most musically exquisite moments of the piece— Konstanze's act 2 aria, no. 10, "Traurigkeit ward mir zum Lose" (Sorrow has become my fate) or Belmonte's act 1 recitative and aria, "O wie ängstlich" (Oh, how anxiously)—the mise-en-scène demonstrates that music functions here not merely as a realm of presence (to use Gumbrecht's term), but as a realm where the claims to presence are represented (to use Gumbrecht's counterterm). Conversely, Selim's concluding—and, of course, spoken— lines approach the condition of music. In one of Neuenfels's most striking textual interventions, Selim's turn from Ottoman despotism to Enlightenment rationality is doubled by a generic turn, from functional spoken text to poetic recitation.

Normally, the singspiel concludes with a *vaudeville* and chorus, both of which celebrate Selim's honor and his beneficence in allowing the Europeans their freedom. In Stuttgart, Selim steps forward and responds to the cascade of adoration. Having been duly celebrated by all,[48] Selim waves off the applause of the crowd onstage and in the auditorium with these words:

> *Selim:* Thank you, thank you, ladies and gentleman. You see, if one is a character in such a work, and one is unable to sing, like the others on stage here, one faces a choice between despair or evil. But then, as I was back in my dressing room, a poem occurred to me that taught a better lesson. The words are, in their way, as lovely as the singers' music. I'd like to recite it here: it's brief, and by Eduard Mörike.

He then continues:

DENK' ES, O SEELE	IMAGINE THAT, O SOUL
Ein Tännlein grünet wo,	A little pine is sprouting somewhere,
Wer weiß, im Walde,	Who knows, in the forest;
Ein Rosenstrauch, wer sagt,	A rose bush, who can say,
In welchem Garten?	Blooms in which garden?
Sie sind erlesen schon,	Already they are destined,

---

48. Strangely enough, Mozart includes Osmin in the refrain that follows the first three stanzas of the *Vaudeville*. On the musical dramaturgy of Osmin's participation in the concluding *Vaudeville*, see Bauman, *Entführung*, 95–97.

Denk' es, o Seele,	Imagine that, o soul,
Auf deinem Grab zu wurzeln	To take root upon your grave
Und zu wachsen.	And to grow there.
Zwei schwarze Rößlein weiden	Two black ponies graze
Auf der Wiese,	In the meadow,
Sie kehren heim zur Stadt	Back to town they go,
In muntern Sprüngen.	Happily cantering.
Sie werden schrittweis gehn	They'll walk step by step
Mit deiner Leiche;	Pulling your corpse;
Vielleicht, vielleicht noch eh'	Perhaps, perhaps before
An ihren Hufen	Their hoofs let fall
Das Eisen los wird,	The iron shoes
Das ich blitzen sehe!	That I see flashing![49]

The poem, first published in 1851, some seventy years after the premiere of *Die Entführung,* reappeared four years later, in 1855, as the concluding lines of Mörike's novella *Mozart auf der Reise nach Prag* (*Mozart on the Journey to Prague*), an account of a day in the life of the composer as he heads from Vienna to Prague to attend the premiere of *Don Giovanni.*[50] In Mörike's novella, Mozart ends up playing piano for a crowd assembled at the *Schloss* of the Count and Countess von Schinzburg, who are celebrating the engagement of their niece Eugenie. In the wake of Mozart's astonishing performance and sudden departure, Eugenie closes the piano and cleans up the assorted music. As she does so, a sheet of music falls to the ground, a "little Bohemian folk song" (*böhmisches Volksliedchen*), the lyrics of which are Mörike's poem.

The poem offers more than yet another intervention in the text of the libretto. In the most immediate sense, it fulfills the terms of Selim's aspiration: in Mörike's novella, the poem is presented as a song text that approaches the condition of musicality (and in particular, the folksy musicality that marks the melody of the concluding *vaudeville*). But beyond that, the text renders in poetic form a recurring claim about Mozart's works, one issued by a number of Mozart critics and staged in turn by the Stuttgart *Ent-*

49. *Friedrich Hölderlin, Eduard Mörike: Selected Poems,* trans. Christopher Middleton (Chicago: University of Chicago Press, 1972), 216–17, translation modified. See also the translation in Eduard Mörike, *Mozart's Journey to Prague and Selected Poems,* trans. and introd. David Luke (London: Libris, 1997), 71.

50. On the poem's publication history, see Eduard Mörike, *Sämtliche Werke in zwei Bänden,* mit einem Nachwort von Benno von Wiese sowie Anmerkungen, Zeittafel und Bibliographie von Helga Unger (Munich: Winkler, 1967), 1:1073, n. 745.

führung: that Mozart's music, even at its most comical, is often also characterized by a sense of despair. The poem rehearses this claim in its repeated movement in each stanza from an initial evocation of a pastoral idyll (in the first quatrain), to a scene of imminent death (in the concluding quatrain). If this movement lands the poem in the dramaturgical territory of *Don Giovanni* (an association borne out by Mörike's novella), the Stuttgart production suggests that it also applies to the dramaturgy of *Die Entführung.* In a general sense, the poem instantiates how, through directorial intervention—but not just that—Mozart's work comes to lose a good deal of its familiar and rather manic comic quality. What emerges in its place is a sense of imminent despair—some of it situational (after all, the Europeans in this piece have been abducted and are being held captive) and some of it a product of human frailty (on the one hand, the recurring and nagging doubts that the Europeans have regarding each other's fidelity, and on the other hand, Selim and Osmin's very different if nonetheless palpable sadness at being spurned by their European love objects). What this production makes clear is that the principals in this piece—Belmonte and Konstanze, in particular, but others as well—are not simply trapped in their rather flimsily constructed roles. Indeed, entrapment may well seem like an odd term for the principals' condition, given that the mise-en-scène splits their roles. But this splitting does not liberate the characters. Instead, it serves to clarify the terms of their constriction. Which brings us to the second effect produced by the Mörike poem—in this case, a local, dramatic effect. For when Selim pipes up with his (re-presentational) poem, and in particular, when he mentions that it is by Mörike, the actor doubles of the Europeans—Pedrillo, Belmonte, and Blonde—perk up noticeably. Here at last is a brief moment of—or at least approaching—discursive parity, a textual contribution that is arguably on par with Mozart's musical invention. In the wake of Selim's reading, Konstanze-Singer, moved, approaches and thanks him.[51]

The final exchange doubles the political turning of the tables with a generic turn: beyond the by now familiar coup de théâtre by which the Turkish despot emerges as more enlightened than the Europeans, here (the sole speaker's) speaking approaches the condition of singing, and for once, the singers (standing here for the condition of singing) are moved by text,

51. The final exchange between Konstanze and Selim echoes the repeated exchanges between the two Belmontes:

Konstanze-Singer: Danke, Selim, danke.
Selim: Bitte, Konstanze, bitte.

[*Konstanze-Singer:* Thanks, Selim, thanks.
Selim: You're welcome, Konstanze; you're welcome.]

rather than the actors (standing here for the condition of speaking) being displaced—or simply rendered superfluous—by singing. In the end, then, the piece is suspended in a kind of discursive interstice between singing and speaking, between presence and hermeneutics, between sensibility and sense, just as it is suspended between enlightenment and barbarism, between Turkey and Europe.

The Stuttgart production does both: it offers us a realm of musical recitation (an avatar of Gumbrecht's culture of presence) at times spatially distinct from and thus implicitly antithetical to spoken drama (an avatar of Gumbrecht's culture of representation), but it also represents this distinction and ultimately suggests the co-imbrication of the two. We might say that the production cultivates a distinct realm of re-presentation while staging its effects in the service of representation. Can poetry constitute a lyrical voice of the father? Is there a presence in *spielen* and a hermeneutics in *singen*? Can music—set apart from and raised above or beyond the space of dramatic enactment—nonetheless serve the cause of a logophilic, if not a logocentric, drama? These are questions raised by the Stuttgart *Entführung*.

5

BETWEEN SUBLIMATION AND AUDACITY

Verdi's *Don Carlos*

Despite their manifold differences, the two Mozart productions considered in chapters 3 and 4 presumed a condition of interpretive mutability—a sense that the work is properly the object of creative engagement, of what detractors will call "directorial license." But if such a license exists—and it should be clear by now that I believe it does—it is fair to ask how it is issued and by whom. Our review of the emergence of dramaturgy and a modern conception of stage direction in chapter 1 suggested that the project of reimagining canonical stage works took form in the nineteenth century and was licensed ultimately by the state, which funded the theaters and therewith granted institutional sanction to the creative, interpretive functions of the dramaturg and the director. As dramaturgy and directing emerged as institutionalized forms of interpretation, so too did a host of operas that reflected upon—or at least allegorically figured—that emergence.[1] In chapter 2, I proposed a reading of the self-referential aesthetic politics of Wagner's *Meistersinger*: the work, I argued, stages the scene of interpretive engagement—a scene of reading—as a moment that separates the wheat from the chaff, or, more precisely, the young and authentic composer-artist of the future (who has no need of the mediation afforded by reading) from the aging, impotent pedant (who is wholly dependent upon that mediation). In Wagner's work, we were reminded that on the one hand, the guardians of aesthetic production, those empowered to grant a license to creative freedom, run the risk of stifling the very freedom of aesthetic expression they are supposed to foster. On the

1. On the artist opera, see John Bokina, "Resignation, Retreat, and Impotence: The Aesthetics and Politics of the Modern German Artist-Opera," *Cultural Critique* 9 (Spring 1988): 157–95. Bokina's essay also appears in his *Opera and Politics: From Monteverdi to Henze* (New Haven, Conn.: Yale University Press, 1997), 128–66.

other hand, Wagner also critiques Walther, the outsider artist-hero whose application for a license has been—unjustly—turned down. Although Wagner certainly sympathizes with Walther's protest against the regime of aesthetic corruption, he chastises his hero's wholesale (and thus properly adolescent) defiance of convention. As a comedy, the forces of aesthetic mutability win out in the end—in this case, a mutability in league with convention. The new folk hero wins the song contest, gets the girl, and is—belatedly—granted his Mastersinger's license, but he also comes to the sentimental recognition that the license is worth something, and that innovation without respect for aesthetic convention (and, with it, the very category of mastery) will not do. The conflict between innovation and convention yields a compromise encompassing the best of both. But as we noted, there is a remainder to this neat resolution, attested to by the discarded piece of paper upon which Walther's song was transcribed and by the discarded "Jew" who failed in his attempt to read it.

Of course, there are other versions of this confrontation between innovation and convention, and in this chapter I propose to consider one of its tragic incarnations. Thus, I would like to return to a question posed in chapter 1, namely, how we might account for the relationship between the thematic concerns expressed in the opera text and their realization in the performance text, onstage. Here, again, I want to consider a work whose themes engage the question of staging, though in less overtly aesthetic terms than in the *Meistersinger*. And yet, the questions posed in and around *Don Carlos* regarding the need to resist or accommodate oneself to discursive norms land us squarely in the midst of the very debates about staging with which this book is concerned.

Throughout this book, I have been arguing for a form of reading whose impetus is dramaturgical as well as philological, where the energies of interpretation extend beyond familiar concerns (e.g., which version of the work to stage) to a concern with the dramaturgical terms of performance (e.g., what to do with the work onstage). So far, my response to this latter question has been threaded through particular productions. That is not the only way to address it. In this chapter, I propose a different sequence of dramaturgical reading, one that begins prior to mise-en-scène. That is, instead of analyzing a particular production, I propose a reading of *Don Carlos*. Which brings us back to the distinction, introduced in chapter 1, between the opera text and the performance text. Let me briefly summarize the terms as employed by Barbara Hodgdon in *The End Crowns All*.[2] In her study, Hodgdon seeks to move beyond

---

2. Barbara Hodgdon, *The End Crowns All: Closure and Contradiction in Shakespeare's History* (Princeton, N.J.: Princeton University Press, 1991).

the impasse between the antitextualist bent in performance studies and the narrowly textual wing of Shakespeare studies. To that end, she distinguishes between textual regimes in performance, where the "playtext" encompasses the material, textual traces of Shakespeare's play, and the "performance text" encompasses the material traces of the work in (and of) performance.

> When I refer specifically to the words that are traditionally construed as "Shakespeare's play," I generally use the term "playtext," both to convey some sense of their indeterminacy and to differentiate them from other, more determinate, textual categories. To further destabilize both the ideal of an established, authoritative text of a Shakespeare play and the notion that the written word represents the only form in which a play can possess or participate in textuality, I refer to theatrical representations as "performance texts," an apparent oxymoron that freely acknowledges the perceived incompatibility between the (infinitely) flexible substate(s) of a Shakespearean play and the (relative) fixity of the term "text."[3]

As I suggested above, my reading of the opera text, while prior to mise-en-scène, is nonetheless conceived with an eye to the possibility of production. In this case, the latter follows upon the former: once we have a clear sense of what is at stake in the opera text, we can consider how best to render those stakes in production. This reverses the trajectory of the preceding two chapters, where our consideration of a particular performance text decisively shaped a reconsideration of the opera text.

In the case of *Don Carlos,* the first question is which version of the work to read. Insofar as the opera text depicts a crisis that stems in part from what I am terming an immutability of discourse, then surely that crisis will be affected by a multiplication of renderings, by what Roger Parker terms the "openness" of the work.[4] The piece exists in many different versions (as *Don Carlos* in French and *Don Carlo* in Italian; in five acts and four; with and without a ballet)—versions prepared over a span of twenty years, from 1866 to 1886, when Verdi's compositional style was undergoing enormous changes.[5] According

3. Ibid., 18–19.

4. Roger Parker, "On Reaching the Beguiled Shore," in *Leonora's Last Act: Essays in Verdian Analysis* (Princeton, N.J.: Princeton University Press, 1997), 10.

5. See, e.g., Budden, who argues that *"Don Carlos's* place in the Verdi canon will probably fluctuate for many years to come. One can never over-estimate its importance in the evolution of the composer's style." Julian Budden, *From Don Carlos to Falstaff,* vol. 3 of *The Operas of Verdi,* rev. ed. (Oxford: Oxford University Press, 1992), 157. *Don Carlos* takes off—geographically and historically—where *Macbeth* leaves off: the recomposition of *Macbeth* encompasses the period from 1847 to 1865, and a trajectory from Florence to Paris; *Don Carlos* premiered in Paris in 1867 and was revised for performances throughout Italy through the mid-1880s.

to Julian Budden, "No other opera of Verdi's contains such a wealth of alternative and superseded material, so little of which can be dismissed out of hand."[6] As a *grand-opéra* in five acts with a French libretto by Joseph Méry and Camille du Locle, *Don Carlos* premiered in Paris at the Théâtre Impérial de l'Opéra on March 11, 1867. Verdi undertook a number of substantial revisions prior to the Parisian premiere and even more—including Italian translations—for Italian productions that followed, in Naples (1872), Milan (1884), and Modena (1886).[7] For the work's production at La Scala in 1884 (originally slated for Vienna), Verdi trimmed the five-act Parisian version in French into a four-act version without a ballet in Italian.[8] By Ursula Günther's calculation, Verdi cut approximately 50 percent of the 1867 version for La Scala, adding additional material that in turn accounted for approximately one-third of the new version.[9] Despite the fact that the opera was originally written for Paris and that Verdi's publisher, Ricordi, published a French edition of the revised work in 1884, it was better known to the world in its Italian incarnations—as *Don Carlo*—until the publication of the new complete edition in 1974. It comes as little surprise when Julian Budden concludes his exhaustive analysis by observing that "there can be no simple answer" to the question of "what the ideal form [is] in which to give *Don Carlos*."[10] The

6. Budden, *From Don Carlos to Falstaff*, 38.

7. Ursula Günther calculates that there were a total of seven versions of the work "conceived or accepted by Verdi." See her extensive explanatory essay and apparatus in *The Complete Edition of Don Carlos by Giuseppe Verdi*, Eng. trans. Lionel Salter (Milan: Ricordi, 1974), 20; hereafter cited as Günther, *Complete* (Eng.). For his part, Budden recognizes five basic versions of the work: (1) the original full-length conception of 1866 preceding the cuts made before the first performance; (2) *Don Carlos* as published in 1867 with five acts and ballet; (3) The Naples version of 1872, identical with (2) except for the alterations in the Posa-Philippe and final Carlos-Elisabeth duets; (4) the new four-act version without ballet of 1884; and (5) the Modena amalgam of 1886, published by Ricordi as "new edition in five acts without ballet." Budden, *From Don Carlos to Falstaff*, 38–39.

8. See Clemens Höslinger, "Dokumente zum Wiener Don Carlos-Projekt (1872–1884): Die Ursachen des Scheiterns von Verdis Oper in Wien, dargestellt auf Grundlage der Opernakten des Haus-, Hof und Staatsarchivs," in *Festschrift Leopold M. Kantner zum 70. Geburtstag*, ed. Michael Jahn and Angela Pachovsky (Tutzing: Schneider, 2002), 185–207.

9. See Günther, *Complete* (Eng.), 3. For a detailed account of the compositional and performance history, see also Budden, *From Don Carlos to Falstaff*, 5–39. On the exigencies of Verdi's revisions to Schiller's play, see Martin Chusid, "Schiller Revisited: Some Observations on the Revision of 'Don Carlos,'" in *Atti del IIo Congresso Internazionale di Studi Verdiani* (Parma: Istituto di Studi Verdiani, 1971), 156–169. Chusid argues that the successive revisions of the opera brought it closer to Schiller's drama than the original opera as performed in 1867.

10. Budden, *From Don Carlos to Falstaff*, 156. Ursula Günther echoes Budden's position: "Which of the many possible versions of *Don Carlos* should be performed today? It is not easy to answer this question according to the composer's intention, since Verdi's opinions about *Don Carlos* in some points changed considerably in the course of the work's twenty year development." Günther, *Complete* (Eng.), 21.

four-act Milan revision of 1882–83 deletes the entirety of the first act, which appears in various forms in the five-act versions for Paris, Naples, and Modena.[11] But as Roger Parker has argued, even smaller-scale interventions, such as the decision whether or not to include the introduction and the wood-cutters' chorus in the first act of a five-act version, resonate in important ways for the logic—and, more important, for our understanding—of the work.[12] Nevertheless, there are some themes that remain largely the same: in each of the versions, Carlos and Elisabeth must come to terms with a devastating reversal in their relationship. The shifting grounds upon which they negotiate this reversal are not just philological (dependent, that is, upon the version of the work being performed); they are also at once political and personal. Indeed, in *Don Carlos,* there is no functional border between the political and the personal.[13] The piece exudes a sense of claustrophobia and surveillance, such that the most intimate scenes are repeatedly and tragically rendered public, and the most public scenes are repeatedly shot through with bitter private disputes.

Like anyone working with the complete edition (in this case, in the form of a piano-vocal reduction) and the multiplicity of possible performance versions it provides, I propose to work with a particular version of the piece. For the purposes of this chapter, then, I will refer to an amalgam of the earliest and latest versions of the work, the five-act version for Modena of 1886 and the five-act version for Paris in 1866–67 prior to the cuts undertaken for the premiere. (Thus, I will retain the woodcutters' chorus from act 1 as it appears in the Paris rehearsal edition of 1866.) During the course of the chapter, I will explain in greater detail the logic behind the editorial choices I propose. In general, the amalgam I consider here offers the fullest and most coherent (and, I hope, the most satisfying) accounting of the problematics that I take to be central to the work. And one final note: in order to spare the reader repeated

11. The five-act version for Modena (1886) deletes the opening prelude and woodcutters' chorus from the first act. For a detailed and exceedingly helpful overview of the distinctions between the various versions of the piece, see the (bilingual) comparative table of contents that serves as part of the prefatory material to the Günther and Petazzoni's edition of the piano-vocal score. See Giuseppe Verdi, *"Don Carlos": Edizione integrale delle varie versioni in cinque e in quattro atti,* 2 vols., ed. Ursula Günther and Luciano Petazzoni (Milan: Ricordi, 1974–1980), 1:XXXVIII–XLIII, hereafter cited as *Don Carlos,* PV. In his essay on *Don Carlos* as *Bildungsoper,* David Rosen provides a cogent overview of the different versions. See table 1, "An Overview of the Principal Versions of Verdi's *Don Carlos,"* in Rosen, *"Don Carlos as Bildungsoper: Carlos's Last Act,"* *Cambridge Opera Journal* 14, no. 1–2 (2002):109–131, at 111.

12. See Parker, "On Reaching the Beguiled Shore," 10–13.

13. See Anthony Arblaster, "Verdi: The Liberal Patriot," in *Viva la Libertà! Politics in Opera* (London: Verso, 1992), 133.

and potentially confusing references to various versions of the opera, I will, in the following, refer to the five-act Paris version of 1866–67 unless otherwise indicated. As previously noted, I derive the spelling of characters' names and the opera's title from the Paris version as well.

No Shelter

Let us begin with a few French words—*hardiesse, audace,* and *oser*—taken from the French text of Verdi's piece. Each is an expression about expression and, more particularly, about expressive limits. *Hardiesse* translates as "audacity" or "cheek" (as when Philippe responds to Elisabeth's protest in act 4: "Vous me parlez avec hardiesse!" [You speak to me with audacity]); [14] *audace* translates, of course, as "audacity" (as when Philippe warns Posa in their duet in act 2, "Je pardonne à l'audace ... Quelquefois" [Audacity is something I can tolerate, sometimes]); [15] and finally, *oser dire* translates as "to dare to say" (as when Posa asks the king, at the conclusion of their duet, "Qu'osez-vous dire?" [What are you daring to say]?). [16] In this chapter, I propose to examine the dramaturgy of expression in *Don Carlos,* considering its logic and implications. For it strikes me that this work is preoccupied with a politics of expression: what people can and cannot express and why. This is, of course, a subject of particular interest to psychoanalysis, and so I will be referring to psychoanalytic theory to elucidate what I take to be some of the salient dramaturgical problems in the work. At the same time, this is an opera—and not, significantly, Schiller's play. So we can expect the forms of expression in this opera—including their suppression—to take hyperbolized form.

Let us begin with the setting. It is winter, it is cold in the forest, and off in the distance we can discern the outlines of a castle. Courtly life forms the backdrop for this opening scene; by contrast, the foreground is marked by a rather stark image of nature: according to the stage directions, "un grand rocher forme une sorte d'abri" (a large rock forms a sort of shelter). [17] The qualification is noteworthy: a *sort* of shelter, *une* sorte *d'abri.* There are all

14. *Don Carlos,* PV, 2:508.

15. Ibid., 1:207.

16. Ibid., 1:224.

17. Ibid., 1:1. For a sketch of the setting for the first scene as envisioned in the third edition (1884) of the *disposizione scenica* for the Paris production, originally published in 1867, see Jennifer Batchelor, ed., *Giuseppe Verdi: Don Carlos/Don Carlo,* Opera Guide 46 (New York: Riverrun, 1992), 35. Because the English translation (by Andrew Porter) provided in Batchelor's volume is a singing translation, I have chosen to refer instead to a recent literal translation by Gwynn Morris published as part of the trilingual libretto accompanying the Sony Classics recording of Verdi, *Don Carlo* (Italian version in five acts), featuring Michael Sylvester as Carlo, Aprile Milo as Elisabeth, Ferruccio Furlanetto as King Philip, and

sorts of shelters to be found in *Don Carlos*—public and private, abstract and concrete, large and small—but few turn out to be substantial. For example, although that rock in the foreground will not crush Elisabeth and Carlos as they fall in love, it will not shelter them when their love is quashed. Or, a bit more abstractly, the king, the queen, and the prince are afforded little protection by their august stations. Thus, although the woodcutters in act 1 can observe wistfully, "Que le sort des rois est heureux!" (the lot of kings is a fortunate one),[18] we soon learn that the crown weighs heavily upon Philippe II: "You've seen me on the throne, but haven't seen into my home," the panicked king explains to Posa near the end of act 2. "Everywhere, rumors of treason! The Queen. A suspicion torments me! My son! . . . "[19] And if political stature affords no apparent protection, a large and familiar part of this piece's polemic is that the church, that shelter of shelters, is a source of immense oppression rather than comfort.[20]

So where is shelter to be found? Certainly not in romance: the piece will depict romantic fantasy as especially treacherous. In revolutionary—or at least resistant—politics, then? Not really. As Paul Robinson has pointed out, the conventionally sentential music of Posa's idealism inflects its appeal as unduly simplistic.[21] And what of sublimation or accommodation—that is, a

Vladimir Chernov as Rodrigo; Metropolitan Opera Orchestra and Chorus, conducted by James Levine, S3K 52 500 (Sony Classics, 1993); hereafter cited as Morris, "Libretto."

18. *Don Carlos*, PV, 1:15; Morris, "Libretto," 50–51.

19. *Don Carlos*, PV, 1:222–23.

20. See Arblaster's claim that "in at least one respect *Don Carlos* is more daring than anything Verdi had done before: it embodies his most unqualified, frontal attack on the Catholic Church. . . . Even as the conflict between nation and papacy was coming to a head in Italy, Verdi sought to dramatize the conflict of Church and State in the most vivid way. And between the two, Verdi leaves us in no doubt that it is the Church that is the more powerful and the more ruthless." Arblaster, "Verdi," 137–38.

21. In Robinson's account, Posa's inflexible idealism is increasingly anathematic to Verdi, who was, at this point in his career, increasingly attracted to a Philippelike *Realpolitik*. See Paul Robinson, "*Realpolitik:* Giuseppe Verdi's *Don Carlo*," in *Opera and Ideas: From Mozart to Strauss* (Ithaca, N.Y.: Cornell University Press, 1985), esp. 180–87. According to Robinson, "It is part of Verdi's musical intention to distance us from Rodrigo's unpsychological view of the world. Therefore we experience his music—with its broad tunes, regular rhythms, and obvious harmonies—as slightly patronizing. Set against the complex musical texture of the opera as a whole, it seems one-dimensional—just as his liberalism is one-dimensional when measured against the *Realpolitiker*'s richly nuanced understanding of human psychology and the intricacies of power." Robinson, "Realpolitik," 183. For his part, Budden notes that Posa, "as Verdi later admitted, was an operatic problem with which he would gladly have dispensed." Budden goes on to suggest that Posa's idealism combined with his "unswerving selflessness makes him musically rather uninteresting. Even at the height of his greatness Verdi can find for him nothing more impressive than a stream of generically noble baritone melody." Budden, *From Don Carlos to Falstaff*, 139. In "On Reaching the Beguiled Shore," Parker takes issue with these characterizations: "In the rather sparse critical writing on *Don Carlos*, Rodrigue, Marquis de Posa, has had a bad

coming to terms with one's lot? It is, after all, a relatively familiar motif in the critical literature on *Don Carlos*.[22] With good reason: the demands placed upon Carlos and Elisabeth to renounce a fervent and suddenly illicit love in the interests of propriety and the state line up with Freud's account of the logic and operations of sublimation. And the piece arguably gives voice to the productive element of sublimation, its affinity with creativity: in this piece, most of the principal characters are at their lyrical best when they're worst off.[23] The king's rumination on his broken marriage, the queen's protest of her invaded privacy, Princess Eboli's reflection on her detested beauty, Elisabeth and Carlos's recollections of their doomed love—the piece appears to invest its expressive force in offering ever more nuanced evocations of misery.

Most of the characters, we might say, seem to be as resolutely lacking in shelter as they are in desperate need of it. And lest we forget, the work keeps reminding us and reintroducing us to a pervading sense of vulnerability. At the outset of the first act (of the five-act version composed for the Paris premiere), for example, the woodcutters catalog their privations: "L'hiver est long! La vie est dure! Le pain est cher! Quand donc finira ta froidure, O sombre hiver! Hélas! Quand finira la guerre?" (The winter is long! Life is hard! Bread is dear! Your frost will never end, o bitter winter! Alas, will the war ever finish?).[24] And then again, at the outset of the second act,[25] the choir of monks informs us that "Charles-Quint, l'auguste Empereur, N'est plus que cendre et que poussière. Et maintenant, son âme altière est tremblante aux pieds du Seigneur!" (Charles V, the supreme Emperor, is nothing but silent dust. At the feet of his Heavenly Maker his haughty spirit now trembles).[26] Until the very end, with its ambivalent coup de théâtre, *Don Carlos* is a work with more than its share of claustrophobia, more than its share of shelters that do not shelter.[27]

---

press, and since I love almost every note Verdi wrote for him, I have sometimes wondered why." See Parker, "On Reaching the Beguiled Shore," 14–19.

22. See Robinson, *"Realpolitik"*; and Heather Wiebe, "Conquering Desire: *Don Carlos* and the Problem of Interiority," in Della Seta, Marvin, and Marica, *Verdi 2001*, 2:545–67.

23. I will consider the exceptions to this condition—Posa (the idealist), on the one hand, and the Grand Inquisitor (the master oppressor), on the other—later in this chapter.

24. *Don Carlos*, PV, 1:3–5; Morris, "Libretto," 49.

25. The four-act version for Milan begins with this scene at the monastery of Saint Just.

26. *Don Carlos*, PV, 1:96; Morris, "Libretto," 79. The Paris version concludes with the first two lines of this refrain as Charles V drags his grandson into the gates of the monastery. See *Don Carlos*, PV, 2:650–51.

27. See Dieter Schnebel's reading of the opera: "Dem Anschein nach ist der Inhalt der Oper ohnehin tief resignativ: alles endet im Aussichtslosen—am Schluß ist Posa tot, Carlos verschwindet in rätselhafter Weise, die Prinzessin geht ins Kloster, der König und die Königin haben keine Zukunft mehr. Nur der selbst schon eigentlich leblose Großinquisitor bleibt—scheinbar der Sieger; und damit ist die alte Ordnung wieder restituiert" (By all appearances, the contents of the opera are in any case deeply resigned: everything ends in futility. By the conclusion of the work, Posa is dead, Carlos disappears

And that, it seems, is the point. In *Don Carlos,* shelters only materialize when it is too late, after all hope of their protection has been abandoned. This is especially true in the realm of discourse. Although characters in the work repeatedly resort to what we might term a sheltering designation— moments where they recognize and designate each other as lovers or friends—these moments are repeatedly and insistently annulled.[28] Thus, and most obviously, Carlos and Elisabeth will have to come to terms with their powerlessness to designate one another as lovers, or indeed, their inability to make such designations stick. But so too will King Philippe learn that he cannot simply designate Posa a friend, that he can neither shelter himself from his "jours d'épreuves" (sorry days) nor Posa from the Inquisition. For his part, Posa offers Carlos the shelter of an unflinching devotion and loyalty—and with it, the promise of honesty and intimacy;[29] but when Posa disarms Carlos in the course of the Infante's public challenge to the king at the conclusion of act 3, it would appear—and it certainly appears to Carlos—that Posa's professed loyalties were a sham. The work, we might

---

mysteriously, the princess is headed to the cloister, the king and queen can have no hope for the future. The only one left standing is the seemingly lifeless Grand Inquisitor—seemingly the victor; and in this way, the old order is once again restored.) Ultimately, according to Schnebel, the sense of resignation is implicitly dissolved by the reemergence of Charles V as the embodiment of a latent aspiration to utopia. See Dieter Schnebel, "Die schwierige Wahrheit des Lebens: Zu Verdis musikalischem Realismus," in *Giuseppe Verdi,* ed. Heinz-Klaus Metzger and Rainer Riehn, *Musik-Konzepte* 10 (Munich: Edition Text + Kritik, 1979), 51–111, here 97.

28. And just to be clear: vindictive nomination is shown to exceed individual control as well: both Eboli and the king will wrongly accuse Elisabeth of infidelity.

29. See the terms of their encounter in act 2, scene 1, where, for example, Don Carlos and Posa engage in the following exchange:

Carlos:	Ah! Mon compagnon, mon ami, mon frère,
	Laisse-moi pleurer dans tes bras!
	Dans tout l'empire de mon père,
	Je n'ai que ce coeur, ne m'en bannis pas!
Rodrigue:	Oh Carlos, mon ami, mon frère,
	Je t'ouvre encor mon coeur!
	Pour le sceptre d'or de ton père,
	Mon coeur, ne changerait pas!

Carlos:	My comrade, my friend, my brother,
	Let me weep in your arms!
	In all my father's empire
	I have only this heart! Do not banish me from it!
Rodrigue:	O Carlos, my friend, my brother,
	Again I open to you my heart!
	For your father's golden sceptre
	My heart would not change!

Don Carlos, PV, 1:120–22; Morris, "Libretto," 56.

say, dramatizes the process of coming to terms with this undoing of (individuated) terms. Put otherwise, the work stages a thoroughgoing immutability of discourse and circumstance, an overarching and often overwhelming sense that names—and, along with them, circumstances—cannot be changed to protect the innocent. Instead, the innocent will have to adapt to discursive and circumstantial imperatives. Thus, in *Don Carlos,* sublimation will figure as a kind of sham shelter of last resort—a position that the piece recognizes and laments. The dramaturgy of audacity will eventually gather us (in the audience) and them (on the stage) around this shelter, in all of its theatrical and visceral ambivalence. Thus, at the work's conclusion, Carlos and Elisabeth have finally abandoned a zone of volatile and uncontrolled expression (such that audacity is, for them, a thing of the past, a matter of shared, sentimental, lyrical reflection). It is at this point that the king and the Grand Inquisitor will show up in yet another melodramatic turn—only to be in turn astonished by the reemergence of that most astonishing of characters, the undead father. I want to explore the ramifications of this bizarre dramaturgical trajectory, not only for the characters within the work but also for the work's disposition onstage.

Ventriloquizing Assent

We first encounter Carlos, son of Spain's King Philippe II, in the forest of Fontainebleau, far from the castle (visible in the distance) and within a stone's throw of that large rock. In a recitative that precedes his only solo aria in the opera, the Infante fashions an account of romantic insubordination: he came to the French forest in defiance of his father and his own princely (and filial) responsibilities, hoping to catch a glimpse of his "belle fiancée," Elisabeth of Valois, daughter of France's Henry II and Caterina de' Medici. His hopes have been realized: he saw her pass by, he reports—"celle qui désormais régnait dans ma pensée" (she who forever more now will rule in my heart). The solo aria that follows sets out Carlos's love in recognizably conventional terms: as Budden observes,

> the rhythmic cut of the melody is characteristic of Meyerbeerian grand opera with its smooth, marching rhythm, its lifting of the second semi-phrase in the manner of *Les Vêpres Siciliennes.* But the form, far from being the expected French ternary, is an old-fashioned a^1-a^2-b-a^2 complete with coda and a rest for the voice at the start of the third phrase.[30]

---

30. Budden, *From Don Carlos to Falstaff,* 47.

The aria is significant for two reasons: it offers an account of Carlos's encounter with Elisabeth, and, less obviously, it demonstrates Carlos's capacity for conventional musical expression. That is, we are introduced to a conventionally romantic young man offering a conventionally romantic account of his newfound love. It won't last.

All of a sudden, Elisabeth comes rushing in again, this time lost and mildly distraught. Carlos, who presents himself merely as a Spanish nobleman, offers Elisabeth protection as her page finally recognizes the castle in the distance and heads off to fetch her mistress's suite. After a scene of ardent flirtation, the prince reveals himself as her intended, and the two take advantage of their remove from the court and its imperatives of decorum—they take advantage, in other words, of the sort of protection afforded by the rock—and allow their nascent love to take flight in song. Their duet alternates between conventions—romantic abandon, on the one hand, and a recurring measure of courtly restraint.[31] That is, as they test the waters of their newfound abandon, they remain on stable expressive grounds. Cannon fire sounds in the distance, marking, it turns out, the onset of peace between Spain and France, and the couple rejoices at "the signal of celebration." But, of course, the canon signals doom: although they don't know it yet, their ascendant love has just been shot down. The page returns to greet Elisabeth as queen: the peace treaty calls for her to marry Philippe, king of Spain and Carlos's father.

At this point, the irony is private: in seeking out Elizabeth, Carlos has "defied" his father's "dread anger" in unimagined ways; having "quit the court," as Carlos put it, the court has come to him. Rapidly, the private scene becomes public, and its primary focus becomes a performative act of discourse: will Elisabeth assent? Her retinue appears along with some pages bearing a litter and "le peuple." It is the people whom we hear before anyone else: they enter, a cappella, having struck up a jaunty choral celebration of the war's end and, in particular, of Elisabeth, "qui va demain sur une trône . . . donner sa main" (who tomorrow, seated upon the throne, will offer her hand). The Spanish ambassador arrives, informing Elisabeth and the assembled crowd that Philippe "ne veut vous devoir qu'à vous-même, / Acceptez-vous la main de ce roi qui vous aime?" (wants to leave the decision entirely up to you: will you accept the hand of this king who loves you?). As the ambassador awaits Elisabeth's response, a chorus of women implores her to have pity upon their suffering and accept the king. Elisabeth is afforded two bars of thinking time, accompanied by total silence on stage and the accumulating pressure of single quarter-note pizzicato chords in the strings: she replies, "d'une voix mourante" (with a dying voice), yes.

---

31. Ibid., 50–51.

Musical Example 5 A quick decision. Elisabeth must decide—in the space of three measures—whether to forsake her love to save her people. With a dying voice, she sacrifices her love.

With a dying voice. If the surprise encounter in the forest provided Elisabeth and Carlos with a newly shared melodic identity and the promise of a new, shared lyrical life, the assent educed from Elisabeth spells doom for that life. The stakes of her assent are underscored by the choral celebration that follows. In the course of their duet in the forest in the preceding scene, the private ecstasy between Elisabeth and Carlos had found its most emphatic expression in E major. The chorus here expresses its profuse joy and relief in the same key.[32] This transaction—its scenic and compositional terms—encapsulates a dramaturgical crux of the piece: the purchase of public satisfaction (and its expression through spectacle) at the expense of private desire. The fine print that enables this transaction, we should note, is an edict of the paternal law: in assenting to her arranged (or indeed, her rearranged) marriage to Philippe, Elisabeth is compelled to ventriloquize an official desire, one dictated by the fathers, Henry and Philippe, and intoned by those pleading women.

Although Elizabeth's voice is dying here, it will return to life over the course of the opera. We will need to attend to this revival, which we can understand as the apotheosis of sublimation.[33] After all, something has to take

32. Ibid., 53–54.

33. Parker pays particular attention to the musical dramaturgy of Elisabeth's extended act 5 aria: "In terms of Carolyn Abbate's now well-known distinction, 'plot-Elisabeth' may indeed remain tied

the place of the shared romantic vision—the false shelter—of a life together that, like Elisabeth's voice, vanished so dramatically at the conclusion of act 1. Lost is the utopian moment—encapsulated in the love between Carlos and Elisabeth that was prescribed by state interests and felt by both—when public duty and private desire were reconciled. In its place, Elisabeth and Carlos must adapt themselves to a new language of courtly relations and familial propriety. *Don Carlos* dramatizes the anguished process of this adaptation. And yet, in the end—and this is part of what makes this piece so dark and truly vexing—even this heroic gesture of accommodation will prove insufficient: even sublimation, it turns out, provides no shelter. In the world of *Don Carlos,* the direct means of fulfilling desire are blocked, and so too are the compensatory, indirect means.

Roger Parker has traced the conflict between public and private desire into the recesses of the work's compositional dramaturgy, offering a compelling and nuanced consideration of the conclusion of the first act, where Carlos must come to terms with a paradise lost even more abruptly than it was won. Left alone, abandoned by his erstwhile fiancée—henceforth his stepmother—Carlos in turn abandons the characteristic triplet figures that had marked his recent passionate exchanges with Elisabeth and eventually adopts instead the dotted rhythm of the chorus in his midst. What, Parker wonders, are we to make of this composed capitulation?

> While a more conventional, noisy close could have held the lovers' musical resistance to the last, in this quiet coda the rebellious anguish, the *difference* expressed in those triplets becomes exhausted, and in their place is a tired acceptance of what the crowd, the public face, the political will decrees; in the most obvious way, then, that dotted rhythm and chromatic lower neighbor mark Carlos's acceptance of public discourse: the exterior world has not retreated with the retreating chorus; it has, rather, invaded all the more completely the individual's affective world, becoming at once a more potent and a more malign force.[34]

As Parker suggests, Carlos's acceptance of the chorus's dotted rhythm here signals a kind of vacancy, a notable expressive pliability in the aftermath of

---

to the stereotype of the passive female heroine; but 'voice-Elisabeth' (or nearer my terms here, 'music-Elisabeth') becomes an important dynamic force in the economy of the opera's world. Unlike Carlos in act I, she is not defeated by the force of history; unlike Philip in act IV, she does not retreat into the interior, private emotion; in fact she becomes most human and alive precisely when she confronts the past and makes it her own present." Roger Parker, "Elisabeth's Last Act," in Smart, *Siren Songs,* 93–117, at 116.

34. Ibid., 98.

losing his love. Following as it does upon the scene of Elisabeth's constrained assent, this moment represents another kind of ventriloquism, another moment when the character accedes to a collective articulation. In both moments, we might say, the characters do not sing so much as they are sung.

There is a further, self-referential dimension to this invasion of the exterior world into the hero's affective world, one that we will explore in the final section of this chapter. For at this very moment of performative ventriloquism, the moment that marks his capitulation to "public discourse," Don Carlos (the character) arguably reiterates the conflict embodied by *Don Carlos* (the work onstage), which in turn reiterates the predicament of many of Verdi's works more generally: whether to submit to unbearable and untenable limitations upon individual expression. The predicament is encapsulated in the cliché concerning the difference between Verdi and Wagner; namely, that while Wagner thoroughly revamped and thus materially altered the discursive norms he inherited, Verdi merely mastered and reproduced those norms.[35] Yet I would argue that Verdi's works repeatedly and inventively raise the question of discursive reproduction, of what it means to occupy an assigned discursive position. In and for *Don Carlos,* the implications are particularly vexing, because, on the one hand, assignment to a discursive position produces the very vulnerability that would provoke the need for shelter, and on the other hand, it constitutes the shelter from that vulnerability.

Don Carlos allows us to refine the notion, proposed in an essay by Peter Brooks, that "operatic aria, like the melodramatic dialogue, speaks the name of desire directly. It may be the most unrepressed speech of desire that art allows."[36] In my reading, *Don Carlos*—the very work to which Brooks turns to elaborate his claim—models the need to restrain speech, most especially the speech of desire. That is, the speech of desire in *Don Carlos* is repeatedly subjected to correctives and controls, such that it ends up bespeaking the functional unspeakability of a desire directly named. In this sense, the dramaturgy of the opera (which leads inexorably to a tragic collapse of the utopian political and personal aspirations that it registers) cancels the expressive aspirations of its component parts.

At this point, it may be useful to offer a brief introduction to Freud's notion of sublimation. As Jean Laplanche and Jean-Baptiste Pontalis point out in *The*

35. See the introduction to *Analyzing Opera,* where this cliché is put to productive use: "But if Wagner's seeming radicalism encouraged his commentators to explore new exegetical methods, the best Italian critics benefited from the other side of the coin, using Verdi's persistence with traditional formal models as a point on which to sharpen their perceptions of his originality and power." Abbate and Parker, "Introduction," 10.

36. See Peter Brooks, "Body and Voice in Melodrama and Opera," in Smart, *Siren Songs,* 118–34, at 122.

Language of Psychoanalysis, Freud's account of sublimation is hardly as comprehensive as one might expect. But throughout his writings, from the early 1900s through the 1930s, we encounter various formulations of the proposition that certain human activities—such as artistic creation and intellectual inquiry—are motivated by the force of the sexual instinct, although they are not overtly connected to sexuality. "The instinct," write Laplanche and Pontalis, "is said to be sublimated in so far as it is diverted towards a new, nonsexual, and socially valued aim."[37] Thus, one must learn to desire a proper object or attend to a proper calling (say, the liberation of Flanders) in lieu of a desire that has been rendered illicit (say, desire for one's mother). As Freud points out, sublimation is a defining mark of civilization, which marshals sexual energies in the service of different, valorized, "productive" ends.[38]

On Posa's repeated prompting, Carlos undergoes a crash course in sublimation, learning to redirect his thoughts and his musical material away from Elisabeth (and the morass of love with which she is associated) and toward Flanders (and the purposive politics with which it is associated). He must learn to sing of Flanders in place of Elisabeth, just as, earlier on, he assumed the chorus's dotted rhythm and chromatic lower neighbor in lieu of holding onto the triplets that had marked his exchange with his newfound love. Upon learning of Carlos's sad and illicit love for Elisabeth at the outset of act 2, Posa instructs the Infante: "Par un effort digne de toi / Brise ton coeur . . . et viens apprendre, / Parmi des malheureux, ton dur métier de Roi!" (Silence your heart, yours will be work worthy of you, now among those who suffer learn to become a king!).[39] The lesson in sublimation that Posa dispenses here does not remove Carlos from an Oedipal scenario, but merely repositions him within it. Posa would evacuate Carlos from a thoroughly illicit station of Oedipal desire (love for Elisabeth as love for his mother) to another, less obviously illicit one (aiding the people of Flanders who are [like him] oppressed by his father; learning to become a king).[40]

The scene takes place in the monastery of St. Just, just before Posa yokes Carlos to the stentorian cabaletta "Dieu tu semas dans nos âmes" (God, who

37. "Sublimation," in J. Laplanche and J.-B. Pontalis, *The Language of Psychoanalysis,* trans. Donald Nicholson-Smith (New York: Norton, 1973), 431.

38. As any number of recent critics have pointed out, sublimation is also a defining mark of opera. For a polemical and amusing account of this condition, see, e.g., Wayne Koestenbaum, *The Queen's Throat: Opera, Homosexuality, and the Mystery of Desire* (New York: Poseidon Press, 1993). For a more dispassionate (or indeed, sublimated) account, see "The Blue Note," in Michel Poizat, *The Angel's Cry,* trans. Arthur Denner (Ithaca, N.Y.: Cornell University Press, 1992).

39. *Don Carlos,* PV, 1:124 and 138; Morris, "Libretto," 88.

40. As a hard-nosed *Realpolitiker* (the term is Paul Robinson's), Philippe will not be fooled: he will refuse Carlos's request outright near the conclusion of act 3. See Robinson, "Realpolitik," 162.

wished to instill love and hope in our souls). In Heather Wiebe's apt formulation: "It is Posa's music, even more than his words, that most powerfully com-
municates his idea of public life as an alternative to Carlos's disintegration,
setting up a discourse of stability and simplicity opposed to the fragmentation
and lack of harmonic direction that characterize Carlos's vocal idiom."[41]
Posa, we might say, is a paragon of bureaucratic sublimation—which, given
the anxiety suffusing those around him, makes him a refreshingly predictable
character: his music is reliably sententious, his ideas fixed and rather mono-
chromatic.[42] Elisabeth, on the other hand, registers the difficulties of acceding
to sublimation, while Carlos's initial (and notably lame) attempts at sublimation fail altogether.

Throughout the work, the problem of Carlos's sublimation is framed as
a matter of designation: Carlos's instability—which is also, as Wiebe demonstrates, an instability of musical telos, a kind of melodic torpor—is marked
by the instability with which he inhabits his assigned designations, including "son" (as opposed to lover) and "prince" (as opposed to romantic or
political rebel).[43] Our first glimpse of this instability, in the second tableau of
act 2, is also our first glimpse of the erstwhile lovers since their jarring separation at the conclusion of act 1. Having been barred access to the discourse of
romantic ardor that he employed to such melodic effect in the forest of
Fontainebleau, Carlos remains at a loss for a viable substitute, despite Posa's
coaching.[44]

Sticking, initially, to the script outlined by Posa, Carlos asks Elisabeth for
help. The Infante claims to be suffocating in Spain and wants Elisabeth to intercede on his behalf and ask the king to allow him to head for Flanders. Elisabeth, "très émue" (very moved), addresses him as "my son," a designation
that Carlos immediately and "vehemently" rejects, insisting instead on "that
other one from back then."[45] In greeting Carlos by his newfound function,
the queen models a successful sublimation and, with it, her submission to the
discourse of propriety. "With very contained emotion," Elisabeth responds
to Carlos's initial request that she intercede on his behalf with the king and
ignores the following "desperate" plea to be renamed.[46]

41. Wiebe, "Conquering Desire," 550.

42. On this point, see Robinson, "Realpolitik," 181.

43. For a helpful definition of Carlos's lack of musical control, see Rosen, "Don Carlos as Bildungsoper," 113 n. 17.

44. Unless, of course, we take his ongoing disorientation, the lack of a viable expressive register,
as constituting a form of expressive register.

45. Don Carlos, PV, 1:183.

46. Ibid., 1:184.

Musical Example 6 A guarded promise. Elisabeth sings, liltingly, to Carlos, promising him that she will take his case before the king but refusing his plea that she call him something other than "son."

As Budden notes, the melodic line of her response is doubled in the cellos and dampened and regularized by an eighth-note triplet accompaniment in the violins: the "restless shifting harmonies on the last pair of triplets betray the effort of will." [47] Which is also to say, the violins render the effort of sublimation as well as its stakes. Elisabeth, for her part, sticks to the script of sublimation—and the cellos second and amplify her resolve. As we would expect, the resulting melody is not especially inventive; instead, it is a model of stability and purposiveness. The violins, on the other hand, render the ongoing—if now marginalized—appeal of the very discourse of authenticity for which Carlos pleads, a wayward harmonic vocabulary that would redirect her purposive melody from its implied formal and psychological resolution.

But in the Freudian account, invention is one of sublimation's hallmarks as well as its payoff, and Elisabeth will model these rewards. Thus, when Carlos assails her for so readily dispensing with the language of their lost love, Elisabeth's response—a brief and intense paean to duty—is anything but dutiful: it is marked by forceful melodic assertion, underscored at its climax by the full martial forces of the brass. If Carlos is shown to be melodically and discursively at a loss, mired in his incapacity either to sustain or replace a private language of intimacy, Elisabeth stands in for a public language of propriety—one that is inflected here as inventive. Thus, Elisabeth's voice has sprung back to life—to a life of sorts—refashioned in the manner and manners of her new station.

Carlos responds with a melodic invention of his own: a saccharine lament to their lost intimacy. He does so, according to the score, "d'une voix mourante" (with a dying voice).[48] As we saw earlier in this chapter, Elisabeth's dying voice in act 1 simultaneously marked the advent of a public language and the loss of a private one. In saying yes to the crowd and, by extension, to Philippe, she marked that moment, however ironically, as affirmative. Carlos's recourse to a dying voice here suggests—if we needed any proof—that he is nowhere near such an affirmation. His dying voice materializes—or, we might say, it melodizes—the threat that was relegated to the margins of (that is, to the violin accompaniment to) Elisabeth's expressed resolution: it represents a last gasp of romance. If her dying voice marked the suppression of her audacity and the advent of sublimation (a transaction that the piece inflects as tragic and noble), Carlos's recourse to a dying voice here serves to resuscitate the audacity it cites.

Carlos's evocation of their lost love proves temporarily irresistible, educing from Elisabeth (or rather, seducing her into) a note-for-note restatement

47. Budden, *From Don Carlos to Falstaff*, 72.
48. *Don Carlos*, PV, 1:187. Compare to Elisabeth's earlier declaration at *Don Carlos*, PV, 1:81.

Musical Example 7a The son's seduction. Carlos seduces Elisabeth with his simple, lilting 4–3–2–1 melody (a), which his stepmother and former fiancée in turn repeats back to him (b).

of his melody as well as a tender invocation of their lost love and his name (thus, "Carlos" rather than "son"). This suspension of the terms of Elisabeth's sublimation—melodic autonomy and its linguistic correlative, a formalized nomination—is brief, and its effects are dire. When Carlos, swooning, announces that "the world [is] forgotten" and, embracing Elisabeth, proclaims his love for her, she lays out the consequences in lurid terms. Breaking free of his lyrical and physical embrace, she recovers her melodic autonomy and stops his advances in their tracks by reversing the downward spiral of his melody (whose initial phrase merely descended a B flat major scale from the subdominant to the tonic), vehemently and rapidly ascending a minor scale and thus spelling out the Oedipal scenario, the implicit—which is to say, the unspoken—master narrative of sublimation: "Eh bien! Donc, frappez votre père! / Venez, de son meurtre souillé, / Trâiner à l'autel votre mère! / Allez,

Musical Example 7a (continued)

allez frapper votre père!" (All right then, so kill your father, and then, spattered with his blood, you can lead your mother to the altar. Go, go and kill your father!).[49]

During the course of her brief encounter with Carlos in this scene, Elisabeth's music travels the stations of sublimation. Initially, neither her mind nor her music is allowed to wander. The result—in her initial response to Carlos—is a generalized constriction of her expressive register, marked, for example, by the doubling of her voice in the cellos and accompanied by an initial clamping down of harmonic invention in the violins. As the scene progresses and her resolve is established, the constraint abates, giving way to an invention in the service of—indeed, an invention impelled by—sublimation. Her seduction by Carlos's melody, which produces a wholesale capitulation, a giving over of that invention, in turn produces a form of reinvention through negation, a turning of the tide from citation to declamation,

49. *Don Carlos*, PV, 1:195–96; Morris, "Libretto," 118.

Musical Example 7b "Well then, kill your father!" Elisabeth explodes at Carlos, imploring him—ironically?—to kill his father if he will not put aside his love for her.

from her participation in his melodic nostalgia to her forceful assertion here of a dissenting and creative counter-melody. Her heated remonstration to Carlos is encapsulated in a highly condensed, rapidly ascending stepwise figure of two sixteenth notes followed by an emphatic dotted quarter (expanded at every third instance by a half note) that quickly takes her from E flat up an octave, first to F, and then eventually to a high B flat. If Carlos earlier protested his unwillingness to occupy the position of (and the

Musical Example 7b (*continued*)

designation as) her son, he now flees at Elisabeth's bald articulation of the terms by which he might reassume the position of her lover.[50] The work's unfolding will depict Carlos's discursive *Bildung,* his accession to a subject position (which is also to say, a speaking and singing position) from which he can more or less stably recognize himself—and inhabit the designation—as her son.[51] But for now, Carlos remains lost between designations: no longer her lover, he is not yet her son; and his music, no longer stably private, is not yet stably public.

Almost everyone else in the work suffers under similar linguistic constraints. Almost everyone, that is, except Posa. The Philippe-Posa duet of act 2 represents a surprising and unusual instance of virtually unfettered exchange and has garnered a substantial amount of critical attention.[52] Verdi returned repeatedly to the Philippe-Posa duet during the course of his revisions to the score, a process that spanned almost two decades.[53] In its various versions, the duet is marked by a strong sense of expressive limits as it stages the transgression of those limits.[54] At various points in the various versions of the duet, the king and the marquis register the singular nature of the marquis's commitment to truth telling. "One day," as Posa puts it to Philippe just before launching into his dire account of conditions in Flanders, "you had to learn the truth." This truth is not just communicated through a marked recourse to language, it also revolves around that recourse. This is true in the broadest dramaturgical sense—that is, in the sense that the marquis does not explore Flanders with the king, but evokes it for him (with a good deal of assistance from the orchestra). But the duet also revolves around language in a

50. In Budden's reading, this moment marks a major turning point for Carlos: "Carlos is sobered immediately; and it is at her exhortation that he decides to sublimate his love by devoting himself to the cause of Flanders and freedom." I certainly agree that the trajectory of the piece will take Carlos to a position—albeit an ambivalent position—of sublimation, but I do not see—and Budden uncharacteristically provides no evidence for his claim—that Carlos arrives at such a decision here. If we have to designate one, I wonder whether we might locate such a moment of Carlos's recognition in the margins of the furious exchange between Eboli and Posa, when Carlos recognizes that he has sullied the name of his mother. See Budden, *From Don Carlos to Falstaff,* 72, 109. Elisabeth's Oedipal exhortation and Carlos's response from musical example 7b, above; Carlos's act 3 recognition comes at *Don Carlos,* PV, 2:367.

51. See Rosen, "*Don Carlos* as Bildungsoper."

52. Roger Parker, "Philippe and Posa, Act II: The Shock of the New," in *Primal Scenes: Proceedings of a Conference Held at the University of California, Berkeley, 30 November–2 December, 2001,* special issue, *Cambridge Opera Journal* 14, nos. 1–2 (2002): 133–47.

53. In "Philippe and Posa," Parker explores the philological and compositional stakes of Verdi's revisions to the score.

54. The duet takes place in the wake of the king's dismissal of the Countess of Aremberg, noted above. The insult that Philippe visits upon the queen is all the more stinging for its indirection: the accusation (of what? of Elisabeth's innate waywardness? of her inevitable propensity to infidelity in the absence of constant supervision?) remains unspoken but audible to all.

rhetorical sense, especially in the later versions of the duet, where Posa's account of life and death in Flanders is augmented not just by his increasingly bold exchanges with the king, but also by a flurry of allusions to allusion. The marquis channels the accounts of others, those who curse the king and would label him a "second Nero." To coin a slight variant of the aptly simplistic language of political agitation, Posa is singing the truth to power.[55] And indeed, the marquis is "un homme au milieu des humains" (a man among humans), as Philippe puts it, on account of the unfettered expression of his convictions. But that directness also explains the untenability of Posa's character in the world of *Don Carlos*. This is the obverse of Carlos's musical and dramatic torpor, although it derives from the same root cause—a commitment to an expression that knows no limits.

At the conclusion of the work, the farewell between Elisabeth and Carlos is markedly reorganized around the public terms of their relations: the love they express for one another has finally come to occupy the sanctioned space of familial relations. He takes leave of his mother; she takes leave of her son. In the revisions undertaken for the Milan premiere in 1884, Verdi clarifies the stakes of this terminological shift—and with it, the terms of Carlos's affective and discursive *Bildung*—by citing melodic material from the doomed encounter between Elisabeth and Carlos in act 2. As Carlos recalls "a lovely dream that vanished," Verdi undergirds his narration with a lush restatement (marked dolcissimo)[56] of the melody by which Carlos, "swooning," had sought to seduce Elisabeth in act 2. Significantly, this return—a kind of return to the scene of the musical crime—comes to bear the signs of a successful "working through" or, indeed, a *singing* cure.[57] If, as we noted, Carlos's earlier use of that musical material had educed from Elisabeth a dangerous romantic echo effect, his return to that material here demonstrates a newfound ability to work through the melody, to bring it to a successful—and entirely autonomous, purposeful, and socially sanctioned—resolution.[58] In Carlos's farewell we can hear (and Carlos himself hears) a fully fashioned statement of sublimation. Thus the music and language of the sweet dream give way to a much more realistic—which is to say, a dire—account of life and death in

---

55. As such, he is a prime exemplar of the dramaturgy of *parrhesia* (fearless speech). See lectures one (on the meaning of *parrhesia*) and two (on the dramaturgy of *parrhesia*) in Michel Foucault, *Fearless Speech*, ed. Joseph Pearson (New York: Semiotexte, 2001), 11–24 and 27–74.

56. See *Don Carlos*, PV, 2:654.

57. In Freud's clinical vocabulary, the "talking cure" effected in the course of analysis would seek to revisit and "work through" traumatic events. This revisitation, Freud theorized, would enable the patient to master the psychic trauma effected by the original experience of the scene.

58. Here I find myself in full agreement with Rosen, *"Don Carlos as Bildungsoper,"* 124–25.

Flanders.[59] When Elisabeth implores him "Va! Va! Va! Monte au Calvaire et sauve, sauve un peuple qui t'attend!" (Delay no longer! Go, mount the hill of Calvary and save a dying people!), Carlos responds that "c'est par votre voix que le peuple m'appelle" (that people calls me with your voice).[60]

In Carlos's account, Elisabeth's voice channels a call from the people of Flanders. In her voice, Carlos can now hear his proper (if not his true) calling. The call of Flanders, and with it, public duty, does not simply drown out the call of personal desire; rather, the former is fashioned out of a reappropriation and reinterpretation of the musical statement of the latter. Having resolved to meet in heaven, where they "trouverons dans la paix du Seigneur, cet éternel absent qu'on nomme le bonheur!" (will find, amid the peace of the Lord, the longed-for bliss that is called happiness),[61] Elisabeth and Carlos finally take leave of each other. Their farewell is fashioned as a proper duet, their first in the opera. We have an expansive account of the fruits of sublimation: Carlos emerges from the morass of melodic purposelessness in which he has been stuck since the conclusion of act 1 to engage in a properly dialogic exchange. He and Elisabeth fashion a melody together, repeat each other's phrases, and conclude each other's melodic and linguistic sentences. Their resolve issues into a final accommodation with their assigned designations: they take leave of each other with the words "Adieu, ma mère!" (farewell, my mother) and "Adieu, mon fils!" (farewell, my son).[62]

In Don Carlos, sublimation does not simply involve a redirection of sexual energies; the redirection in turn enables a creative accommodation with (and ultimately, a return of sorts to) the very terms of oppression that produced the need for sublimation in the first place. Here we glimpse the strange logic of discursive shelter: in the end, the paternal script that dictated the oppressive, traumatic shift in terms between Elisabeth and Carlos is not rejected or even rewritten; instead, Elisabeth and Carlos appropriate it, reinflecting it as the script of their delayed gratification.

Ever the terrible reader, Philippe mistakes the scene of Elisabeth and Carlos's accommodation to his law as compelling evidence of their ongoing disregard for it. Thus, he enters with the Grand Inquisitor as Elisabeth and Carlos exchange their properly fashioned goodbyes ("adieu, ma mère," "adieu,

59. Thus, whereas at the initial statement of the melody in act 2, Carlos heard Elisabeth's voice and, swooning, his spirit turned to heaven ("Mon âme, à votre voix, rêve du paradis" [Don Carlos, PV, 1: 187–88; Morris, "Libretto," 112]), now, at the conclusion of the work, he sees a river of blood, abandoned villages, and a people in death throes begging him to save them in their day of disaster.

60. Don Carlos, PV, 2: 612–13; Morris, "Libretto," 206.

61. Don Carlos, PV, 2: 629–31 and 664–65; Morris, "Libretto," 210.

62. Don Carlos, PV, 2:632–33 and 666; Morris, "Libretto," 210.

mon fils") and hands both of the purportedly traitorous sinners over to the Inquisition. This final confrontation—when Carlos and Elisabeth are met by the king and the Grand Inquisitor—is more elaborated, its terms more emphatic, in the earlier versions for Paris and Naples. There the king explicitly renounces his son, whose illicit seductions are inflected as both political and familial. In Philippe's words, Carlos has seduced the queen and the people: thus, he hands Carlos to the Grand Inquisitor with the ferocious words, "À vous, ce fils ingrat que de moi Dieu fit naître! Un détestable amour le brûle à vous ce traître!" (To you the unworthy son whom God allowed to be born of me! An abominable love blazes in him. . . . To you, this traitor!)[63] and, a few moments later, "A vous ce séducteur de mon peuple fidèle, cet ennemi des Rois et de Dieu! ce rebelle!" (To you this seducer of my faithful subjects, this enemy of kings and of God . . . this rebel!).[64] This adds irony as well as dramaturgical sense to the terms of Charles V's surprising appearance at the conclusion of the opera, where he enfolds Carlos as "my son." There is a bizarre proliferation of familial appellations here: Carlos quickly becomes the best object and the worst, the favorite and most detested son. The irony is clear: having accepted his erstwhile lover as his mother, Carlos is denounced for the treachery that he has just renounced. At the very moment Carlos has assumed his proper position as Philippe's (and Elisabeth's) son, Philippe intervenes to cancel that very appellation with "Mon fils n'est plus!" (my son is no more).[65] Philippe hands his guilty (ex-) son over to the church, which would sacrifice him (of course, as the Grand Inquisitor had pointed out in the preceding act, this is the church of a God that willingly sacrificed his only son). But before that can happen, Charles V intervenes, presumably, although not clearly, with the effect of saving his (grand-)son. As Charles gathers Carlos into the shelter of the cloister, he addresses him as "mon fils," which, predictably, produces an astonished "mon Père!" from Philippe.[66] The undead grandfather emerges as father to his grandson, whose own father has just renounced him.

What are we to make of this? I am particularly interested in the aesthetic implications of the generational politics here. In Wagner, power almost always resides in the young: the Wanderer cannot "hold back" his defiant grandson Siegfried, who shatters the old man's staff in the process. At best, the older generations in Wagner have wisdom to dispense, but they rarely have phallic power. As we saw in chapter 2, Hans Sachs can teach a

63. *Don Carlos*, PV, 2:635–36.
64. Ibid., 2:637–38.
65. Ibid., 2:648.
66. Ibid., 2:649.

reluctant Walther the importance of tradition, but he can't himself win the song contest or Eva, its ultimate prize.

In *Don Carlos,* phallic power is and remains paternal. And the only contestants for that power left standing at the work's conclusion are old (Philippe), older (the Grand Inquisitor), and oldest (Charles V). For their part, Don Carlos and Elisabeth are surprised in the course of a tender summation of their accommodation: again, they are betrayed by the fathers (Elisabeth by her father at the outset of the piece; Carlos by his here at the conclusion). It is left to the grandfather to come to the rescue. To the extent that it is provided at all, the unexpected shelter materializes out of a backward rather than a forward impetus: the undead good grandfather reemerges in defense of the grandson's accommodation with the imperatives of sublimation and the father's unjust misrecognition of that accommodation. And yet there is something aptly unsatisfying, even ambivalent to this resolution. After all, who is Charles V? And what is his political and emotional valence? Beyond the vocal fact of his intervention as a kind of deus ex machina (or indeed, a "reus ex machina"), the nature of his intervention remains entirely unclear. What is he up to? On whose behalf? He drags Carlos into the cloister, but it is hard to discern what this might mean in the piece's political and discursive economy. At best, Carlos is saved (although the nature of his salvation remains entirely mysterious). But what about Elisabeth? In the best-case scenario, she is doomed to continue to lead the life she has been leading—a life of enforced and performed submission, playing the affectionate wife. At worst, and more likely, she will be sacrificed by Philippe as Carlos is sacrificed by the Inquisitor.

If the opera text portrays the all-encompassing authority of what I have been terming wholesale discursive and personal accommodation (to the laws of propriety rather than the inclinations of the heart), it also ends up inflecting that accommodation as entirely inadequate. No one is happy. The king and the Grand Inquisitor remain suspicious, Carlos and Elisabeth remain unfulfilled, Posa is dead, the Countess of Aremberg is on her way back to Paris, and Eboli is off to a cloister. What are we to make of this? And, to put the question in the most general terms, how is the piece to be staged?

In important ways, *Don Carlos* is ambivalent and claustrophobic; it suggests that there is no way out. As it registers the allure of resistance to the imperative of sublimation, it also dramatizes the untenability of such resistance. The conclusion of the work is shot through with a similar ambivalence. On one reading, the conclusion of the work does not rescue Carlos or anyone else from the imperative of sublimation; rather, it would shelter him in the wake of his successful internalization of its terms. It could be that he is saved from the Inquisition, but he is certainly not saved from a renunciation of his affections for Elisabeth. Having sublimated desires (i.e., for his mother) that the work cannot tolerate (although it can understand them), he must be saved from an ecclesiastical rabble that would destroy him for harboring views that the work celebrates. But we keep returning to the question: Is Carlos saved? And if so, in what sense?

From Opera Text to Performance Text

So far, my argument has addressed the dramaturgy of the opera text, suggesting that it charts the interrelated effects of a thoroughgoing lack of shelter, an overwhelming sense of discursive immutability, and an overriding imperative of accommodation and sublimation. For the remainder of this chapter, I want to consider the implications of this argument for a staging of the work. In doing so, I will not just be asking functional questions, such as how to conceive of individual characters or to render particular situations. Rather, I also want to ask a more abstract set of questions, about how we conceive of the work onstage and how we imagine the relationship of the piece's thematics to its disposition onstage. What, then, is the relation of the staging of discourse within the opera text to a conceptualization of the piece's position within a discourse of performance? How might we describe the relationship between the imperatives of sublimation elaborated within the opera text and the imperatives of operatic naturalism that have characterized the work's appearance onstage? In order to address these questions, we need to locate Verdi in a history of operatic staging.

According to the British director Mike Ashman, audiences and critics have historically been much more tolerant of experimentation when it comes to productions of works by German composers (Wagner in particular, but not just him) than the works of Verdi. With Verdi, critics and the public "remain less willing to tolerate attempts to move beyond historically informed fourth-wall naturalism." [67] Here, then, we encounter another variation of the clichéd distinction between Wagner (as compositional innovator) and Verdi (as compositional conservative) to which I alluded earlier. In this case, the purported compositional aesthetics produce a corresponding aesthetics of performance, with Wagner's works regularly taking off into uncharted territory while Verdi's works are more commonly restricted to

---

67. "Critical and public outrage at novel Verdi productions both outstrips that at like-minded Wagner (or other German-composer) productions—where it is currently regarded as *de rigueur*—and remains less willing to tolerate attempts to move beyond historically informed fourth-wall naturalism." Mike Ashman, "Misinterpreting Verdian Dramaturgy: History and Grand Opera," in *Verdi in Performance,* ed. Roger Parker and Alison Latham (Oxford: Oxford University Press, 2001), 42–46, at 43.

established routes and familiar grounds. (Wagner, in this account, is the Posa to Verdi's Carlos.)

In the course of this book, we have examined the emergence of operas in mise-en-scène. The formulation is intentionally awkward, for what "emerges" in the stagings we have been considering are facets that have largely gone unnoticed, often rendered invisible by convention, by the kind of naturalism to which Ashman alludes. As Ashman suggests and as I argued in chapter 2, naturalistic staging practices in opera houses today have come to serve as a bulwark against interpretive adventurism, tending to constrain operatic signification within its borders—borders that have become so familiar (we might say, naturalized) that they are hardly noticed. On the other hand, mise-en-scène can be exhilarating when it uncorks (and alerts us to) an unruly surfeit of expressive means that I take to be emblematic of opera. Although the work of performance is famously contingent, and thus difficult to grasp and theorize, it is essential to the expression—in provocative, gripping forms—of that surfeit. As an opera text, *Don Carlos* renders an audacity of expression as well as its containment; as a performance text, *Don Carlos* has tended (with some important exceptions) to render containment alone.[68]

Since the late nineteenth century, the operatic canon has shrunk drastically, such that, on the whole, fewer and fewer works are performed with greater and greater frequency.[69] To the extent that new productions tend to be reproductions of familiar, canonical works, we can conceive of mise-en-scène in terms of reiteration. But reiteration in what form? Should a performance text reiterate a consensus about the work's meaning and appearance (reiteration understood as repetition), or should it reinflect the work's meaning and appearance (reiteration understood as revision)?

An example may help to clarify the distinction. It is one thing—indeed, it is something familiar—when a new production reproduces a consensus about the work's meaning and appearance: in this case, a new production (say, of *Aida*) is often best understood as a rerun. It is something else when a production reflects anew upon the work and enacts that reflection: thus, we might imagine a new production of *Aida* that, say, attends to (and thus

68. We find important exceptions in early-twentieth-century Germany (where, even during the Nazi era, stage directors at times subjected Verdi's opera to intense interpretive pressure) and, increasingly, on contemporary opera stages, mostly in Europe. See Gundula Kreuzer, "Voices from Beyond: Verdi's *Don Carlos* and the Modern Stage" in *Cambridge Opera Journal* 18, no. 2 (July 2006); and on adventurous stagings of *Don Carlos* and *Aida*, see Risi, "Shedding Light."

69. For a polemical reconsideration of this condition, see chapter 4, "The Opera Museum," in David Evans, *Phantasmagoria: A Sociology of Opera* (Brookfield, Vt.: Ashgate, 1999). On the philosophical implications, see Lydia Goehr, *The Imaginary Museum of Musical Works* (Oxford: Clarendon Press, 1992), chapter 1.

reinflects) the aspiration to mise-en-scène within the opera text, a mise-en-scène organized around a conjunction of melodramatic fantasies involving the Orient as a space where so much is staged, from grand war (along with grand send-offs and even grander returns) to impossible loves (including the spectacle of that impossibility).[70]

Opera allows us to revisit and refine Jacques Attali's distinction between representation and repetition. In Attali's account, "Representation in the system of commerce is that which arises from a singular act; repetition is that which is mass-produced. Thus, a concert is representation, but also a meal à la carte in a restaurant; a phonograph record or a can of food is repetition."[71] In opera, the live performance may constitute a representation, but the mode of a given production's mise-en-scène, its dramaturgical politics, revisits the distinction and may well refashion it. Thus, a live production (Attali's representation) that rehearses and reiterates a conventional sense of a work is arguably more of a repetition than a televised broadcast of the same work (Attali's repetition) that drastically reshapes our understanding. Our ability to determine whether a work is properly understood as representation or repetition is as much a function of its dramaturgical politics as of its medial disposition.

Until very recently, and with a few notable exceptions, Verdi has served as a model—or, indeed, a prisoner—of the operatic culture of reiteration as repetition.[72] Over the course of the past century, stagings of Verdi's works have often served as a visible symptom of an interdiction on certain types of (nonnaturalistic) theatrical invention. Verdi and his publisher, Ricordi, no doubt bear some responsibility for this. The tendency to present Verdi's works in naturalist terms surely derives historical sanction from the *disposizioni sceniche,* the staging manuals, owned and rented out by Ricordi, that denote the stage action of the work at its premiere.[73] The prescriptive force

70. On *Aida,* see Said, "Imperial Spectacle," later published as "The Empire at Work," as well as section 1 of Weber, "Taking Place." Mary Ann Smart takes issue with some of the basic terms of Said's argument in "Ulterior Motives: Verdi's Recurring Themes Revisited," in Smart, *Siren Songs,* 135–59.

71. Jacques Attali, *Noise: The Political Economy of Music,* trans. Brian Massumi (Minneapolis: University of Minnesota Press, 1985), 41. Philp Auslander discusses Attali's claim in *Liveness,* 26.

72. On some of the exceptions, see n. 68, above.

73. For an early introduction to the *disposizioni sceniche,* see David Rosen, "The Staging of Verdi's Operas: An Introduction to the Ricordi *Disposizioni sceniche,*" in *International Musicological Society: Report of the Twelfth Congress, Berkeley, 1977,* ed. Daniel Heartz and Bonnie C. Wade (Kassel: Bärenreiter, 1981), 444–53. More recently, scholars have begun to incorporate the manuals into discussions of the stage aesthetics of Verdi's works. See, e.g., chapter 13, "From the Score to the Stage," in Philip Gossett, *Divas and Scholars: Performing Italian Opera* (Chicago: University of Chicago Press, 2006); as well as Parker, "Reading the *Livrets,*" 126–48. Gossett discusses the French origins of the *disposizioni sceniche* in "From the Score to the Stage," 443–86, and notes that "it was through Giuseppe Verdi's contact with Paris that the idea of publishing staging manuals passed from France to Italy" (457). As

of the staging manuals is a matter of debate, and lately the debate has been simmering in the academy.[74] A number of academics have been wondering what to make of the instructions recorded in the staging manuals: Are they most relevant to work on the stage or in the library? That is, are they effectively prescriptive or primarily of historical, philological, or scholarly interest?[75] The terms of this debate mirror the debate about modes of iteration: seen as fixed and prescriptive, the staging manuals materialize the sense of reiteration as repetition; read as texts, as objects of creative interpretation, the staging manuals contribute to the project of reinflection.

The question of the *disposizioni sceniche* gets to the very heart of how we imagine — or fail to imagine — the place of mise-en-scène in our conceptualization of opera. What is a stage director, dramaturg, or scholar to do with this material? We seem to be suspended between two equally unappealing alternatives, an eminently Verdian predicament. Do we follow instructions and do what we are told (the programmatically deferential model), or do we read and stage the work as we see fit (a more audacious model)? The deferential model has the appeal of the Master's authorization but runs the risk of stultification and ossification; the audacious model has the appeal of freshness and invention but runs the risk of recklessness or inscrutability.

---

noted above, Jennifer Batchelor incorporates material from the third edition (1884) of the *disposizione scenica* for the Paris production, originally published in 1867, into the extensive notes to the libretto that appears in her ENO Guide to *Don Carlos*. See Batchelor, *Giuseppe Verdi: Don Carlos / Don Carlo*, 29–156. Michaela Peterseil considers the particularities of the *disposizione scenica* for *Don Carlos* in her "Die 'Disposizioni sceniche' des Verlags Ricordi: Ihre Publikation und ihr Zielpublikum," *Studi Verdiani* 12 (1997): 147–49. In addition, English-speaking readers may want to consult, among the many other sources, Hans Busch's translation of the complete *disposizione scenica* for *Aida* in his *Verdi's Aida: The History of an Opera in Letters and Documents* (Minneapolis: University of Minnesota Press, 1982). In the early 1990s, Ricordi began to republish a series of Verdi *disposizioni sceniche*. For a facsimile of the original *disposizione scenica* for *Otello* as well as an extensive critical apparatus, see James A. Hepokoski and Mercedes Viale Ferrero, *Otello di Giuseppe Verdi: Collana di disposizioni sceniche*, vol. 1 (Milan: Ricordi, 1990).

74. The extent of the prescription necessarily depends upon the precision of its formulation. As Gossett points out: "As the century went on, the *disposizioni sceniche* grew longer and more elaborate. The book for the 1858 *Un ballo in maschera* fills 38 pages; those for Boito's *Mefistofele* (published in 1877), the 1881 revision of *Simon Boccanegra*, and the 1887 *Otello*, 109, 58 and 111 pp., respectively. All three were prepared by Giulio Ricordi on the basis of stagings at Milan's Teatro alla Scala. In the *disposizione scenica* for *Otello*, the level of detail is staggering, indicating each movement during a dialogue, commenting on motivation, tone, and facial expression." Gossett, "From the Score to the Stage," 460.

75. See, e.g., Parker, "Reading the *Livrets*," and the concluding paragraphs of Parker, "Philippe and Posa," as well as the debates published in *Verdi in Performance* and *Verdi 2001*. If we were to pursue the national angle of this debate, we would need to inquire whether the prescriptive force of the *disposizioni sceniche* has any *more* authority than, say, Wagner's assiduously recorded instructions on the staging of his works.

By framing the question broadly, we quickly find ourselves at the heart of Verdi's dramaturgy—not simply because Verdi's works are rife with such hyperbolized, Manichaean alternatives, but more particularly because the condition of calcified power and the possibilities of resistance to it constitute a recurring theme in his works.[76] There are a number of works from the Verdian corpus that explore the conflict between an unruly, impatient, largely disempowered figure (usually inflected as youthful) and an inflexible, unmovable figure of power (often inflected as parental).[77] No work, however, presents this conflict with such verve, such a sense of intractability, as *Don Carlos*.

In my account, the crisis rendered in the opera text involves an intractability of discourse. The performance text poses a similar problem. The opera text figures the effects of a severe constriction of expression: throughout, the threat of an unbridled expression produces a pervasive sense of anxiety and dread.[78] And as I suggested in chapter 1, this anxiety in turn produces a regime of quotidian surveillance, according to which language and bodies are kept carefully in check. The anxiety obtains on both levels—it is produced within the opera text and recurs in its deployment, as performance text, onstage.

The thematics of the work and the problematics of mise-en-scène are related. Let me cite an example. In *Don Carlos*, power requires a script to emerge as properly powerful. The pervading sense of suffocation in the work is attributable to a fossilization of political power and its discursive correlative, an extreme rigidity of interpersonal exchange. This rigidity is scripted; indeed, its scriptedness accounts for its rigidity. Thus, for example, the Flemish deputies are not granted a royal hearing when they make an unscheduled

---

76. On melodrama and the "manichaeistic," see Peter Brooks, *The Melodramatic Imagination: Balzac, Henry James, Melodrama, and the Mode of Excess* (New Haven, Conn.: Yale University Press, 1976), 12.

77. On the various configurations in Verdi of the relationships between parents and their offspring, see de Van, *Verdi's Theater*, 157–67. Paul Robinson argues that the preoccupation with the family that characterizes Verdi's works of the early 1850s (i.e., *Rigoletto, Il trovatore, La traviata*) reflects the composer's temporary withdrawal from politics: "The failure of the revolution of 1848, and with it the hopes for a united Italy, led to a sudden withdrawal of Verdi's interests from politics. From 1851 to 1853, he composed a series of three operas whose concerns are largely domestic or romantic: *Rigoletto, Il trovatore,* and *La traviata*. In *La traviata* politics are banished entirely, while in *Rigoletto* and *Il trovatore* they are relegated very much to the periphery. At the emotional center of these operas is the family, and their most powerful scenes examine, in a manner that sometimes anticipates Freud, the tensions between parents and children. During the immediate postrevolutionary years, then, politics appear to have been driven from Verdi's artistic consciousness." Robinson, "Realpolitik," 156.

78. As de Van notes, "In fact, all the characters in this opera are stifled in their roles, and their deepest nature, if they have an opportunity to reveal it, consists of nothing but vertigo and confusion. This disintegration of the character's inner life and moral consistency creates a crisis in melody as the embodiment of a clear, defined psychological attitude." De Van, *Verdi's Theater*, 306.

Musical Example 8 A shift in sympathy. The melody of the Flemish "heretics" is pronouncedly lyrical as opposed to the stark and bureaucratic music of Philippe and the monks that preceded it. Upon hearing the cries of the Flemish, the crowd—joined by Elisabeth, Posa, Carlos, and Thibault—suddenly and severely shifts its sympathies in favor of them.

appearance during the auto-da-fé in act 3, even when they are granted a (heavily sentimentalized, almost saccharine) unison choral voice.[79] The work stages their exclusion from the diegetic realm of political discourse and the in-justice of that exclusion in musical terms. The envoys' plea is granted lyrical license, representing a notable exception to the scripted alternation of

79. Here again, public, political purposiveness—the kind embodied by Posa and marshaled here by Carlos—is invested with the trappings of straightforward rhythmic, harmonic, and melodic fo-cus. The question—derived from Heather Wiebe's astute consideration of the compositional aes-thetics of public and private lives in *Don Carlos*—is how to read this purposiveness. Is the conven-tionality of the chorus of Flemish deputies, for instance, to be understood as simple and, say, earthy (a kind of *compositional* purposiveness) or is it to be seen as simplistic and thus ironic? That is, how are we to account for the fact that the world of introspection and irresolution—which the opera clearly inflects as less desirable and functional than the public world of Rodrigo's idealism—pro-duces the more interesting and complicated music? See Wiebe, "Conquering Desire," esp. 550–52.

Musical Example 8 *(continued)*

monastic rigor and raw declamatory force that characterizes the auto-da-fé. All of a sudden, King Philippe's carefully staged event is at risk of coming unglued: the people, who were just singing Philippe's praises according to script, are suddenly moved to implore the king to have mercy on Flanders. And they are joined in their plea by that latent gang of four, Elisabeth, Posa, Carlos, and Thibault.

Musical Example 8 *(continued)*

Carlos's appearance with the deputies violates multiple scripts: he is interrupting the carefully staged spectacle of the auto-da-fé and publicly abandoning his assigned role as loyal son in the process. Posa's surprise move to restore order—the paternal order as well as the scripted spectacle of the auto-da-fé—reinstates not merely the king's authority, but along with it the primacy of the script by which that authority finds expression.[80] The massive choral hymn to the spectacle and the king's power that authorizes it is reprised at (and as) the conclusion of the act, signaling the collapse of the Oedipal coup d'état (and its musical correlative, what we might term the lyrical *coup de la mélodie*) and the return of the musical and political status quo *ante*.[81] Joachim Herz is certainly right to note that the auto-da-fé does not critique "the Christian faith so much as its perversion via a terrorism of belief on the part of a voracious power structure that lets people burn under the sign of the cross" (Nicht der christliche Glaube wird hier angetastet, sondern seine Pervertierung in den Gesinnungsterror einer raffgierigen Hierarchie, die unter dem Zeichen des Kreuzes Menschen verbrennen läßt).[82] What he might have added is that this perversion ends up carrying the day. Although the extraordinarily sweet soprano voice from heaven promises redemption to the victims of the flames, the nature of power on display here is (and needs to be shown as) horrific: a mass spectacle of—and a mass hymn to—political torture. Here, then, we have the piece's object lesson in resistance. Those who resist are burned at the stake.

This raises a fundamental point about the function of spectacle in Verdi's works. Very frequently in Verdi, the advent of spectacle coincides with and even signals the advent of irony.[83] The victory march in *Aida*, to name the most familiar example, is as much a harrowing spectacle as an opportunity for grandiloquent display. It is harrowing in part because of its grandiloquence: it treats us to the spectacle of what we might, adjusting Walter Benjamin's formulation, describe as "history being staged by the victors."[84] In act 3 of *Don*

---

80. Verdi's relationship to paternal order is a matter of some debate. See esp. Luigi Baldacci, who explores the mirroring effect between figurations of paternity in Verdi's works and those in the Italian domestic sphere. Luigi Baldacci, "Padri e figli: Parole e musica, etc.," in *Libretti d'opera e altri saggi* (Florence: Vallecchi, 1974), as quoted in de Van, *Verdi's Theater*, 160.

81. In the end—or, more precisely, by the second scene of the fourth act—it will emerge that Posa's gesture of apparent complicity with the king was in fact an act of solidarity with—and self-sacrifice on behalf of—Carlos. This constitutes a different, intentionally secret script.

82. Joachim Herz, "Neue Dimensionen gegenüber dem Drama: Notizen zu Verdis *Don Carlos*" (1967), in Walter Felsenstein and Joachim Herz, *Musiktheater: Beiträge zur Methodik und zu Inszenierungskonzeptionen*, ed. Stephan Stompor, 2nd ed. (Leipzig: Reclam, 1976), 266–68, at 267.

83. Compare Gilles de Van, "War, Festivity, Pomp," "Ambivalence and Irony," and "Friezes and Tableaux" in de Van, *Verdi's Theater*, 199–202, 245–50, and 256–62, respectively. As de Van points out, "*Don Carlos* is an opera marked throughout by [the] oscillation between French ceremonial spectacle and Italian concision, which explains the coexistence of several versions that revise but never quite replace each other." De Van, *Verdi's Theater*, 291.

84. Walter Benjamin, "Theses on the Philosophy of History" [1940], trans. Harry Zohn, in *Critical Theory and Society: A Reader*, ed. Stephen Bronner and Douglas Kellner (New York: Routledge, 1989), 255–66, at 257. Published in German as "Über den Begriff der Geschichte," in *Gesammelte Schriften*, ed. Rolf Tiedemann and Hermann Schweppenhäuser, Werkausgabe Bd. 2 (Frankfurt am Main: Suhrkamp, 1980), 2:696.

Carlos (though not just there) we are given a strong sense of how entrenched authority depends upon scripted reiterations of its power. As I have suggested, the opera text of *Don Carlos* fashions the imperative of sublimation as a matter of learning a new script and then sticking to it. At the risk of being obvious, I will point out that there are two components here: the text must be learned (say, by Elisabeth, who must learn her new role as queen and wife), and then, to be effective, it must be performed (say, in public displays of queenliness and wifeliness). The performance text needs to render this fashioning, but it need not reiterate its terms. That is, the performance text needs to stage the effects of the imperative of sublimation, but it need not submit to or replicate them: in Attali's vocabulary, it can represent those terms without repeating them. But for us to arrive at this insight, we need to reread Verdi, being careful to distinguish between opera texts and performance texts. We need to subject the scripts — including both the scripts embedded within the opera text (e.g., the scene of the auto-da-fé) and those overlaid upon the performance text (e.g., the *disposizioni sceniche*)—to interpretive scrutiny, in theory and onstage.

Conceptualizing Mise-en-Scène

I imagine that we can all agree that the drama of Verdi's *Don Carlos* (and, I would add, its musical affect) elaborates a critique of entrenched, inflexible authority. And yet, the sanctioned means of depicting that critique (and the institutionalization of those means via the *disposizioni sceniche*) has come to rest upon the very grounds of entrenched, inflexible authority that the opera text seems intent upon exposing.[85] (An inventive mise-en-scène might reflect its own ironic condition, namely, the sense that it too is subject to the very pressures of discursive and representational accommodation that it would render in the opera text.) Over time, the scripts of the *disposizioni sceniche* have come to model a form of discursive propriety—an accommodation with representational norms—whose toll and effects are arguably rehearsed in turn in the opera text. Beyond registering the performative irony of this conjunction, I wonder how we might track its implications for our conceptualization of the work in production—and our conceptualization of the work of mise-en-scène.

I want to close by sketching some ideas for the work in performance. According to my argument, a mise-en-scène would need to chart the opera text's terms of oppression, including the dramatic trajectory of sublimation. This

---

85. Like Philippe and the Grand Inquisitor, the *disposizioni sceniche* were not always entrenched. See Peterseil,"Die 'Disposizioni sceniche,'" 135–36.

would mean staging the full arc of sublimation, from its prehistory (Elisabeth and Carlos as living a conventionally carefree, privileged existence: Carlos as impressionable rebel, Elisabeth as unsuspecting, sheltered girl) through its imposition (Elisabeth's voice dies only to be reborn in its affinity with propriety; Carlos's concomitant and thoroughgoing disorientation, including his failed attempts at giving voice to romance and resistance, result in his existential torpor) and its eventual apotheosis (Carlos's ambivalent accession to Posa's protocol of sublimation; the farewell between Carlos and Elisabeth as a product and a statement of sublimation, as well as the misrecognition that follows upon that statement). Posa, as my argument has already suggested, bears the markings of a single-minded ideologue, wavering between demagoguery and idealism. There is something distinctly presentable about him (his melodies are so catchy, he is so smooth), while at the same time there is something simplistic and even suspicious to that presentability. As Posa's impressionable friend, Carlos wavers between a conscious—if unconsciously conventional—defiance (e.g., his initial appearance in the forest at Fontainebleau; his subsequent appearance at the auto-da-fé with the Flemish deputies) and an even more conventional romantic sentimentality and incapacitation. We should—as Carlos invariably does—linger on this point. Once his romantic identity has been shattered in act 1, there are very few points in the piece where Carlos actually does anything. And those few instances where he attempts to do something—most memorably, interrupting the auto-da-fé in order to challenge his father's authority—fail miserably. I wonder whether Don Carlos is best understood as a romantic hero or as the shell of a romantic hero, a moored vessel of romantic torpor. (If this is the case, then Posa would be his peppy little tugboat). Elisabeth needs to bear the traces of her enforced accommodation; it should be clear that she has been compelled to take a sudden turn from being quite unencumbered at the outset of the opera to being thoroughly weighed down by her assigned position. One way to imagine this transformation is to suggest that Elisabeth has been forced to grow up overnight, catapulted from early adolescence to late middle age. (Here we encounter one of the problems of presenting the work in four acts: if we lop off the first act, Elisabeth's transformation cannot be shown; it is a fait accompli.) While her music suggests that she navigates this jump with remarkable dignity, her dramatic situation suggests that she does so with considerable difficulty, a product of the passivity to which she is largely conscripted. For example, she must endure the king's banishment of her lady-in-waiting, the Countess of Aremberg, and she must attend—and comport herself with dignity at—the auto-da-fe. Her suffering is not entirely silent (she is given a *scena* in act 4 to protest to the king, who eventually wallops her), but it is largely public, which makes it all the more difficult to pull off. As for Philippe, the terms of his attempt to befriend Posa in act 2, his famous act 4 aria "Elle ne m'aime pas!," and his lament in the wake of the Inquisitor's demands all suggest that he is suffused with self-pity. But that in no way diminishes the king's implication in power politics. Instead, it underscores that implication: he is the brutal and ruthless victimizer convinced of his own victimization. And Eboli? Hers is a difficult character to fathom. In a sense, she embodies more than anyone the piece's dramaturgy of ambivalence: on the one hand, she is utterly devious (in her dealings with Elisabeth), and on the other, she is altruistic (in her determination to save Carlos); on the one hand, she is musically frivolous and effervescent (in the courtyard aria that she sings to the ladies in waiting), and on the other, she is relentlessly purposive (in a remarkable series of arias, culminating, of course, in "O don fatal"). But who *is* she? She is hard to pin down: she would be the Infante's lover but was (is still?) the king's mistress; she is a member of the queen's retinue but is also her secret rival. In each of these identities, she *acts* decisively— she arranges to meet Carlos secretly at the outset of act 3, she places Elisabeth's casket in the king's hands in act 4, and she hustles Carlos away from the Inquisitor's rabble at the end of the act. In this, she is remarkably different from Carlos, a tragic player to his tragic torpor.

To sketch some ideas for the setting: It strikes me that a production would need to account for the pervading atmosphere of constriction and surveillance at the Spanish court, the overwhelming sense that a public life is shelterless because it is unresponsive to individual desire, which is to say, the overwhelming sense of public life as scripted and the concomitant annulment of private desire. The Spain of *Don Carlos* is, after all, not quite the tourist destination that so many productions make it out to be. For one thing, there is the matter of the Inquisition. Is it clear what this means? After all, we are shown what is at stake, if you will. Or rather, we ought to be shown. As the Inquisitor makes clear in his act 3 duet with Philippe, anyone is liable to be next. And the crowd, far from protesting, loves it! It is a veritable party: "Maintenant à la fête!" as Philippe puts it when he assumes his place in the grandstand to a trumpet fanfare at once overtly celebratory and deeply sinister. This is terrifying also because it *is* presented as a festival. Despite the bright lights called for in the *disposizione sceniche,* the auto-da-fé is an exceedingly dark affair: these are the bright lights of a concentration camp gallows or a Ku Klux Klan mass rally and lynching. In performance this demands to be harrowing—a cross between the enforced solemnity of a Stalinist show trial and the gleeful festivity of an Independence Day celebration. (In that, it is not far removed dramaturgically from the victory march in *Aida*).

But spectacle is not the only forum for this terror. There is an everyday quality to it, and a production needs to make that clear. Hardly anyone sings without encumbrance in the world of *Don Carlos*. Not even the queen can be left alone. So a production needs to render the everyday sense of this constriction: life in the world of *Don Carlos* is life in a culture of thoroughgoing surveillance. Whether that sense of constriction needs to be materialized or abstracted is not clear to me: it might work to populate the stage with a surveillance apparatus (e.g., low-tech flunkies or high-tech surveillance cameras); but it also might work, it might be more sinister and oppressive, to render the *internalization* of that sense of Big Brother watching—a sense of constriction, suffocation, and generalized oppression.

And herein lies an irony to be staged: For Elisabeth and Carlos, the only tenable shelter is to be found in their embrace of the script of sublimation, and yet, as the rest of the work suggests, it is this very preponderance of scripts— including the script of sublimation—that impels their search for shelter in the first place. And in the end, of course, it hardly matters, since sublimation offers no shelter at all. The Grand Inquisitor and the king surprise Elisabeth and Carlos in the act of consummating their sublimation, of taking their leave, as mother and son—*pour toujours, per sempre*. Verdi's opera text lays out the terrible, terrifying irony of this deeply unsettling resolution.

6

BEYOND THE CANON

Zemlinsky's Der König Kandaules

In the first five chapters of this book, I have sought to reconceive of canonical operas as unsettled in and through performance. In this chapter, I want to consider how this project might apply to new or rediscovered works that have yet to enter the repertory, let alone the canon. How would we go about unsettling what is not yet settled? And what would be the point? On the one hand, the trajectory of this chapter will strike the reader as quite familiar: I want to consider the dramaturgy of a work in order to ask how that dramaturgy might best find expression onstage, in production. A work that has yet to hit the stage or that has been staged very rarely is not (yet) burdened by the history of interpretation that accumulates around—and settles—canonical works. And yet, engaging with a new or rediscovered work will require some new terminology, since it hardly seems useful to distinguish, as I have throughout this book, between modes of rearticulation when the work in question demands an initial articulation rather than a secondary one.

Beyond allowing us to distinguish between modes of articulation, a new or rediscovered work also enables us to focus upon the locations and exigencies—the wheres and wherefores—of settling and unsettling. Just as settledness is not an intrinsic quality of canonicity, but one of its recurring features, a work is not necessarily unsettled simply by virtue of its newness or unfamiliarity. (There are plenty of new works that are suffused with an aspiration to settledness.) Furthermore, there is no necessary correspondence between the condition of the work and that of its mise-en-scène: a settled work can find expression in an unsettled mise-en-scène and vice versa. In the course of this chapter, I propose to revisit and refine my claim, first proposed in chapter 2, that unsettledness is a dramaturgical quality that variously characterizes the opera text and the performance text.

I propose to focus on a work that is multiply unsettled: Alexander Zemlinsky's *Der König Kandaules,* composed in 1935–36 but left unfinished upon
the composer's death in 1942. (Indeed, for years it was presumed lost.) In
1990, the British musician and musicologist Antony Beaumont was able to
reconstruct the short score to the opera and a portion of its orchestration
from among Zemlinsky's papers at the Library of Congress. Within two
years of his discovery, Beaumont had been commissioned by the Hamburg
State Opera to complete the orchestration of Zemlinsky's work. *Der König
Kandaules* premiered in Hamburg on October 6, 1996, sixty years following
its partial composition.[1] Since then, the work has received a modest number
of productions in Europe—including, in 2002, a television broadcast on the
German cable channel SAT 3—but for the most part it remains unknown.[2]
The work's philological unsettledness is in turn amplified by its thematics.
That is, the opera is not just unsettling (involving psychological and physical violation, voyeurism, and regicide); it is, in important ways, fundamentally mysterious. How might we account for this unsettledness in theory
and onstage?

In pondering the indeterminate space of *Der König Kandaules,* it is worthwhile to begin with a brief consideration of the instability of Zemlinsky's career. Although he enjoyed a good deal of success as a composer, he was most
successful as a conductor. In 1904, shortly before turning thirty-three, Zemlinsky accepted a position as a resident conductor at the Vienna Volksoper;
then, in 1911, he was appointed music director at the Neues Deutsches Theater in Prague.[3] In 1927, Otto Klemperer asked Zemlinsky to join him as a

1. On the composition history, see Uwe Sommer, "Alexander Zemlinsky, *Der König Kandaules:*
Analyse und Deutung," *Musik-Konzepte* 92–94 (1996): 78–84. As early as the 1950s, Zemlinsky's
widow, Louise, was interested in seeing the score of *Kandaules* completed. Anton Swarowsky, son of
the conductor Hans Swarowsky and an assistant to the collector Robert Owen Lehmann, to whom
Mrs. Zemlinsky had sold her husband's papers, offered his services, but she declined. Many of the
preceding details are recounted in Uwe Sommer, "Alexander Zemlinskys Oper *Der König Kandaules:*
Zur Entstehung eines integrativen Spätwerks," in *Jahrbuch des Staatlichen Instituts für Musikforschung
Preussischer Kulturbesitz* (Berlin: De Gruyter, 1997), esp. 237–38.

2. In addition to the Hamburg premiere, conducted by Gerd Albrecht and directed by Günther
Krämer, the work has also been presented at the Vienna Volksoper, where Zemlinsky worked for
many years as a conductor (the Vienna production was by Hans Neuenfels) and in 2002 in a production at the Salzburg Festival, conducted by Kent Nagano and directed by Christine Mielitz.

3. In Vienna, Zemlinsky conducted the Viennese premieres of Puccini's *Tosca* and Dukas's *Ariane
et Barbe-bleue;* in Prague he conducted the world premiere of Schoenberg's *Erwartung.* For a duly extravagant *laudatio* on Zemlinsky as a conductor, see Ernst Rychnovsky, "Über Alexander Zemlinsky,"
originally published in 1924, reprinted in Curjel, *Experiment Krolloper,* 207–9. See also Arnost Mahler,
"Alexander Zemlinsky: Das Porträt eines großen Musikers," in *Alexander Zemlinsky: Tradition im
Umkreis der Wiener Schule,* ed. Otto Kolleritsch, Studien zur Wertungsforschung 7 (Graz: Universal

principal conductor at the Kroll Opera in Berlin, the opera house whose legendary commitment to radical productions I noted in chapter 2. Zemlinsky was on the podium for many of the Kroll's most controversial productions, including an extraordinary constructivist staging, premiered in 1929, of Offenbach's *Contes d'Hoffmann,* directed by Ernst Legal, with sets and costumes by László Moholy-Nagy; and an equally astonishing, abstract production of Puccini's *Madama Butterfly* that premiered shortly before the house was shut down in 1931, directed by Hans Curjel and again designed by Moholy-Nagy.[4] Zemlinsky, then, was at the center of one of the most important institutions in the history of opera in the twentieth century—a place where opera was visibly transformed into a vehicle for exceedingly provocative innovations, a forum for modernism.

In terms of his professional biography, Zemlinsky's assigned place at the center of these innovations was on the conductor's podium. But a number of critics—including Theodor Adorno, Alban Berg, and Arnold Schoenberg, as well as, more recently, Antony Beaumont, Jens Malte Fischer, and Uwe Sommer—have argued that Zemlinsky properly occupies a place in the history of twentieth-century music as a major composer. Like Zemlinsky's career, which makes it difficult to pin him down to a single professional identity, his compositions are characterized by hybridity, occupying a volatile space between Wagner, Brahms, and Schoenberg. He never met Wagner (who died in February 1883, a year before Alexander, then thirteen, enrolled at the Vienna Conservatory), but he had a number of important interactions with Brahms, who was an early and enthusiastic supporter.[5] As for Schoenberg, Zemlinsky was his composition teacher, mentor, friend, and brother-in-law: Zemlinsky's sister Mathilde was Schoenberg's first wife.[6]

Edition, 1976), 13–26, at 17–20. For an exhaustive account of Zemlinsky's tenure in Prague, see Pamela Tancsik, *Die Prager Oper heißt Zemlinsky: Theatergeschichte des neuen Deutschen Theaters Prag in der Ära Zemlinsky von 1911 bis 1927* (Vienna: Böhlau, 2000). A much briefer account of Zemlinsky's initial experiences as a conductor in Prague can be found in Jiří Vysloužil, "Zemlinskys Prager Antrittsjahre," *Alexander Zemlinsky: Ästhetik, Stil und Umfeld,* ed. Hartmut Krones, Wiener Schriften zur Stilkunde und Aufführungspraxis (Vienna: Böhlau, 1995), 237–46.

4. Over the course of his four years at the Kroll house, Zemlinsky conducted a remarkable range of new productions, including works by Smetana, Puccini, Weber, Strauss (both Richard and Johann), Ravel, Milhaud, Ibert, Verdi, Schoenberg, and Gustave Charpentier. On Zemlinsky's tenure and reception at the Kroll, see Antony Beaumont, *Zemlinsky* (Ithaca, N.Y.: Cornell University Press, 2000), 349–54.

5. Brahms was quite taken with Zemlinsky's music and urged (successfully) that his publisher Simrock publish the young composer's Clarinet Trio op. 3. On Zemlinsky's enrollment in music school, see Horst Weber, *Alexander Zemlinsky: Eine Studie* (Vienna: Elisabeth Lafite, 1977), 10–11. On his relationship with Brahms, see ibid., 12.

6. See Weber, *Alexander Zemlinsky,* 12–15; See also Beaumont, *Zemlinsky,* 164–66; 323–25.

Any listener will immediately recognize that Zemlinsky's music is not as radical as Schoenberg's.[7] Here is how Adorno defined the difference:

> If in Schoenberg's works the most divergent impulses of the age met, culminating in the idea of constructivist composition, it was Zemlinsky who defined the cultural space which made it possible to compare those different impulses in the first place: apart from Wagner and Brahms, [the cultural space encompassed by Zemlinsky's music includes], above all, Mahler, Debussy and Schoenberg.[8]

If Schoenberg is immediately recognizable as a modernist, Zemlinsky is something very different. Adorno brands it eclecticism—suggesting that Zemlinsky's works characteristically and brilliantly encompass strikingly disparate musical tendencies. This makes it doubly hard to pigeonhole Zemlinsky—that is, once we have decided to pigeonhole him as a composer, it is hard to know where to place his compositions. (And indeed, for the thirty-five or so years between his death in 1942 and the rediscovery of his works in the late 1970s, Zemlinsky's works were hardly placed at all, having been largely forgotten.) Some critics and historians characterize him as a *Jugendstil* composer, while Alfred Clayton characterizes him as an impressionist because Zemlinsky's works—especially his works for the stage—bear a number of defining impressionistic traits, including a new, antinaturalist inwardness, the priority accorded to nuance, and a profusion and variety of eroticism.[9] Although Adorno does not use the term impressionism, his account certainly runs along similar lines:

> [Zemlinsky's operas] are primarily *lyrical* in nature, he scorns all shrill, overemphatic gestures; in this respect he was a true disciple of the French. Above all, the content has a . . . wholly unfeigned *warmth*. It is the *direct* proclamation of feeling, not its imitation. To that extent and despite his use of largely traditional methods, Zemlinsky may be classified along with the *post-Straussian* generation.[10]

---

7. See, in this respect, "Arnold Schönberg über Alexander Zemlinsky," originally published in 1921, reprinted in Curjel, *Experiment Krolloper*, 209–10. See also Ernst Hilmar, "Zemlinsky und Schönberg," in Kolleritsch, *Zemlinsky*, 55–79; and Rychnovsky, "Zemlinsky."

8. Adorno, "Zemlinsky," in *Quasi una fantasia: Essays on Modern Music*, trans. Rodney Livingstone (New York: Verso, 1992), 117.

9. See Alfred Eberhard Stephan Clayton, "The Operas of Alexander Zemlinsky" (Ph.D. diss., Queen's College, Cambridge, 1982), 15.

10. Zemlinsky's "modernity," Adorno concludes, is marked by "the very pride his music takes in refusing to project itself." Adorno, "Zemlinsky," 122.

In 1931, political support for the Kroll Opera's program of innovation evaporated, and the house was shut down. Zemlinsky had just finished composing his seventh opera, *Der Kreidekreis* (The Chalk Circle [1930–31], based on a drama by Klabund). Most of the operas Zemlinsky had composed prior to the *Kreidekreis* had premiered at prestigious European houses, albeit with only modest success. But that was about to change—or so it seemed. *Der Kreidekreis* had been accepted for a high-profile set of simultaneous premieres in Berlin, Frankfurt, Cologne, and Nuremberg late in 1933.[11] The premieres were then abruptly canceled when the National Socialists took power in April 1933. At the same time, Zemlinsky was dismissed from his teaching post at the Hochschule für Musik in Berlin—his principal place of employment after the Kroll Opera was closed—because his marriage violated the newly instituted racial laws for civil servants.[12]

In September 1933, Zemlinsky, his wife, Louise, and his daughter, Johanna, (from Zemlinsky's first marriage) fled to Vienna, the city of his youth and early career.[13] It is here, "in the face of the abyss," as Jens Malte Fischer puts it, that he began work on *Der König Kandaules,* fashioning the libretto from an 1899 play by André Gide.[14] Gide's play is something of a palimpsest, based on multiple and diverse sources including Herodotus, Plato, and a novella by Théophile Gautier.[15] Zemlinsky began work on *Kandaules* in the

11. *Der Kreidekreis* is a three-act work mingling Orientalist, modernist, and fairy-tale effects. The Orientalist effects include extensive use of the pentatonic scale and the gong; the modernist effects include the incorporation of jazz and epic recitation; the fairy-tale effects include the happy ending and the magical power of the chalk circle. See Weber, *Alexander Zemlinsky,* 64–65; Beaumont, *Zemlinsky,* 368–76.

12. Zemlinsky served as director of the chorus and the oratorio school. Jens Malte Fischer sees the fact that he was not invited to teach either conducting or composition as a direct affront. See Fischer, "'Das ist keine Stadt für's Exil': Alexander Zemlinskys letzte Wiener Jahre," in *Der König Kandaules,* program book to the Salzburg Festival production (Salzburg, 2002), 28–35, at 29. In lieu of the simultaneous premieres in Germany, *Der Kreidekreis* premiered in Zurich in October 1933. On the fate of the work in production, see Beaumont, *Zemlinsky,* 402–7. On Zemlinsky's religious identity, see Beaumont, *Zemlinsky,* 3–10, esp. 3.

13. Zemlinsky married Ida Guttmann in 1906. Their only child, Johanna, was born two years later. Ida died in 1929 in Berlin; just over a year later, Zemlinsky married Louise Sachsel, a thirty-year-old singer from Prague. See Weber, *Alexander Zemlinsky,* 23; Beaumont, *Zemlinsky,* 368.

14. Fischer, "Exil," 29.

15. Herodotus, *The Histories,* trans. Aubrey de Sélincourt, rev. A. R. Burn (New York: Penguin, 1972), 43–46. The tale of Candaules's overthrow appears early on in book 1 of *The Histories* in order to account for the overthrow of the Heraclids in Lydia by the Mermnadae. Plato, *The Republic,* trans. Richard W. Sterling and William C. Scott (New York: Norton, 1985), bk. 2, verses 359–60, which offers a version of the tale of Gyges (as a shepherd) and his ring; Théophile Gautier, *The Wife of King Candaules* (New York: Wisdom House, 1942). For an extensive discussion of the source material for Gide's drama, see Sommer, "Aspekte der Stoffgeschichte," in *Zemlinsky,* 41–43. Of the numerous reworkings of the Gyges/Kandaules material, the best known is Friedrich Hebbel's drama *Gyges und sein Ring* (in Friedrich Hebbel, *Sämtliche Werke: Historisch kritische Ausgabe,* ed. Richard

early summer of 1935 and completed a first draft of the short score just before New Year's 1937.[16] In the following months, he reworked the first half of the opera, completing 885 bars of a new short score by March, at which point the *Anschluss,* Germany's annexation of Austria, brought his revisions to a halt.[17] By the time the composer and his family fled Vienna—heading first, in September 1938, to Prague, and then, in December, to New York—he had completed only approximately one-third of the work's orchestration.

Zemlinsky had hopes of completing *Kandaules* in the United States and seeing it premiere at the Metropolitan Opera, where one of his former students, Artur Bodanzky, was the principal conductor of German repertoire. Alas, no Met production was forthcoming, and Zemlinsky never completed the orchestration: supposedly the bedroom scene was too risqué for the Met of the late 1930s.[18]

The libretto to *Der König Kandaules* takes few liberties with André Gide's play (trimming the text, but otherwise leaving it largely intact), so it makes sense to devote some attention to Gide's work. There is an additional reason to do so. At this point, we have a reconstructed score to Zemlinsky's opera, but not much else: there are no supplemental documents that would enable us to discern Zemlinsky's precise intentions—no diary, letters, or essays. Gide, on the other hand, wrote a good deal about his intentions—and Zemlinsky had access to some of the most important of those writings, since they were included in Franz Blei's German translation.[19]

Gide wrote the three-act verse play *Le roi Candaule* in 1899, two years before writing *L'immoraliste* and almost a half a century before receiving the Nobel Prize for Literature in 1947. It is unclear how—in Vienna, in 1935—Zemlinsky got his hands on a library copy of Blei's German translation. Nor is it clear whether Zemlinsky was aware that Gide had been blacklisted.

Maria Werner [Berlin: B. Behr, 1903–7], 12 vols., vol. 3: Dramen III, 1851–58). For a more detailed discussion, see Eva Walch, "Von Platon zu Zemlinsky: Zur literarischen Entfaltung des Kandaules-Stoffes," in *Der König Kandaules,* program book to the Salzburg Festival production (Salzburg, 2002), 15–27. The purview of Walch's essay encompasses a host of additional renderings of the Kandaules material, including Hugo von Hofmannsthal's scenario for a tragic drama (1903) as well as various—mostly comical—operatic renderings beginning in the seventeenth century.

16. See Sommer, *Kandaules,* 79–84.

17. See Beaumont, *Zemlinsky,* 425.

18. Early in 1939, Zemlinsky began work on another opera, *Circe,* to a libretto by Irma Stein-Firner, but it too remained unfinished at the composer's death in March 1942. For an exceptionally detailed and informative account of Zemlinsky's years in America, see Antony Beaumont and Alfred Clayton, "Alexander Zemlinskys amerikanische Jahre," in Krones, *Zemlinsky,* 247–67. See also Beaumont, *Zemlinsky,* 458–66.

19. Blei was a Francophilic editor, translator, and literary critic who, among other things, prepared the libretto for Paul Hindemith's *Das Nuschi-nuschi.* See Sommer, *Kandaules,* 9.

Zemlinsky had been blacklisted as well: indeed, he and his work were routinely defamed in much the same terms as Gide. But Zemlinsky's biographers suggest that he was resolutely apolitical—and it is by no means clear that he would have perceived Gide's play as inflammatory in any political sense.[20]

Gide, for his part, knew his work was inflammatory, although he predicted that it would offend for all the wrong reasons. Here is how he characterized the problem in a typically witty preface to the first edition of the play:

> I should first excuse myself for writing this preface if I were not writing the preface to excuse myself for having written the play. I fully realize that if the play is good, it has no need of a preface to sustain it; and if the play is bad, the greatest mistake, next to having written it, is to try to explain it. Therefore, up to the present, I have denied myself prefaces; and I should certainly continue to do so were it not for the *strangeness* of this play and the *misunderstanding* it is liable to arouse.
>
> Not knowing what sort of reception awaits it, I can and indeed *must* imagine every possibility—must even imagine that it may be applauded. That would be the first misunderstanding. For, seeing the noisy success with which the public has greeted the plays of Mons. Rostand, for instance, I may not pretend for an instant that any applause my play may receive will be for its *literary* merits; rather if there should be a burst of applause, it will certainly be for that which those who do *not* applaud will consider *scandalous;* it will be for that which I should have *suppressed* in my play, if that had not meant suppressing at the same stroke the *whole* play, and if I did not believe, as I confess I do, that a dramatic work should offer *all sorts* of attractions in addition to its deeper meaning, should be a spectacle *and a fine* spectacle, should not fear to "speak to the senses." But the more this *latter* aspect of the work, which, after all, is secondary here, is likely to please the public, the greater is my need to exonerate myself at once, in order to avoid at least prolonging the misapprehension.[21]

The scandal that Gide sought to avoid is, as he suggests, nonetheless central to the piece. And what is that scandal?

In order to address that question, let me offer a thumbnail sketch of the drama. Kandaules, king of the Lydians, professes insistently and repeatedly to be an extremely happy and wealthy man—among the happiest and wealthiest on Earth. And he is happiest, he says, when he is sharing his

20. See Beaumont, *Zemlinsky;* Weber, *Alexander Zemlinsky;* Sommer, *Kandaules.*

21. André Gide, "Preface to the First Edition," *King Candaules,* in *My Theater: Five Plays and an Essay,* trans. Jackson Mathews (New York: Knopf: 1952), 163–68, at 163–64; my emphasis. "Noisy success" is a slap directed at Edmond Rostand (1868–1918), whose *Cyrano de Bergerac* premiered to great and lasting success in 1897.

wealth with others. When we first encounter him, Kandaules is in the process of expanding his definition of shareable wealth to include his wife, Nyssia, a legendary beauty. Kandaules has Nyssia appear at a court banquet, where he forces her to remove her veil before the assembled guests. During the ensuing feast, one of the members of the court almost chokes on a ring embedded in the fish that is the banquet's main course. Upon inspection, the ring is found to bear the inscription "I conceal happiness/good fortune." Duly perplexed, King Kandaules sends for the fisherman who delivered the fish to the palace. Near the conclusion of act 1, Gyges, the impoverished fisherman, finally appears at the banquet along with his wife, Trydo. Trydo, it turns out, had spent the preceding night with one of the courtiers, who recognizes her—to his own delight and to the horror of both Trydo and Gyges. Confronted with the revelation of Trydo's infidelity, Gyges stabs her to death in front of the assembled guests. Nyssia is appalled and flees, but Kandaules is impressed and asks Gyges to stay at court as a newfound friend. At the outset of act 2, Kandaules suggests that his new friend don the ring retrieved from the fish (a ring that bears magical properties, rendering its wearer invisible). Kandaules suggests that this will (and indeed, it does) enable Gyges, unobserved, to see the queen undress in the royal chambers— to which the king has invited him. And once Gyges has seen the queen undress, Kandaules orders him, still unobserved, to spend the night with her. The consequences are cataclysmic.

In a sense, then, the scandal is perfectly obvious. Indeed, a number of things are recognizably scandalous here: first, the king's perversity in displaying and then pimping the queen (let alone conceiving of her that she might be thus displayed and pimped); second, the physical fact of that display, that is, the queen's nudity; finally, Gyges's brutal murders, of Trydo in act 1 and of Kandaules in act 3. We might call this the theatrical version of the scandal—the sort of moral outrage that tends to garner political and public attention. *That* element of scandal, Gide claims, is entirely beside the point. There is, then, a further scandal to be found here, the *real* scandal, according to Gide's prefatory note. And what is it? Strangely enough, the scandal is and remains mysterious. Which is to say, the scandal is hard to specify (and I will explain why), but also, and more important, the scandal has to do with this lack of specificity—it is the scandal of mystery itself.

Let me put the point somewhat differently. Like Gide's play, Zemlinsky's opera is about veils and veiling—about veils being raised and lowered, respected and violated.[22] Zemlinsky tells us as much from the very outset of

---

22. As Fadwa El Guindi points out, "the single convenient Western term 'veil' . . . is indiscriminate, monolithic, and ambiguous." For an etymology of veiling and an introduction to its ideolog-

Musical Example 9 Prologue to *Der König Kandaules*. As the orchestra intones the major motifs of the opera, Gyges intones his law: "He who possesses happiness [or good fortune] should conceal himself well. And better yet: conceal his happiness [or good fortune] from others. Here Kandaules will show his friends how to get rich off of his riches. I cannot flatter; my arms are stronger than my tongue."

the opera, in its first few bars. Gyges appears in an epic prologue and speaks the opera's opening line: "Der, der ein Glück hält, soll sich gut verstecken! Und besser noch, sein Glück vor andern" (he who possesses happiness [or

cal history, see El Guindi, "Etymology of Veiling," in *Veil: Modesty, Privacy and Resistance* (Oxford: Berg, 1999), 7. Among the various meanings that have accrued to it are "a covering" as well as "a piece of light fabric hung to separate or conceal or screen what is behind it; a curtain."

good fortune] should conceal himself well. And better yet: conceal his happiness [or good fortune] from others).[23]

The prologue introduces us to a number of themes, both musical and dramatic, that will become familiar during the course of the opera. These themes have been catalogued much in the manner of Wagnerian leitmotifs—corresponding to individual characters, such as the Trydo, Kandaules, or Gyges motif; or groups of characters, such as the flatterers' motif; or things of particular dramatic importance, such as the ring motif.[24] Yes, a ring motif. In this case, the motif is indistinct—which makes sense, since that is precisely the property of the ring: it renders its wearer invisible. The flatterers' motif, on the other hand (see bar 7 in musical example 9), is gratingly memorable, obnoxiously ingratiating. And therewith an important pattern emerges: in this work, what is readily discernible, even superficially appealing, is suspect—indeed, suspect by virtue of its superficial, discernible appeal. For that reason, we would be wise to attend to Gyges's opening lines, alerting us to the importance of veiling. These lines, accompanied quite distinctly and programmatically by the veil motif (bars 3–4), set out a paradoxical lesson of this piece, a lesson that proffers the importance of withholding; a lesson that would reveal the importance of hiding, of stanching revelation. It is a lesson—at once moral and dramaturgical—that will be refashioned as it reemerges, inscribed on the ring contained within the fish served at the court banquet in act 1: *Ich verberge das Glück;* I conceal good fortune or happiness.

There is, according to this opera, a fundamental integrity to invisibility; conversely, as I suggested above, the visible is repeatedly inflected as fraught with danger and worthy of suspicion. But this is an entirely counterintuitive claim, especially for an opera—which, as a genre, is all about visibility, audibility, and palpability. An opera that touts modesty? Invisibility? Hiding? One that endorses mystery over revelation? This is a scandal! Indeed, we might term it the scandal of mystery. This, presumably, is the true scandal to which Gide alludes; and if Gide was concerned that the scandal would derive from nudity or an excess of display, Zemlinsky's opera clarifies that the scandal derives instead from an insistence on modesty, a refusal of display.

Which is to say that the opera bears some of the attributes of its thematic preoccupation: it is not just interested in an exposition of veiling but is itself suffused by it. Given this programmatic interest in modesty and veiling, we

---

23. The text of the libretto is taken from the piano-vocal score. See Alexander Zemlinsky, *Der König Kandaules,* piano-vocal score by Antony Beaumont, text arranged and music composed by Alexander Zemlinsky (Munich: Ricordi, 1993), 5.

24. See Sommer, *Kandaules,* 98–111.

might expect the opera to be impenetrable. But it is not—it is simply mysterious. And like all mysterious masterpieces, it proffers a variety of possible explanations. In the following, I will not settle for one of those explanations, insisting that it solves the mystery. Instead, I propose to explore three of them. We gain a better understanding of the work by attending to the particularities and varieties of its veiling than by unveiling it, and I propose to account for the work's unsettledness in order to sustain rather than resolve it. And once we have settled upon some of the terms of that unsettledness, we will need to determine how they might be rendered on stage.

Why, then, does Kandaules do what he does? How does *Kandaules* do what it does? And how should we think about the relationship between these two questions? The first explanation I propose is psychological (involving the question of generosity); the second is political (involving the politics of appearance); and the third is allegorical (involving various analogies—e.g., between Kandaules and Zemlinsky, between Gyges and the Nazis, and between life at Kandaules's court and life in mid-1930s Vienna). All are plausible; none is conclusive.[25] These three approaches will help, however, to illuminate the piece insofar as they illuminate the ongoing vitality of its mystery.

The Psychological Explanation

In the opera (as in the play), Kandaules is too generous. Indeed, he is neurotically generous: he gives effusively (hosting lavish banquets for the court), and his effusions (his arias, his musical outbursts) often concern his generosity. Two of these effusions about effusiveness occur in act 1, scene 3, when Kandaules explains the nature of "mein Glück, mein *unverborgenes* Glück" (my happiness, my *unconcealed* good fortune), as he terms it. It is unclear which is more important, the "Glück" or the fact that it is unconcealed.

In this case, the character's effusion also takes compositional form: Zemlinsky's indications here are a study in hyperbolization. At the outset, the aria is marked "leidenschaftlich bewegt" (passionately moving). From there, it takes off on an upward spiral, becoming "immer gesteigerter" (ever more intense) and then "immer exaltierter und leidenschaftlicher" (ever more exalted and passionate).

In the aria, Kandaules is directly contradicting the rule intoned by Gyges at the outset of the piece. When it is first announced, the import of Gyges's Law—that he who has good fortune should conceal it, and himself, before

---

25. And of course, there are other possible avenues of exploration and explanation—feminist or allegorical interpretations, for instance, have figured in the few productions of the work that have taken place since its reconstruction in Hamburg in 1996.

Leidenschaftlich bewegt (♩ = ♪)

Doch weil mein Glück, mein un - ver - borg' - nes

Glück im an - - dern sei - ne Kraft___ und sei - ne Hef - tig - keit zu

immer gleich bewegt im Ausdruck

schöp - fen scheint, so kommt's mir vor, oft

Musical Example 10 Kandaules breaks Gyges's law. In this aria, Kandaules hysterically extols his own good fortune—ever more intensely, ever more exaltedly, according to Zemlinsky's hyperbolic markings.

others—is completely unclear.[26] But at this point, in act 1, scene 3, it begins to make sense. It does so, I suspect, because Kandaules's aria does not: that is, Kandaules's hymn to his own fortune and his need to share it comes off as distinctly odd, all the more so given the extraordinary orchestral emphasis it is accorded. Indeed, in the wake of his emphatic and euphoric explanation, it remains unclear *why* Kandaules is so intent on sharing. On the one

26. At the outset of the opera, it is merely an aesthetic rule and not yet a political one.

Musical Example 10 *(continued)*

hand, we can say that Kandaules doth profess too much concerning his wealth and his happiness. But in another sense, he hardly professes enough, insofar as his account explains very little. How, then, are we to make sense of his claim that his unconcealed joy derives its strength and intensity from others?

There is an obvious and generative tension in the piece between the king's fervent commitment to display (the unconcealedness of his "unconcealed joy") and the queen's preference for modesty. In the preface to his play, Gide invokes Nietzsche to account for this tension: "It is a curious thing to note," Nietzsche writes, "that excessive generosity does not go without loss of

Musical Example 10 (*continued*)

modesty."[27] This tension has a dramatic and generic correlative. Dramatically, it produces a noteworthy distinction in modes of expression. Until the very end of the opera, Nyssia's lyricism emerges in the private sphere (e.g., in her exchanges with Kandaules in act 2, scene 2; and in act 3, scene 2), which is, of course, precisely where we would expect it to emerge, given her wariness of publicity. The opposite is true for Kandaules. In this scene as elsewhere in the opera, Kandaules reverses the conventional distinction between the public and private. On the one hand, as in this aria, Kandaules expresses within

27. Gide, preface to *Candaules*, 166 n. 2.

Musical Example 10 (*continued*)

the public sphere sentiments that would normally be expressed in private. But more interesting is the sense that for Kandaules a conventionally private sentiment (such as love or desire) can only emerge as such when routed through the public sphere: its integrity depends upon its public validation. In thus reversing the conventional sense of private and public, the aria rehearses in lyrical form the king's later actions, when he will smuggle Gyges (a more or less random representative of the world "out there") into the innermost recesses of the king's private sphere, the royal bedroom. Kandaules, it would appear, presents Nyssia to the court, and then to Gyges, in order eventually to withhold her (so he announces, too late, in act 3); he shares in order to

Musical Example 10 (*continued*)

comprehend possession; he giveth, we might say, as an exercise, in order to prepare for the day when he taketh away.

Part of what makes this aria particularly disquieting is that it is not inflected as disquieting. That is, Zemlinsky underscores the king's effusion before the courtiers with a full-throttle lyrical expressiveness. Rather than splitting the aria into divergent voices, such that the orchestra would audibly assume some distance from the king's effusions, the lush, emphatic orchestral accompaniment is marshaled quite conventionally in support of the

Musical Example 10 *(continued)*

king's expression.[28] The aria's rhetorical consolidation and its status as a monologue enact a kind of royal remove, a characteristic solipsism that isolates the king musically and dramatically from his more properly socialized surroundings. The aria recalls Peter Brooks's observation (encountered

28. Sommer's account of the aria is uncharacteristically scant, noting the connection between the aria's "glowing tone" and that of Zemlinsky's works between 1915 and 1923, and proposing that the aria locates Kandaules in the realm of ritual: Kandaules (as a character, not a work), he argues, "is one single ritual." Sommer, *Kandaules*, 144.

above, in chapter 5) about the way in which some operatic arias seem to speak desire:

> The operatic aria, like the melodramatic dialogue, speaks the name of desire directly. It may be the most unrepressed speech of desire that art allows. And yet, it can have something of the weirdness of hysteria as well. The hysteri-cization of voice in opera, especially in the aria, derives, I think, from . . . both the extremity of the situation in which the character finds himself—more pertinently, usually, herself—and also that extremity that comes from the paradoxical conjunction of artifice and naturalism in the genre itself. The extremity of the character's situation is obvious enough: operatic libretti exist to move characters from one moment of excruciating crisis to another with a minimum of necessary development in between, and the moment of crisis is the place for musical illustration, where a few words can be unpacked into a major piece of song. The extremity of the genre, I've tried to suggest, is inherent in the very risk of a sung drama, that impossible heightening of life where it takes on the form of dreams (and don't we all from time to time dream of our lives transmuted into opera?), in a world where one can sing, over and over again, with all the possible embellishments, "I love you" or "he betrayed me." [29]

The king gives full voice here to an unconstrained expression of desire (which is, as I have noted, a desire for that lack of constraint): as Uwe Sommer puts it, "The king intoxicates himself, as it were, in his own emphasis." [30] And yet, this very lack of constraint is symptomatic. Instead of emanating from what Brooks terms "the moment of crisis"—the moment that in turn marks "the place for musical illustration"—Kandaules's aria emerges as a symptom that would alert us to that crisis, which is otherwise hidden. In an important sense, then, the aria is also about the rhetorical function of an aria, the condition of excess that I earlier termed "the operatic": it does not represent an *exceptional* condition of expressive fullness for the king but is instead the expressive norm to which he aspires, the expressive territory over which he would reign. His aria, like his character, aspires to a quotidian condition of the exceptional, one where the reserves (of expression, of wealth, of resources) are limitless, and thus generosity can be unbounded.

---

29. Peter Brooks, "Body and Voice in Melodrama and Opera," in *Siren Songs*, 118–26, at 122.
30. Sommer, *Kandaules*, 137. The entirety of Sommer's passage reads: "in seinem großen Glücks-Monolog (T. 820–74) [legt der König] ein Selbstbekenntnis [ab], in dessen Verlauf sich der ange-staute Konflikt entlädt und der König sich gleichsam an einer eigenen Emphase berauscht" (In his great happiness monologue [bars 820–74], the king issues a confession in the course of which the accumulated conflict erupts and the king intoxicates himself, as it were, in his own emphasis).

To return to Nietzsche, we might say that the aria offers various explanations of the king's generosity, each of which (like the aria itself) attests to his lack of modesty. First, he explains that his good fortune and happiness, his "Glück," seems to derive its power and intensity from others; indeed, it strikes him that it only exists in the knowledge others have of it; finally, he feels his wealth only when others partake of it. In this sense, Kandaules arguably aspires to embody the condition of representation itself—in particular, its logic of exchange, its derivation from and dependence upon a scene of sharing. I will explore the implications of such an allegorical interpretation a bit later in this chapter; for now, I propose to move on to a consideration of the politics of appearance in the work.

The Political Explanation

The aria suggests that Kandaules is pathological, but it hardly tells us why. Gide, for his part, offers an explanation that encompasses psychology and politics. In so doing, he helps move us along to a second explanatory model. Gide suggests that his play dramatizes "the *defeat,* almost the suicide, of an aristocracy whose too noble qualities first easily undo it and then keep it from defending itself."[31] In Gide's account, Kandaules stands in for an entire class, a class that is *too* noble. This excess of nobility in turn produces a symptomatic undoing. In the play, this defeat-verging-on-suicide is extraordinarily bleak. Kandaules's reign is replaced by that of Gyges—and if the new king's first (and only) act is any indication, his regime will not be a pleasant one. Immediately upon being named king by Nyssia (who also declares herself the new king's new queen), Gyges observes that the queen is not veiled. As in the opera, Nyssia responds that Kandaules tore away her veil. But in the play, the new king will have none of it: according to the stage directions, he "brutally covers her face with part of her garment" as the courtiers drink to his happiness. Curtain. Welcome to the Gyges regime!

The opera is less relentlessly bleak—and, as a result, less politically transparent, and more mysterious. In the opera, Nyssia has the last word: the work concludes with her observation that Kandaules tore her veil. Zemlinsky girds her proclamation—which encompasses her naming Gyges as Kandaules's successor—with an emphatic march, reminiscent both dramaturgically and musically of the scene of Parsifal's return to the Grail realm, his inaugural procession, in act 3 of Wagner's *Parsifal*. The stentorian solemnity of Wagner's music for his hero's return (woven, as Ernest Newman points

31. Gide, preface to *King Candaules*, 166.

out, out of the motive of the funeral procession)[32] will eventually give way to a much less strident accompaniment to the new Grail King's inaugural address. Wagner's orchestration for Parsifal's first executive order, "Enthüllet den Gral, öffnet den Schrein!" (Uncover the grail, open the shrine!), is more ethereal than emphatic, an effect derived in part, as Newman observes, from Wagner's "crossing and recrossing of the Faith motive in strings, woodwind and harps."[33] And Wagner stages the terms of ambivalence, suggesting that there is a cost to Parsifal's ascension. The stage directions that outline these costs constitute a thorn in the side of any halfway sensitive stage director: Kundry, recovering temptress, "sinkt, mit dem Blicke zu [Parsifal] auf, langsam vor [ihm] entseelt zu Boden" (sinks lifeless to the ground in front of Parsifal, her eyes uplifted to him). The price of male ascension, it would appear, is heterosexual partnership: Parsifal's rule in the all-male confines of the Grail knights will be unencumbered by his female companion with the shady past.

The dramatic and musical terms of Zemlinsky's conclusion are quite the opposite, although the effect of ironic ambivalence is arguably similar. Zemlinsky's music for the conclusion of the work is unrelentingly emphatic, and it is Nyssia, not Gyges, whose words mark the new king's inauguration. It is as if Wagner had sustained the march to the Grail and given the last word to Kundry. Nyssia's last words (encompassing both a question and a pronouncement) and their musical setting (as the rhetorical culmination of a march) only add to the sense of bewilderment. Are we hearing the march of history as we see the effects of a radical *Realpolitik?* (The score indicates that Nyssia's last lines are spoken *verächtlich* [scornfully]). Or does the march figure the terms of the catastrophe, registering in its figuration of externalized power (the fortississimo marking of the accompaniment), the extermination of Nyssia's regime of modesty, its replacement with a new economy of audible, visible force? It is entirely unclear: the opera text's conclusion can be read as a statement of ascension (after all, Nyssia has impelled Gyges to kill Kandaules and has named him king; and here she has the last word— arguably a word of defiance). At the same time, however, her words can be understood as a statement of remorse, or even capitulation (after all, hers was the rule of the veil, and that rule—like the veil—has been discarded). The work leaves the question unresolved.

32. Ernest Newman, *The Wagner Operas* (New York: Knopf, 1981), 718. See Richard Wagner, *Parsifal*, ed. Egon Voss and Martin Geck, Bd. 14 (3 vols.) of Wagner, *Sämtliche Werke*, general ed. Carl Dahlhaus, published in cooperation with the Bavarian Academy of Fine Arts, Munich (Mainz: B. Schott, 1972–73), 3:90–101 and 136.

33. Newman, *Wagner Operas*, 721.

Of course, the politics of the work are not restricted to its ambiguous conclusion. Indeed, it strikes me that the piece is haunted by Pierre-Joseph Proudhon's revolutionary slogan "Property is theft." [34] That slogan has, of course, reverberated throughout the western world, not just on the streets, but even in the theaters. It raises the question, what is property? What is ownership? And what responsibilities do the haves bear to the have-nots? Let's recall Gide's observation:

> If Candaules was too great and too generous, if he forces himself to the ex-treme in permitting the ignorant Gyges first to see, then to touch and share that which he learns, slowly and all too quickly, to enjoy—then to what point, to what person, can such *communism* be carried?

The outlines of the problem are beginning to emerge. It involves conflict-ing imperatives. We can clarify the terms of the conflict with reference to Gyges's opening exhortation: "If you've got something, hide it!" This is a di-rect contradiction of Kandaules's spirit. His motto, although it is never ex-pressed as such, is "If you've got it, flaunt it!" But the king hardly means this in a selfish, entitled sense. Indeed, in Kandaules's case, the motto would pre-sumably be "If you've got it, flaunt it, but flaunt it in order to share it; and share it in order to know you've got it!" (Admittedly not much of a motto.) But got what, flaunt what? And most important, share what? For instance, how about wives? Are wives "things" that one possesses and flaunts? This is precisely Nyssia's angry remonstration when, in act 1, Kandaules explains to the assembled court his determination to share her beauty (we will consider this exchange shortly). In some sense, of course wives are *not* property; but in another sense (indeed, a hidden, veiled sense), of course—wives *are* pos-sessions. And if we have any doubts about this, we need look no further than the inversion of the veiled wife (which is precisely what the king has in mind): the trophy wife.

A trophy, any trophy, is the physical embodiment of an object of desire. It requires an audience that recognizes it (and what it stands for) as desirable, such that Kandaules would be recognizable as a winner in winning it. The trophy wife is a trophy insofar as she embodies what everyone wants, but only very few—those who win the trophy—can actually have. We don't need to delve into the insight too deeply to recognize its economic and po-litical qualities: it relies upon an economics of scarcity (the most valuable

---

34. Pierre-Joseph Proudhon (1809–1865), *Qu'est-ce que la propriété?*, published in English as *What Is Property?*, ed. and trans. Donald R. Kelley and Bonnie G. Smith (New York: Cambridge University Press, 1994).

trophies are the hardest to win) and a politics of display (since a trophy is only valuable if it is recognizably desirable). This brings us to a nodal point of *Der König Kandaules*. For the king insists that he is desperately, utterly, completely happy on account of his ravishing queen. But the queen insists on maintaining her privacy—she is not interested in public display. Kandaules, it seems, has an invisible trophy—and at the outset of the opera, it is clear that he is desperate to display her.

The opera offers an oddly corporeal corollary to the by now familiar adolescent query: if a tree falls in the forest and no one is there to see it, does it fall? In Zemlinsky's opera, Kandaules insistently, manically asks whether his beautiful wife—and the happiness he experiences in the face of her beauty—can be said to exist (as beauty, as happiness) if they are not seen? Or, put otherwise: Is beauty properly located in the eye of the beholder, or is the equation perhaps more complicated than that? Does the beholder perhaps require another, third element—becoming, then, a beholder whose beholden is in turn beheld by one who could ratify the apprehension and thus affirm the estimation? Zemlinsky's opera, then, is not merely about visibility and the bedroom, but about a particular networking of visibility. The most compelling account of that network derives, I think, from various accounts of triangulation—by Claude Lévi-Strauss, René Girard, Gayle Rubin, and Eve Kosofsky Sedgwick.[35] In each of these accounts, the triangulation of desire (usually between two male rivals for a female) has important consequences not just for the disposition of desire, but for what Gayle Rubin has termed "the traffic in women." Here is Sedgwick's succinct gloss on Rubin's intervention:

> Gayle Rubin has argued . . . that patriarchal heterosexuality can best be discussed in terms of one or another form of the traffic in women: it is the use of women as exchangeable, perhaps symbolic, property for the primary purpose of cementing the bonds of men with men. For example, Lévi-Strauss writes, "the total relationship of exchange which constitutes marriage is not established between a man and a woman, but between two groups of men, and the woman figures only as one of the objects in the exchange, not as one of the

---

35. See René Girard, "'Triangular' Desire," in *Deceit, Desire, and the Novel: Self and Other in Literary Structure*, trans. Yvonne Freccero (Baltimore: Johns Hopkins University Press, 1965); Claude Lévi-Strauss, *The Elementary Structures of Kinship* (Boston: Beacon, 1969); and Gayle Rubin, "The Traffic in Women: Notes Toward a Political Economy of Sex," in *Toward an Anthropology of Sex*, ed. Rayna Reiter (New York: Monthly Review Press, 1975), 157–210. For a discussion of Girard, Rubin, and Lévi-Strauss on triangulation, see Sedgwick, "Gender Asymmetry and Erotic Triangles," in *Between Men: English Literature and Male Homosocial Desire* (New York: Columbia University Press, 1985), 21–27.

partners." Thus . . . Lévi-Strauss's normative man uses a woman as a "conduit of a relationship" in which the true partner is a man. Rejecting Lévi-Strauss's celebratory treatment of this relegation of women, Rubin offers, instead, an array of tools for specifying and analyzing it.[36]

Over the course of the opera we are introduced to various forms of triangulation. At the outset of act 1, scene 3, when Kandaules presents Nyssia to the court, the triangulation reads as though it has been scripted by Lévi-Strauss: the exchange is not between the king and queen, but between the king, the queen, and the (male) courtiers. The queen figures primarily as an object in the exchange. In terms of the politics of triangulation, it is arguably less significant that Kandaules insists that Nyssia remove her veil than that he insists that she remove her veil *before his male friends.* Similarly, it remains unclear whether his happiness merely derives from "others"—that is, from its rerouting into a mediated, indirect form—as he explains in his aria in act 1, scene 3, or whether it derives from other men—according to which its rerouting is effective by virtue of the unannounced specificity of its gendered address. But that is not enough. Kandaules's desire, as he explains in this aria, is fundamentally conditioned by the logic of capitalism: his ability to recognize himself as a have (that is, one who has great wealth and happiness) is dependent upon his ability to recognize someone else as a have-not (that is, one who aspires to the wealth and happiness he possesses). Although the logic of this desire seems clear (and it is reiterated often enough in the opera for it to become so), its nature and its object remain fundamentally mysterious.

An earlier moment in act 1, scene 3, when Kandaules is toasted by the courtiers, offers a further example of the logic and nature of triangulation in the opera. Initially, the courtiers—who, we should note, take the form of a male chorus—toast "der vollendeten Schönheit von Kandaules Weib" (the ultimate beauty of Kandaules's wife) before toasting Kandaules himself, who, they say, "ein so köstliches Gut sein Eigen nennt und, statt es zu verbergen und für sich allein zu halten, erlaubt, daß unsre ehrfurchtsvollen und entzückten Blicke sich daran berauschen" (lays claim to such a valuable property and, rather than hiding it and keeping it all to himself, allows our respectful and enchanted gazes to be enraptured by it).[37] Kandaules's response is characteristically (which is also to say, predictably) perplexing, offering a duly lyrical account of the suffering he experienced in the course of his earlier, exclusive enjoyment of the wealth of Nyssia's beauty.

36. Sedgwick, *Between Men,* 25–26. The quoted material appears in Lévi-Strauss, *Elementary Structures,* 115; Rubin, "The Traffic in Women," 174.

37. *Kandaules,* PV, 35–36.

Musical Example 11 Kandaules breaks Gyges's law again. Kandaules expresses the pain of keeping his beautiful wife all to himself.

The explanation explains as much as it mystifies. In the wake of Kandaules's explanatory outburst, it remains unclear whether his desire is economic (e.g., for an experience of wealth) or sexual (e.g., for Nyssia), and whether he desires Nyssia in particular or the experience of observing her desired (which finds expression here in the courtiers' toast, as it will again later in Kandaules's invitations to Gyges first to see the queen undress, and then to "stay" with her). Each of these explanations is plausible; none is definitive.

Musical Example 11 (*continued*)

One thing that *is* clear in Kandaules's account is that Nyssia is a desirable property—one that he intends to share. Indeed, this is also clear to Nyssia, who protests these very terms. Zemlinsky inflects her intervention as both forceful and restrained: it markedly interrupts the gathering momentum of Kandaules's monologue, but the melodic affect of her intervention is demure, even introspective, rather than strident or obviously enraged. The logic may be perverse, but it should be clear. Insofar as Nyssia is one of Kandaules's greatest, loveliest possessions, he can revel in *possessing* her great

Musical Example 11 (*continued*)

loveliness only by having it generally recognized, which is to say, by sharing it. According to this logic, sharing is a necessary step en route to exclusive ownership, since no private possession is satisfying unless it is generally desired, and a generalized desire depends upon public display.

If the king, in presenting an endless series of bounteous banquets, appears to be interested in challenging the distinction between private and public *property,* his actions within the opera suggest that he is determined to challenge the distinction—equally familiar, equally entrenched—between the public and the private *spheres.* A private experience, absent its public

Musical Example 11 (continued)

validation, does not exist. But beyond its fundamentally odd psychology, there is something aesthetically odd about this equation. Part of it is architectural: the distinction between the bedroom and the theater seems to have vanished. It is not that the stage has become a bedroom (which is familiar enough, at least since *Othello*); rather, it is that the distinction between them seems to have disappeared altogether. The sharing Kandaules has in mind is

Musical Example 11 (continued)

a peculiarly theatrical one, in which everyone will see (and thus desire) Nyssia, but only, presumably, in order for him then to reclaim his possession; this is an artificial form of display, one without apparent real-life effects. The analogy goes further, for the protagonist's situation onstage maps onto that of the operatic spectator in the audience: the otherwise disempowered spectator (Gyges onstage and we in the auditorium) is unexpectedly granted a certain power of invisibility in order to observe unobserved and ultimately partake in the purportedly private display of regal intimacy.

The Allegorical Explanation

There is, no doubt, a strong temptation to read Kandaules (as a work and as a character)—like many of Zemlinsky's works and characters—as a proto-autobiographical condensation of the composer's own historical and personal predicament.[38] If Kandaules is the entitled, aristocratic liberal who would share his possessions with those in his midst who are comparatively impoverished; then one might read him—like the composer—as an embodiment of modern Jewish enlightenment aspirations or assimilationist practices. Similarly, if Kandaules is somewhat ridiculous, crazily idealistic, and socially self-conscious, one might read into him prominent aspects of Zemlinsky's character. Along the same lines, some critics have suggested that one might map onto Gyges the brutish, disenfranchised qualities of Nazi thuggery.[39] Perhaps the most plausible case for an allegorical reading of the opera comes from Eike Rathgeber, who suggests that Zemlinsky tragically found his true hometown not in any particular city, indeed not in this world, but in contemporary art.[40] We might say the same of Kandaules. Conceiving of Kandaules as an aesthete helps us to understand his fundamentally mysterious relationship to sharing and publicity, because, as I suggested earlier, the impulse to share, to display beauty publicly, is a condition of aesthetic production. Conceiving of the king as an aesthete also clarifies the tragedy of his situation, the radical discrepancy between his assigned and elected station. Kandaules, after all, is not just the wayward inhabitant of some "hometown"—he is its absolute ruler. Or at least that is his title. Beyond the king's frequent recourse to the rhetoric of ruling (he bosses around people at court), there is very little to suggest that Kandaules actually rules over anything. Indeed, the rhetoric of delusion in the piece, marked by a recurring glissando figure in the strings and accompanied by rapidly descending

---

38. This is Horst Weber's position (Weber, *Alexander Zemlinsky*, 130). Weber's argument is quoted—but not cited—in Peter Ruzicka, "Zu Zemlinskys *Kandaules*-Projekt," in *Erfundene und gefundene Musik*, ed. Thomas Schäfer (Hofheim: Wolke, 1998), 180–85, at 183.

39. For a sensitive discussion of this position, see Sommer, *Kandaules*, 246–53.

40. "Gegründetsein als solches war damals in Frage gestellt worden; und zutiefst verwurzelt in eben jenem Zweifel scheint Zemlinskys eigentlicher Heimatort der der Kunst dieser Zeit zu sein" (At that time, being grounded as such was called into question. Deeply rooted in precisely this doubt, Zemlinsky's true home town may well have been the contemporary art of that time). Eike Rathgeber, "Alexander Zemlinsky: Varianten zur Ruhelosigkeit," in Krones, *Zemlinsky*, 259–67, at 266.

forte horns, suggests that Kandaules is more a captive of his thoughts than their master. Thus, as Kandaules hits upon each step in his plot to invite Gyges into the royal palace, the royal bedroom, and the royal bed, he addresses himself to his thought, which, he says, is whispering to him. He may be the king, but it is entirely unclear what he is the king of. Far from ruling over the aesthetic realm, Kandaules's wholesale absorption suggests that he is less an aesthete-king than an aesthetic subject, more in thrall to than in control of the pleasures of aesthetic apprehension.

And yet, as I have been arguing, while the opera is readily legible in relatively familiar terms—be they political (reflecting the advent of Nazism or communism), biographical (encompassing Zemlinsky's fate), allegorical (alluding to the fate of the artist in the modern world), or psychological (as an account of modern pathologies), I think Zemlinsky's opera remains oddly, steadfastly resistant to ready encapsulation. This represents a particular challenge to any stage director, for a production of the work needs to make sense of it, and yet, in my view, the best production would offer a cogent account of the piece's programmatic mysteriousness. It is hard for a director to stage a work as intentionally mysterious; after all, the audience might well mistake the lack of resolution as a reflection of directorial incompetence (an inability to tie up loose ends) rather than sophistication (a determination to leave them untied). And yet, the alternative, it seems to me, is more troubling: it would involve a narrowing of the work, a decision to allow one of these explanatory models to be controlling when it is their contradictory interaction that makes this piece most interesting. A successful production would do nothing to make the work less mysterious, but would instead render and therewith clarify many of its terms. If the preceding argument has done anything, I hope that it may have done something like such a production: helping to explain—but not to resolve—some of the terms of this mystery.

Ethics, Dramaturgy, and Mise-en-Scène

There is an ethical component to the argument outlined in this chapter and, more generally, in this book. I have argued at length for a conception of opera as a generic vehicle whose component parts tend to take it in very different directions. But my argument in favor of the unsettledness of opera in performance goes beyond a plea for calibrating performance to generic identity. Rather, I am convinced that great works of art (be they works of cinema, literature, music, painting, photography, or opera) are not just documents of powerful expressive forces, but of powerfully *antithetical* expressive forces. In performing and theorizing these works, we bear an ethical as well as an aesthetic responsibility to attend to the terms of antithesis.

An account of *Der König Kandaules* (onstage or in a book) as an allegory of its composer's condition might well be convincing; but in my view it risks being inadequate, not merely in some impressionistic sense, but inadequate to the work's expressive range and thickness. The questions I have been posing involve the extent of homogenization. Opera in performance—be it Mozart, Verdi, Wagner, or Zemlinsky—is not just capable of encompassing and sustaining a diversity of expression, it is most thrilling and rewarding when that formal diversity of expression in turn finds expression onstage. Of course, that expression can take many forms, and thus opera onstage remains a forum for surprise, dismay, and delight—sonic as well as scenic. The point derives from—and in so doing, returns us to—a position we encountered in chapter 1, the notion of opera's ineffability. In Carolyn Abbate's gloss, Vladimir Jankélévitch poses the question of musical—and by extension, operatic—ineffability in ethical terms:

> Jankélévitch defines music's ineffability (for some, an uncomfortable word) at times rather neutrally as music's indeterminacy, its mutability when submitted for contemplation, its range of effects, which include seeming to be strange or beautiful noise as well as firing up social or poetic or visual or other associations. It is this that frees us. A coherent stance towards the situation would involve not taking advantage of it, hesitating before articulating a terminus, or restricting music to any determinate meaning within any declarative sentence. And, perhaps, drawing back. At least a coherent stance might mean not saying what musical configurations mean without simultaneously signaling a deficit in seriousness or without proposing too many alternative meanings at the same time.[41]

In this chapter, and in this book, I have sought to suggest some of the perils and possibilities of the freedom of which Abbate speaks. *Der König Kandaules* is a fine work with which to revisit Abbate's claim, for it arguably proposes on a diegetic level what it encompasses as a musical work—that is, a surfeit of mystery. And yet, the fact that this work–or indeed, as Abbate suggests, *any* work—can be made to signify almost anything does not mean that anything goes. In her account, Zemlinsky's piece would stand in for a more general condition, since music's ineffability renders it fundamentally, constitutively mysterious.[42] We bear an ethical responsibility to account for that mystery—not to resolve it, but to account for it. There are any number of ways to do so, and in the course of this study we have encountered a few. The moment, during the finale, in act 4, of the Peter Sellars production of *Le nozze di Figaro*, when the principals are suddenly suspended in slow motion, attending to the music, arguably renders the (mysterious, nonsignifying) eruption of music upon the scene. As we have seen, a similar (and, to use Jankélévich's terminology, a similarly drastic) moment transpires in the extended quartet (no. 16) that concludes act 2 in Hans Neuenfels's production of Mozart's *Entführung aus dem Serail,* when Belmonte, Pedrillo, Konstanze, and Blondchen briefly become dancers, or when the orchestra is elevated to the level of the stage and the dramatic scene is transformed into a concert space.[43] These strike me as various moments when the dramatic scene becomes a site—what Abbate would term an *event*—of listening. Each offers a local instance where the drama is suspended, given over to a state of nonsignification. These instances arguably respond to Abbate's call to draw back—they look before the productions leap into the interpretive fray. Or indeed, they are leaps into looking and listening. For when it comes to opera onstage, leap we must—even if, or precisely because, the results can be unsettling.

42. Jankélévitch's formulation is cogent and apt: "Music means nothing and yet means everything. One can make notes say what one will, grant them any power of analogy: they do not protest. In the very measure that one is inclined to attribute a metaphysical significance to musical discourse, music (which expresses no communicable sense) lends itself, complaisant and docile, to the most complex dialectical interpretations." Vladimir Jankélévitch, *Music and the Ineffable,* trans. Carolyn Abbate (Princeton: Princeton University Press, 2003), 11.

43. There are other forms of staging—the work of Robert Wilson comes to mind—that render the mystery in global terms. In Wilson's productions, singers tend to employ highly idiosyncratic and nonrepresentational gestures, akin to the highly stylized vocabulary of the kabuki theater. See, e.g., Dean Wilcox, "Sign and Referent in the Work of Robert Wilson: Reconstituting the Human Form," in *Essays on Twentieth-Century German Drama and Theater: An American Reception, 1977–1999,* ed. Hellmut Hal Rennert (New York: Peter Lang, 2004), 37–45; Arthur Holmberg, *The Theatre of Robert Wilson* (New York: Cambridge University Press, 1996).

Following are synopses of the operas discussed in this book. The plot summaries for *Der fliegende Holländer, Die Meistersinger von Nürnberg, Le nozze di Figaro, Die Entführung aus dem Serail,* and *Don Carlos* are slightly modified from *The New Grove Dictionary of Opera* (Oxford, 1992). The summary for *Der König Kandaules* is provided courtesy of the Vienna Volksoper.

Richard Wagner, *Der fliegende Holländer* (*The Flying Dutchman*)

Romantische Oper in three acts by Richard Wagner to his own libretto after Heinrich Heine's *Aus den Memoiren des Herren von Schnabelewopski;* Dresden, Königliches Sächsisches Hoftheater, 2 January 1843.

Daland, a Norwegian sailor, bass
Senta, his daughter, soprano
Erik, a huntsman, tenor
Mary, Senta's nurse, contralto
Daland's Steersman, tenor
The Dutchman, bass-baritone
Norwegian sailors, the Dutchman's crew, young women
Setting: The Norwegian coast

The supposedly autobiographical inspiration of the *Holländer,* vividly described in *Mein Leben*—according to which the work took shape during the Wagners' stormy sea crossing in July and August 1839—is in part a fantasy. If any musical sketches were made in the months following the voyage on the *Thetis,* they have not survived. The first numbers to be composed were Senta's Ballad and the choruses of the Norwegian sailors and Dutchman's crew, some time between 3 May and 26 July 1840. The poem was written in May 1841 and the remainder of the music during the summer, the overture being completed last, in November 1841. Heine's retelling of the nautical legend provided Wagner with his chief source, but the composer, who identified himself with the persecuted, uprooted, sexually unfulfilled protagonist, introduced what was to become the characteristic theme of redemption by a woman. The purchase of Wagner's original prose scenario in July 1841 by Léon Pillet, the director of the Paris Opéra, led ultimately to a commission not for Wagner (as he had hoped) but for Pierre-Louis Dietsch. Contrary to what is frequently stated, Dietsch's librettists, Paul Foucher and Bénédict-Henry Révoil, based their opera, Le vaisseau fantôme, not primarily on Wagner's scenario but on Captain Marryat's novel The Phantom Ship, as well as on Sir Walter Scott's The Pirate and tales by Heine, Fenimore Cooper, and Wilhelm Hauff. However, the appearance of Le vaisseau fantôme on the stage at the Opéra in the same month (November 1842) as rehearsals for the Holländer began in Dresden was undoubtedly one reason for the eleventh-hour changes in Wagner's score. Until just a few weeks before the premiere, Wagner's opera was set off the Scottish coast, with Daland and Erik named Donald and Georg respectively. Other factors in the change may have been Wagner's desire to reinforce the autobiographical element and to distance himself at the same time from the Scottish setting of Heine.

Wagner originally conceived his work in a single act, the better to ensure its acceptance as a curtain-raiser before a ballet at the Opéra; his later claim that it was in order to focus on the dramatic essentials rather than on "tiresome operatic accessories" may be retrospective rationalization. By the time he came to write the music, the first consideration no longer applied, his proposal having been rejected by the Opéra. He therefore elaborated the scheme in three acts, but at this stage to be played without a break. Then, some time after the end of October 1842, when he retrieved his score from the Berlin Opera (and possibly acting on advice from that quarter), he recast it in three discrete acts—the form in which it was given in Dresden and subsequently published. Following Cosima Wagner's example when she introduced it at Bayreuth in 1901, the work is now often given, both there and elsewhere, in the single-act version. There is, however, an ideological element in Bayreuth's preference for the version that presents the work most convincingly as an incipient music drama (as Wagner himself viewed it in retrospect), and both versions have some claim to authenticity.

Wagner made revisions to the score, largely in the orchestration, in 1846 and again in 1852. In 1860 (not, as sometimes stated, in 1852) the coda of the overture was remodeled (and the ending of the whole work accordingly), introducing a motif of redemption; the textures of the 1860 revision also reflect Wagner's recent preoccupation with Tristan.

The premiere in Dresden was conducted by Wagner, with Wilhelmine Schröder-Devrient as Senta and Johann Michael Wächter as the Dutchman. The first performance in London was in 1870 (in Italian); it was given there in English in 1876 and in German in 1882. The American premiere (1876, Philadelphia) was also in Italian; it was first given in New York the following year and at the Metropolitan in 1889.

Act 1

A steep, rocky shore. The curtain rises to a continuation of the stormy music of the overture, but now in B flat minor, in contrast to the overture's D minor/major. Daland's ship has just cast anchor. The cries of the Norwegian sailors ("Johohe! Hallojo!") as they furl the sails allude to their chorus first heard in its entirety in act 3. The crew is sent to rest and the steersman left on watch. His song, "Mit Gewitter und Sturm aus fernem Meer," begins confidently, but the phrases of its second stanza are repeatedly interrupted by orchestral comments as he succumbs to slumber. Immediately the storm begins to rage again, and open-fifth "horn calls," string tremolos, and a shift of tonality (from B flat major to B minor) signify the appearance of the Flying Dutchman's ship with its blood-red sails.

The Dutchman's monologue that follows begins with a recitative, "Die Frist ist um," in which he tells how he is permitted to come on land once every seven years to seek redemption from an as yet unnamed curse. A section in 6/8, marked "Allegro molto agitato," "Wie oft in Meeres tiefsten Schlund," projects a powerfully declaimed vocal line against a storm-tossed accompaniment. An earnest entreaty for deliverance is then sung over relentlessly tremolo strings, in a manner criticized by Berlioz, and the monologue ends with a broadly phrased section, "Nur eine Hoffnung," in which the Dutchman looks forward to Judgment Day. From their ship's hold, his crew distantly echo his last words.

Daland comes on deck, sees the strange ship, and hails its captain, whom he sees on land. The captain introduces himself simply as "a Dutchman," going on to give a diplomatically compressed account of his voyaging, "Durch Sturm und bösen Wind verschlagen." The regular four-bar phrasing of the latter section, contrasted with the freer phrase structures of "Die Frist ist um," signify what is to become a characteristic of the score: the "exterior," public world of Daland, Erik, and the Norwegian sailors and maidens is represented by traditional forms and harmonies, while the "interior," self-absorbed world of the Dutchman and Senta frequently breaks out of the straitjacket of conventionality.

The Dutchman offers Daland vast wealth in exchange for a night's hospitality. Daland, who cannot believe his ears, is no less delighted by the wealthy stranger's interest in his daughter, and in the ensuing duet, "Wie? Hört' ich recht?," the Dutchman's rugged individuality is entirely submerged by Daland's triteness. Daland's greedy, meretricious character is perfectly conveyed both here and in the duet's continuation, with its jaunty rhythms and elementary harmonic scheme. With the Dutchman preparing to follow Daland to his house, the Norwegian sailors steer the tonality back to B flat major for a full-chorus reprise of the Steersman's Song.

Act 2

A large room in Daland's house. To cover the scene change in the original continuous version, Wagner wrote a passage in which the virile double-dotted rhythms of the sailors are transformed into the humming of the spinning wheels in the opening chorus of the second act, "Summ und brumm." The full dramatic effect of that transition is lost when the work is given in three separate acts, though the repetition of music from the end of act 1 at the beginning of act 2 has a deleterious effect only when the opera is heard on gramophone records, not in the theater with an intervening interval. (A similar situation arises between acts 2 and 3.)

The repetitive figures (both melodic and accompanimental) of the Spinning Chorus evoke not only the ceaseless turning of the wheels, but also the humdrum (if contented) existence of the young women. Urged on by Mary, Daland's housekeeper and Senta's nurse, the women spin in order to please their lovers who are away at sea. Senta is meanwhile reclining reflectively in an armchair, gazing at a picture hanging on the wall of a pale man with a dark beard in black, Spanish dress. She is reproached for her idleness by Mary and mocked in onomatopoeic cascades of laughter by the other women. Senta retaliates by ridiculing the tediousness of the Spinning Chorus, asking Mary to sing instead the ballad of the Flying Dutchman. Mary declines and continues spinning as the other women gather round to hear Senta sing it herself. Senta's Ballad, "Johohoe! Johohohoe!," begins with the same bracing open fifths on tremolo strings that began the overture, and with the "horn-call" figure of the Dutchman heard first as a pounding bass and then in the vocal line itself. The startling effect of these opening gestures is enhanced, in the version familiar today, by the unprepared drop in tonality from A major to G minor; however, the ballad was originally in A minor, and Wagner transposed it down at the end of 1842 for Schröder-Devrient. The strophic structure of Senta's Ballad sets it firmly in the early-nineteenth-century operatic tradition of interpolated narrative songs; indeed, there is a direct link with the song sung by Emmy in Marschner's *Der Vampyr*, which Wagner had prepared for performance in Würzburg in 1833. Each of Senta's three turbulent stanzas (in which we learn that the Flying Dutchman's curse was laid on him for a blasphemous oath) is followed by a consolatory refrain featuring the motif associated with redemption; the final refrain is taken by the chorus, but in an abrupt breach of precedent, Senta, "carried away by a sudden inspiration," bursts into an ecstatic coda expressing her determination to be the instrument of the Flying Dutchman's salvation. Wagner's retrospective account of the genesis of the *Holländer*, representing Senta's Ballad as the "thematic seed" or conceptual nucleus of the whole work, was designed to depict the opera as an incipient music drama. But although some elements of the ballad appear elsewhere in the work, and even in some of its central numbers, the use of the various motifs bears little relation to the closely integrated structural organization of post–*Oper und Drama* works such as the *Ring*.

Erik, who is in love with Senta, is horrified to hear her outburst as he enters. He announces that Daland's ship has returned, and the young women busily prepare to welcome their menfolk. Erik detains Senta and launches into a passionate protestation of love, "Mein Herz voll Treue bis zum Sterben," whose conventionality of utterance and regularity of period scarcely commend themselves to Senta in her present mood. She struggles to get away but is forced to endure another stanza. After an exchange in which Senta alarms Erik by telling of her empathy with the strange seafarer in the picture, the huntsman recounts a dream whose ominous significance he now dimly discerns: "Auf hohem Felsen." From several points of view, Erik's Dream Narration represents the most advanced writing in the work. Where in his previous song the regular phrases had frequently forced normally unaccented syllables on to strong beats, in the dream narration the length of phrases is determined by the rhythms of the lines. The lack of melodic interest is an indication of how far Wagner had yet to go to achieve the subtle musicopoetic synthesis of his mature works; nevertheless it is a worthy precursor of the narrations of Tannhäuser and Lohengrin. As Erik recounts how he dreamt that Senta's father brought home a stranger resembling the seafarer in the picture, Senta, in a mesmeric trance, relives the fantasy, her excited interjections latterly adopting the rising fourth of the Dutchman's motif.

Erik rushes away in despair and Senta muses on the picture. As she croons the "redemption" refrain of the ballad, the door opens and her father appears with the Dutchman. Recognizing him as the seafarer in the picture, Senta is spellbound and fails to greet her father. Daland approaches her and introduces the Dutchman in a characteristically breezy, four-square aria, "Mögst du, mein Kind."

Daland retires and, after a coda based on themes associated with Daland, the Dutchman, and Senta, the long duet that occupies most of the rest of the act begins. Its unconventionality is signified by the opening statements of both characters in turn, each absorbed in his and her own thoughts. The voices eventually come together and there is even a quasi-traditional cadenza. A new plane of reality is signaled by a slight increase in tempo and a shift from E major to E minor. The pair now address each other, and in response to the Dutchman's inquiry, Senta promises obedience to her father's wishes. She goes on to express her desire to bring him redemption, and in an agitato section he warns of the fate that would befall her if she failed to keep her vow of constancy. Against an accompaniment of repeated wind chords redolent of a celestial chorus, Senta pledges faithfulness unto death, and the final exultant section of the duet is launched with the singers heard first separately and then together. Although not free of the constraints of traditional opera, the duet is the musical and emotional high point of the work.

Daland reenters to ask whether the feast of homecoming can be combined with that of a betrothal. Senta reaffirms her vow and the three join in a rapturous trio to bring the act to an end.

Act 3

A bay with a rocky shore. Daland's house stands in the foreground, to one side. In the background the Norwegian ship is lit up and the sailors are making merry on the deck, while the Dutch ship nearby is unnaturally dark and silent. According to Wagner's account in Mein Leben, the theme of the Norwegian Sailors' Chorus, "Steuermann! Lass die Wacht!," was suggested to him by the call of the sailors as it echoed round the granite walls of the Norwegian harbor of Sandviken, as the Thetis took refuge there on 29 July 1839. After the first strains of the chorus, the men dance on deck, stamping their feet in time with the music. The women bring out baskets of food and drink and call out to the Dutch ship, inviting the crew to participate. Men and women cry out in turn, but a deathly silence is the only response. The lighthearted appeals of sailors and womenfolk, again in alternation, become more earnest, and tension is accumulated in the orchestral texture too. A forte and then a fortissimo cry are both unanswered, and the Norwegians only half-jestingly recall the legend of the Flying Dutchman and his ghostly crew. Their carousing becomes more manic, and the Dutchman's motif in the orchestra, accompanied by sinister chromatic rumblings, builds to a climax. A storm rises in the vicinity of the Dutch ship, and the crew finally burst into unearthly song, the wind whistling through the rigging. The Norwegian sailors attempt to compete, in a powerful piece of writing for double chorus, but they are eventually subdued.

Senta comes out of the house, followed by Erik, who demands to know why she has changed her allegiance. In a cavatina of conventional cut, "Willst jenes Tags du nicht dich mehr entsinnen," he reminds her that she had once pledged to be true to him. The Dutchman, who has overheard, makes to return to his ship and releases Senta from her vow to him. She protests her fidelity and the Dutchman, Erik, and Senta all voice their emotions in a trio (often needlessly cut).

In a recitative, the Dutchman tells of his terrible fate and how he is saving Senta from the same by releasing her. He boards his ship, and Senta, proclaiming her redeeming fidelity in a final ecstatic outcry, casts herself into the sea. The Dutchman's ship, with all its crew, sinks immediately. The sea rises and falls again, revealing the Dutchman and Senta, transfigured and locked in embrace.

The first work of Wagner's maturity, *Der fliegende Holländer* brings together several ingredients characteristic of the later works, notably the single-minded attention given to the mood and color of the drama, and the themes of suffering by a romantic outsider and of redemption by a faithful woman. The initial stages of a tendency toward dissolution of numbers and toward a synthesis of text and music also endorse Wagner's assertion that with the *Holländer* began his career as a true poet.

BARRY MILLINGTON

Richard Wagner, *Die Meistersinger von Nürnberg* (*The Mastersingers of Nuremberg*)

Music drama in three acts by Richard Wagner, to his own libretto; Munich, Königliches Hof- und Nationaltheater, 21 June 1868.

Hans Sachs, cobbler, bass-baritone
Veit Pogner, goldsmith, bass
Walther von Stolzing, a young knight from Franconia, tenor
David, Sachs's apprentice, tenor
Eva, Pogner's daughter, soprano
Magdalene, Eva's nurse, soprano
A night watchman, bass

Mastersingers:
Kunz Vogelgesang, furrier, tenor
Konrad Nachtigal, tinsmith, bass
Sixtus Beckmesser, town clerk, bass
Fritz Kothner, baker, bass
Balthasar Zorn, pewterer, tenor

Ulrich Eisslinger, grocer, tenor
Augustin Moser, tailor, tenor
Hermann Ortel, soapmaker, bass
Hans Schwarz, stocking weaver, bass
Hans Foltz, coppersmith, bass

Citizens of all guilds and their wives, journeymen, apprentices, young women, people
Setting: Nuremberg; about the middle of the sixteenth century

Wagner conceived *Die Meistersinger* in 1845 as a comic appendage to *Tannhäuser,* in the same way that a satyr play followed a Greek tragedy. His first prose draft for the work was written in Marienbad (Mariánské Lázně) in July that year, using Georg Gottfried Gervinus's *Geschichte der poetischen National-Literatur der Deutschen* of 1835–42 for historical background. Other relevant volumes in Wagner's Dresden library include Jacob Grimm's *Über den altdeutschen Meistergesang* (1811), J. G. Büsching's edition of Hans Sachs's plays (1816–19), and Friedrich Furchau's life of Sachs (1820). The second and third prose drafts date from November 1861 (the former probably 14–16 November, the latter, containing minor revisions, prepared on 18 November for Schott). At this point, Wagner found J. C. Wagenseil's *Nuremberg Chronicle* of 1697 a particularly rich source of information on the ancient crafts and guilds and on other aspects of Nuremberg. Also evident are motifs from such contemporary stories as E. T. A. Hoffmann's *Meister Martin der Küfner und seine Gesellen,* which is set in sixteenth-century Nuremberg. Wagner completed the poem of *Die Meistersinger* on 25 January 1862 and began the composition in March or April. The full score was not completed until October 1867.

Even after the immensely successful premiere under Bülow in Munich, *Die Meistersinger* was taken up first by theaters of medium size, such as Dessau, Karlsruhe, Dresden, Mannheim, and Weimar (all in 1869). The court operas of Vienna and Berlin followed in 1870. The work was first given at Bayreuth in 1888 under Richter. The first performance in England was also under Richter, at the Theatre Royal, Drury Lane, in 1882, and in the United States under Seidl, at the Metropolitan in 1886. The prelude opens the work in an emphatic, magisterial C major, with a theme that celebrates the dignity of the Masters, at the same time possibly hinting at their air of self-importance. A more pensive idea gives way to a pair of themes, the first, of a fanfarelike nature, standing for the Masters and their guild. An elaborate modulation to E major introduces Walther and the theme of his passion, later to form a part of his Prize Song. After an episode in E flat depicting the chattering, bustling apprentices, three of these themes are expansively combined before a grandiloquent coda.

Act 1

Inside St. Katharine's Church. The act opens with the congregation singing a sturdy C major chorale (of Wagner's invention), the phrases of which are interrupted: Walther is urgently trying to communicate with Eva. At the end of the service, the church empties and Walther addresses Eva. He wishes to know whether she is betrothed, and though Eva sends away Magdalene to find first her handkerchief, then the clasp, and then her prayer book, she never quite manages to stem Walther's impassioned flow with an answer. Magdalene finally tells him that Eva will marry the mastersinger who wins the song contest to be held the next day. Walther is left to be instructed in the rules of the mastersingers by David, Sachs's apprentice, with whom Magdalene is in love.

In scene 2 David, after some ribbing from his fellow apprentices, proceeds to initiate Walther into the secrets of his own master's art: a properly fashioned song is, after all, he says, like a well-made pair of shoes. His catalog of the tones that have to be learnt ("Mein Herr!"), along with the appropriate rules (mostly taken by Wagner from Wagenseil), overwhelms Walther, but he sees that his only hope of winning Eva is by composing a mastersong in the approved manner. The apprentices, who have erected the wrong stage, put up the right one under David's supervision, to the accompaniment of their bustling semiquavers.

Eva's father, Pogner, now enters with the town clerk, Beckmesser (scene 3). Two tiny motifs are heard here, later much repeated both together and individually. Pogner assures Beckmesser of his good will and welcomes Walther to the guild, surprised as he is that Walther wishes to seek entry. Kothner calls the roll. Pogner then announces the prize he intends to award to the winner of the song contest the next day ("Nun hört, und versteht mich recht!"). The first part of his address is based entirely on a new motif. Then he changes to the style of an old-fashioned recitative, accompanied by sustained chords, to tell how burghers such as they are regarded in other German lands as miserly. He proposes to counter this slander by offering all his goods, as well as his only daughter, Eva, to the winner of the song contest. His proviso that she must approve the man is not welcomed by all the Masters. Sachs's proposal, however, that the winner be chosen by the populace, as a means of renewing the traditional rules with the good sense and natural instincts of the common people, is laughed out of court.

Walther is introduced by Pogner and asked about his teacher. His reply ("Am stillen Herd") is that he learnt his art from the poetry of Walther von der Vogelweide and from nature itself. In formal terms, the song is a piece of gentle mockery, on the composer's part, of the Bar form so prized by the Masters. Of the three stanzas, A-A-B, the last (*Abgesang*) is intended to be a variation of the others (*Stollen*), but in "Am stillen Herd" the variation is so florid that no one is able to contradict Beckmesser's opinion that it is but a "deluge of words."

Beckmesser withdraws into his Marker's box, ready to pass judgment on the young knight's formal attempt to enter the guild. The syncopated motif accompanying him both here and elsewhere is a churlish version of the dotted motif that first introduced Walther, as befits Beckmesser's cantankerous character. The rules of the *Tabulatur* are read out by Kothner in a style that (as Robert Bailey has pointed out) parodies that of Handelian opera, complete with coloratura (given, unusually, to a bass, for comic effect).

For his Trial Song, Walther takes up the command of the Marker: "Fanget an! So rief der Lenz in den Wald." A passionate celebration of the joys of spring and youthful love, it again fails to find favor with the Masters. It is, in fact, a complex Bar form in which each *Stollen* is in two parts—A-B-A'-B'-C—though Beckmesser interrupts after A', assuming that the form is ternary (A-B-A). Beckmesser's critical scratching of chalk on slate provokes Walther's angry outburst about envious Winter lying in wait in the thorn bush. (That this is intended as a reference to the Grimm brothers' anti-Semitic folktale "Der Jude im Dorn" is clear from the parallel situation: in the Grimm tale a bird flies into the thorn bush, in Walther's song it flies out again in an image of liberation. The matter is put beyond doubt by Wagner's pun "Grimm-bewährt," which suggests both "guarded with anger" and "authenticated by Grimm." The identification here of Beckmesser with the stereotypical Jew of folklore has profound implications for the interpretation of the character and of the work as a whole.)

Beckmesser leads the chorus of opposition to Walther; only Sachs admires his originality. Walther mounts the singer's chair (a gross breach of etiquette) to complete his song. The hubbub increases as he does so: the Masters, by an overwhelming majority, reject his application to the guild, while the apprentices revel in the commotion. With a gesture of pride and contempt, Walther strides from the stage, leaving Sachs to gaze thoughtfully at the empty singer's chair.

Act 2

In the street in front of the homes of Pogner and Sachs. The orchestral prelude takes up the main theme of Pogner's Address in a joyous celebration of midsummer's eve: trills and glissandos abound. The curtain rises to reveal a street and a narrower adjoining alley in Nuremberg. Of the two corner houses presented, Pogner's grand one on the right is overhung by a lime tree and Sachs's simpler one on the left by an elder. The apprentices are tormenting David once again. Magdalene asks him how Eva's paramour fared at the Song School and is vicariously disconsolate at the bad news. Sachs arrives and instructs David to set out his work for him by the window. Pogner and Eva return from an evening stroll and sit on a bench under the lime tree. The new motif to which he expresses his satisfaction with Nuremberg and its customs is reminiscent rhythmically of the main theme of Pogner's Address. Pogner belatedly realizes that Eva's questions about the knight are not idle curiosity.

As Eva follows her father inside, Sachs has his work bench set up outside his workshop. The tender reminiscences of a phrase from Walther's Trial Song suggest that the knight's celebration of spring and his embodiment of vital youthful passion have made a great impression on him. Sachs's relishing of the scent of the elder in this solo, "Was duftet doch der Flieder," has given it the name of the "Flieder Monologue": it develops into an exquisite evocation of the joys of spring.

Eva approaches Sachs's workshop (scene 4) and, in a long, delicately woven exchange, tries to elicit from him the likely winner of the next day's contest. Sachs playfully parries her questions until Magdalene enters to tell her that her father is calling, and that Beckmesser intends to serenade her.

Walther now turns the corner (scene 5) and an impassioned duet ensues, based largely on a demonstrative variant of one of the themes from the previous scene. They are at a loss as to how to obviate her father's conditions for obtaining her hand. Walther suggests eloping, but he gets carried away by his loathing of the Masters' pedantry until he is interrupted by the sound of the Nightwatchman's horn: a single blast on an F sharp that launches an exquisite transition to the B major of the Midsummer Magic music. Although an F sharp is sustained over many bars as a dominant pedal, the night watchman's warning to the citizenry, when it starts, is in a conflicting F major. A second blast of F sharp on his horn then reestablishes B major. Eva has meanwhile followed Magdalene into the house and now reemerges, having changed clothes with her.

Eva and Walther are about to make their escape when Sachs, who has realized what is afoot, allows his lamp to illuminate the alley they are in. They hesitate and are then pulled up short by the sound of Beckmesser tuning his lute. Walther is for settling his score with the Marker and has to be restrained by Eva: "What trouble I have with men!," she sighs. She persuades him to sit quietly under the lime tree until Beckmesser has finished his song. But Sachs has other ideas, launching into a noisy, vigorous song of his own ("Jerum! Jerum!"). A simple, balladlike structure with augmented harmonies spicing the basic B flat major, Sachs's song is permeated with references to the biblical Eve and to shoemaking that are not entirely lost on the listeners. Beckmesser has less time for the poetic subtleties; seeing what he believes to be the object of his wooing come to the window (in fact Magdalene in Eva's clothes), he begs Sachs to stop his clattering. Reminding him that he had been critical of his workmanship earlier in the day, Sachs suggests that both would make progress if Beckmesser were to serenade while he, Sachs, marked any faults with his cobbler's hammer. (The coloratura of Beckmesser's Serenade, "Den Tag seh' ich erscheinen," is a parody of an old-fashioned bel canto aria. It is also notable for its obvious and stilted rhymes and its grotesque violations of meter and misplaced accents. Clearly Beckmesser provided a target for Wagner's ill-will toward what he perceived as hostile, insensitive critics—not least Eduard Hanslick, whose name was commandeered for the Marker in the 1861 prose drafts—and other reactionary practitioners. But Beckmesser's artistic failings are also precisely those ascribed to the Jews in Das Judenthum in der Musik, and it may be argued that the serenade is also a parody of the Jewish cantorial style.)

The commotion caused by Sachs's hammering and Beckmesser's attempts to make himself heard above it brings the populace out on to the streets. A riot ensues (scene 7), during which David, under the impression that he is courting Magdalene, cudgels Beckmesser. The music of the Riot Scene, which takes up the theme of Beckmesser's Serenade, and which contains more than a dozen polyphonic lines, is notoriously difficult to perform; a simplified version, initiated by Toscanini, is used in many houses. At the height of the pandemonium, the Nightwatchman's horn is heard again. Everybody disperses, and by the time he arrives on the scene the streets are empty; he rubs his eyes in disbelief.

Act 3, Scenes 1–4

Sachs's workshop. The prelude to the third act, familiar as a concert item, opens with a broadly phrased theme on the cellos, taken up contrapuntally by the violas and, in turn, second and first violins; the theme has earlier been heard as a countermelody to Sachs's "Jerum! Jerum!" in act 2. The horns and bassoons then intone the solemn chorale that is to become the ode of homage to Sachs sung by the assembled townsfolk at the end of the opera. Announced by the characteristic semiquavers of the apprentices, David enters the workshop. Sachs, deep in thought, at first ignores him but then asks him to sing the verses he has learnt for the festival of St. John, celebrated on midsummer's day. His mind still on the events of the previous evening, David begins his ditty to the tune of Beckmesser's Serenade and has to start again: "Am Jordan Sankt Johannes stand." David belatedly realizes that it is also his master's name-day (Hans = Johannes). When the apprentice has left, Sachs resumes his philosophical meditation on the follies of humanity: "Wahn! Wahn! Überall Wahn!" (The concept of *Wahn*, which includes the notions of illusion, folly, and madness, lies at the heart of *Die Meistersinger*: by the 1860s, Wagner had come to believe that all human endeavor was underpinned by illusion and futility, though art, he considered, was a "noble illusion.") The "Wahn Monologue," as it is often known, begins with the theme of the prelude to act 3; the Nuremberg motif is heard as Sachs's thoughts turn to Nuremberg and its normally peaceful customs. The memory of the riot returns, but the agitated quavers are banished by the serene music of the Midsummer Magic. The last part of the Monologue, the dawning of midsummer's day, brings back the main theme of Pogner's Address.

The end of Sachs's reverie, and the beginning of scene 2, is signified by a modulation with harp arpeggios, rather in the manner of a cinematic "dissolve"; similar gestures occur later too in connection with dreams and reveries. Walther appears and tells Sachs of a wonderful dream. Sachs urges him to recount it as it may enable him to win the Master's prize. (Wagner had readily become a convert to the Schopenhauerian view that creativity originates in the dream world.) Walther's resistance to the demands of the Masters is overcome in the name of love, and he embarks on his Morning Dream Song—what is to become the Prize Song: "Morgenlich leuchtend in rosigem Schein." He produces one *Stollen* and then, at Sachs's bidding, another similar, followed by an *Abgesang*. Under Sachs's instruction, Walther goes on to produce another three stanzas. The last part of the overall structure (A-A-A), each section of which is in Bar form (A-A-B), is not supplied until scene 4.

In the third scene, Beckmesser appears alone in the workshop. After his beating the night before, he is limping and stumbling, and prey to nightmarish memories and imaginings. All this is depicted in a "pantomime" notable for its anarchically progressive musical style. Picking up Walther's freshly penned song, he pockets it on Sachs's reentry. He adduces it as proof that Sachs means to enter the song contest, but Sachs denies such a plan and offers him the song. Beckmesser's suspicions are eventually allayed, and he delightedly retires in order to memorize the song.

Eva enters (scene 4) and under the cover of a complaint about the shoes Sachs has made for her, she expresses her anxieties about Walther and the coming contest. Sachs affects not to understand, and pretends not to notice Walther's arrival, in spite of Eva's passionate cry and the orchestra's thrilling tonal shift on to a dominant ninth chord in B major. Walther delivers the final section of his song and Eva, moved to tears, sobs on the shoulder of Sachs, until the latter drags himself away, complaining about the lot of the cobbler. Eva, emotionally torn between the avuncular shoemaker and her younger lover, draws Sachs to her again. Sachs reminds her of the story of Tristan and Isolde and says he has no wish to play the role of King Mark; the themes of the opening of Wagner's *Tristan* and of King Mark are recalled here.

Magdalene and David arrive, and Sachs, with a cuff on his ear, announces David's promotion to journeyman, in time to witness the baptism of "a child" (the themes of the Masters and of the opening chorale are heard at this point). The progeny turns out to be Walther's new song. The music moves to a plateau of G flat major, a tritone from the C major of the surrounding scenes, for Eva's introduction to the celebrated quintet, "Selig, wie die Sonne."

Act 3, Scene 5

An open meadow on the Pegnitz. The themes associated with Nuremberg and midsummer's day effect a transition to the fifth scene. The townsfolk are all gathered and, to the accompaniment of fanfares on stage, greet the processions of the guilds: first the shoemakers, then the tailors and bakers. A boat brings "maidens from Fürth" and the apprentices begin dancing with them; David, at first reluctant, is drawn in.

At last the Masters arrive, to the music of the first-act prelude. Sachs is hailed by the populace with the chorale from the third-act prelude to the words with which the historical Sachs greeted Luther and the Reformation: "Wach auf, es nahet gen den Tag." Sachs modestly acknowledges the homage and exhorts people and Masters to accord the coming contest and prize their due worth. Beckmesser, who has frantically been trying to memorize Walther's song, is led first to the platform. His rendering of the song, to the tune of his own serenade, is marked by grotesque misaccentuations and violations of meter, but it is his garbling of the words, producing an absurd, tasteless parody of the original, that provoke a crescendo of hilarity in the audience. He presses on in confusion, but only makes a greater fool of himself. Finally he rushes from the platform, denouncing Sachs as the author.

Sachs refutes that honor and introduces the man who will make sense of it for them. Walther's Prize Song, "Morgenlich leuchtend in rosigem Schein," compresses his earlier dry run into a single Bar form of three stanzas (A-A-B) but with each stanza expanded. In several details, including the heartwarming plunge into B major (from a tonic of C) in the second stanza, Walther's prizewinning entry is a greater infraction of the rules than ever. But the Masters are evidently swept away by Walther's artistic integrity and impassioned delivery, for he is awarded the prize by general consent.

When Pogner proffers the Master's chain to Walther, he impetuously refuses, and Sachs delivers a homily about the art that the Masters have cultivated and preserved throughout Germany's troubled history: "Verachtet mir die Meister nicht." Sachs's address concludes with a celebration of the sovereignty of the German spirit—a theme dear to Wagner's heart in the 1860s; that spirit, it is proposed, can never be exterminated so long as the great German art that sustains it is respected. The salient themes of the opera's prelude are recalled for the final choral apostrophe to Sachs and "holy German art."

The only comedy among Wagner's mature works, *Die Meistersinger* is a rich, perceptive music drama widely admired for its warm humanity but regarded with suspicion by some for its dark underside. Its genial aspect is immensely enhanced by the technical mastery displayed by Wagner at the height of his powers.

BARRY MILLINGTON

Wolfgang Amadeus Mozart, *Le nozze di Figaro* (*The Marriage of Figaro*)

Opera buffa in four acts, K492, by Wolfgang Amadeus Mozart to a libretto by Lorenzo da Ponte after Pierre-Augustin Beaumarchais's play *La folle journée, ou Le mariage de Figaro* (1784, Paris); Vienna, Burgtheater, 1 May 1786.

Count Almaviva, baritone
Countess Almaviva, soprano
Susanna, her maid, betrothed to Figaro, soprano
Figaro, valet to Count Almaviva, bass
Cherubino, the count's page, mezzo-soprano
Marcellina, housekeeper to Bartolo, soprano
Bartolo, a doctor from Seville, bass
Don Basilio, music master, tenor
Don Curzio, magistrate, tenor
Barbarina, daughter of Antonio, soprano
Antonio gardener, Susanna's uncle, bass
Villagers, peasants, servants
Setting: Aguasfrescas near Seville, the Almavivas' country house; the action is contemporary with the play and opera.

The operatic version of Beaumarchais's *Le mariage de Figaro* may have been a timely notion of Mozart's own. Although the play was banned from the Viennese stage, it was available in print and Paisiello's opera on the earlier play, *Le barbier de Séville,* had triumphed in Vienna in 1783 (and all over Europe). Mozart evidently studied Paisiello's handling of the same personalities and included deliberate references to it. Composition began late in 1785 and the opera may have been drafted in only six weeks. After some opposition attributed to the Italians, and (if Da Ponte is to be believed) after the librettist had overcome the emperor's objections, it was produced in May with an outstanding cast whose character and skills, as well as their performance in Paisiello's *Barbiere,* contributed to its conception: Francesco Benucci (Figaro), Nancy Storace (Susanna), Luisa Laschi (countess), Stefano Mandini (count), Dorotea Bussani (Cherubino), Maria Mandini (Marcellina), Francesco Bussani (Bartolo and Antonio), Michael Kelly, who discussed the event in his reminiscences (Basilio and Curzio), and Anna Gottlieb (Barbarina). Mozart may have expected Storace to sing the countess; he rearranged the act 2 trio and other passages so that Susanna took the upper line.

Contrary to what is often stated, *Figaro* was generally liked, as is indicated by the emperor's ban on excessive encores (only arias were to be repeated). There were, however, only nine performances in 1786; the Viennese preferred other works, such as Martín y Soler's *Una cosa rara.* Figaro was next given in Prague, where according to Mozart's report (letter of 15 January 1787) it created a furor and led to the commission for *Don Giovanni.* The successful Vienna revival (26 performances in 1789) preceded the commission for *Così fan tutte:* Susanna was confirmed as the prima donna's role when Mozart wrote two new arias for Adriana Ferrarese del Bene, Da Ponte's mistress and the first Fiordiligi.

By this time *Figaro* had received isolated performances in Italy (acts 1 and 2, the rest composed by Angelo Tarchi, Monza, autumn 1787; Florence, spring 1788), and had been translated into German for performances in Prague (June 1787), Donaueschingen (1787), Leipzig, Graz, and Frankfurt (1788), followed by other German centers over the next few years. These performances used spoken dialogue, as did the first performance in France (Paris Opéra, 1793, using Beaumarchais). Many productions were given in French-speaking centers during the nineteenth century. Other premieres included Amsterdam (1794, in German); Madrid (1802, in Spanish); Budapest (1812, in German); London (1812, in Italian, following interpolations of numbers into other operas by Storace and Benucci; 1819, in English, reduced to three acts and arranged by Bishop); and New York (1824, in English, and 1858, in Italian). Numerous translations have been used during the nineteenth and twentieth centuries. Figaro is now Mozart's most popular opera, displacing *Don Giovanni*. No major company lets many years elapse without presenting it; Glyndebourne opened with it in 1934.

In *Il barbiere* Almaviva wooed Bartolo's ward Rosina with the aid of Figaro, now his valet. He has also, despite his Don Juanesque tendencies, abolished the *droit de seigneur* whereby he had the right to deflower every bride among his feudal dependants.

For the overture Mozart abandoned a planned middle section, leaving an electrifying sonata without development which perfectly sets the scene for the "Crazy Day."

Act 1

An antechamber. The pacing motif and lyrical response in the opening duet ("Cinque, dieci") belong respectively to Figaro, who is measuring the room, and Susanna, who is trying on a new hat. She finally entices him from his work to admire her, and to sing her motif, suggesting that she may prove to be the stronger personality. Figaro tells her the count has offered them this room, but she reacts with alarm. In the ensuing duet ("Se a caso madama") she mocks Figaro's imitation of the high and low bells of count and countess: the convenience of answering them will also make it easy for the count to visit Susanna when she is alone. Figaro's confidence is shaken, but if the count wants to dance, it is he, Figaro, who will call the tune (cavatina, "Se vuol ballare"), first offering a minuet, then a Presto contredanse. Figaro has promised to marry Marcellina if he cannot repay money he owes her. By helping her Bartolo will avenge himself on Figaro (who thwarted his plans to marry Rosina in *Il barbiere*) and rid himself of an embarrassment (Marcellina). His exit aria ("La vendetta") has a full orchestra with trumpets, in the opera's principal key, D major. His vaunted legal knowledge brings formal counterpoint (and a phrase from *Lo sposo deluso*), but his fury also vents itself in comically undignified patter. Susanna finds Marcellina, and hustles her out, the music poised, the exchange of compliments venomous (duettino, "Via resti servito"). Cherubino confides in Susanna. In a lyrical arch of melody over a sensuously muted accompaniment, he impulsively babbles of his love for all women ("Non so più"), an enchanting musical image of adolescence. The count is heard; Susanna hides Cherubino behind a chair. Basilio's voice interrupts the count's amorous proposals; while he too hides behind the chair, Cherubino nips onto it and Susanna covers him with a dress. Basilio's malicious (but accurate) observation that Cherubino adores the countess rouses the count. Gruffly, in an ascending line, he demands an explanation (trio, "Cosa sento!"); Basilio, his motif unctuously descending, disclaims knowledge; Susanna, turning to the minor dominant, threatens to faint. The men officiously come to her aid (a new, ardent motif with a chromatic cadence). The count describes his discovery of Cherubino in Barbarina's room, hidden under a cloth . . . at which he is again revealed, to the count's self-righteous indignation, Basilio's delight, and Susanna's horror. Sonata form perfectly matches the action, the recapitulation fraught with irony (or, from Basilio, sarcasm). Figaro ushers in a rustic chorus praising the count's magnanimity in renouncing his extramarital right, but the count refuses to be trapped into marrying the couple then and there, and banishes Cherubino with an officer's commission. While apparently sending him on his way to a bold march rhythm ("Non più andrai": no more frolicking and flirting; he is off to death or glory), Figaro detains the page for purposes of his own.

Act 2

The countess's chamber. In an achingly tender larghetto, sharing clarinet-based instrumentation with "Non so più," the neglected countess prays to the god of love to restore her husband's affections (cavatina, "Porgi, Amor"). But she listens eagerly to Susanna and Figaro's plotting (Figaro leaves to a snatch of "Se vuol ballare"). Cherubino is to be dressed as a girl, take Susanna's place, and compromise the count. His ardor is formalized, in a song of his own composition, sung to Susanna's "guitar" accompaniment, but it breaks into recondite modulations before the reprise; Mozart miraculously suggests, but evades, the clumsiness of a tyro (canzona, "Voi che sapete"). Susanna tries to dress him but he keeps turning his gaze toward the countess ("Venite, inginocchiatevi": an action aria replaced in 1789 by the strophic "Un moto di gioia"). Alone with the countess, Cherubino is close to winning her heart when the count demands admittance: he has returned precipitately from the hunt because of an anonymous letter (part of Figaro's ill-laid plot). In confusion the countess thrusts Cherubino into her closet; the count asks questions; Susanna enters unseen. The countess says Susanna is in the closet. The count's jealous fury, his wife's terror and Susanna's anxious assessment of the situation again outline a sonata form, although the action does not advance (trio, "Susanna, or via sortite"). When the count leaves (to fetch tools to break down the door), taking the countess, Susanna thrusts Cherubino through the window (duettino, "Aprite, presto aprite") and enters the closet.

Mozart's most consummate comic finale begins by resuming the fury and anxiety of the trio (E flat, "Ecci omai, garzon malnato"). The countess confesses that Cherubino is in the closet but protests his innocence; the count is ready to kill. But it is Susanna who emerges, to a simple minuet which mocks the nobles' consternation. Explanations and further confusion occupy an extended Allegro which deploys its thematic wealth with marvelous inventiveness. Although puzzled, the count has to ask forgiveness. At the single abrupt key-change of the finale (B flat to G) Figaro enters, again asking for an immediate wedding. Recovering his sangfroid (C major, gavotte tempo), the count poses questions about the anonymous letter; Figaro prevaricates. Antonio charges in to complain of damage to his garden caused by the page's precipitate exit (Allegro molto, F major). The count senses more chicanery; Figaro claims it was he who jumped. The tempo slows to andante (in B flat) and with measured calm the count questions Figaro about a paper the page has dropped: the music emerges from an harmonic cloud to a shining recapitulation as Figaro (prompted by the women) identifies it as the page's commission, left with him (he claims) to be sealed. The count is baffled, but revives when Marcellina, Basilio, and Bartolo rush in demanding justice (E flat).

Act 3

A large room decorated for the marriage-feast. The countess urges Susanna to make an assignation with the count; they will exchange cloaks and compromise him with his own wife. Susanna approaches him, explains her previous reticence as delicacy, and offers to meet him that evening. In a rare outburst in the minor (duet, "Crudel! perchè finora") the count reproaches her; changing to major, he sings of his coming happiness with exuberant syncopation. She tries to join in but trips over the right replies ("Yes" for "No," etc.), correcting herself at a melodic high point. Leaving, she encounters Figaro and carelessly shows her satisfaction: "without a lawyer we've won the case." The count is again suspicious and angry (the first obbligato recitative and aria, "Vedrò, mentre io sospiro"). Must he sigh in vain while a mere servant wins the prize? The martial orchestration and key, even the contrapuntal language, recall Bartolo's aria, but the music snarls with aristocratic jealousy, not pompous self-importance: within the social structure of this opera it is a truly menacing utterance.

At the trial of Marcellina's case Curzio is finding for the plaintiff. Figaro protests that he cannot marry Marcellina without his parents' consent. It emerges that he is the lost son of Marcellina, and Bartolo reluctantly admits paternity. Marcellina embraces Figaro (sextet, "Riconosci in questo amplesso") and the three express delight while the count and Curzio mutter their annoyance. Susanna misinterprets the embrace and boxes Figaro's ears. The comical explanation leads to a quartet of satisfaction against which Curzio and the count fling out a defiant phrase of anger.

The countess, waiting for Susanna, muses on the past and wonders if there is hope for her marriage. This set piece (obbligato recitative and rondò, "Dove sono i bei momenti," which, it has been argued, may have been intended to precede the previous scene) shows her as profoundly tender yet impulsive; it reaches a glowing a″ at the climax. Antonio tells the count that Cherubino is still in the castle. The countess dictates a letter from Susanna to the count confirming their rendezvous (duettino, "Che soave zeffiretto"), their voices mingling in an expression of the love they feel, each for her own; the honeyed music shows none of the deviousness of their intentions.

During a choral presentation to the countess, Cherubino is unmasked, but allowed to stay for the wedding as he (and Barbarina) are tempted to make revelations embarrassing to the count. During the finale, the necessary action is cunningly woven into the sequence of dances. During the march the two couples (Marcellina and Bartolo have decided to regularize their union) are presented to the count and countess. The bridesmaids' duet and chorus (contredanse) precede the alluring fandango, during which Susanna slips the letter to the count, sealed with a pin (to be returned as a sign of agreement); Figaro notices with amusement that the count has pricked himself.

Act 4

The garden, at night; pavilions on either side. Barbarina, the go-between, has lost the pin (a mock-tragic cavatina, "L'ho perduta"). Figaro, hearing her tale, concludes that Susanna is unfaithful; an abyss seems to open beneath him. Marcellina is inclined to warn Susanna; she must have a good reason for meeting the count, and women should stick together ("Il capro e la capretta"). Barbarina is preparing to meet Cherubino in a pavilion. Figaro summons Basilio and Bartolo to witness the betrayal. Basilio moralizes about the wisdom of not resisting one's superiors, adding a tale of his own hot youth ("In quegl'anni"). Figaro's monologue (obbligato recitative and aria, "Aprite un po' quegl'occhi") uses raw musical gestures to convey the terrors, for a clever but emotionally simple man, of sexual betrayal. Disconnected phrases witness to his anxiety, and horn fanfares mock him without mercy. He overhears but cannot see Susanna, who is disguised as the countess (obbligato recitative and aria, "Deh vieni, non tardar"). The floating line and titillating woodwind cadences with which Susanna confides her amorous longing to the night perfectly capture the blended love and mischief with which she deliberately rouses Figaro's passion (in 1789 Mozart replaced the aria with the elaborate rondò "Al desio").

From now on all is confusion; the characters mistake identities and blunder into each other in the dark, receiving kisses and blows intended for others, before nearly all of them end up in the pavilions (finale). Cherubino begs Susanna (actually the disguised countess) for a kiss; Susanna watches anxiously as the count and Figaro drive the pest away. The count begins to woo "Susanna," who responds shyly; Figaro's impotent rage is highlighted in the bass. He contrives a temporary interruption. As the key changes from G to E flat a serenadelike melody ironically evokes the peace of the night. Seeing the countess (actually Susanna), Figaro tells her what is going on; then recognizing her by her voice, he pays "the countess" passionate court. Enraged, Susanna boxes his ears again, blows which he greets with rapture. This scene unfolds to a frantic allegro, replaced at the reconciliation by pastoral 6/8. Now they enact Figaro pleading passionate love to the countess; on cue, with a second abrupt key change (B flat to G), the count bursts in on them, calling witnesses, dragging everyone including the false countess from the pavilion, shouting accusations. The entry of the real countess (in Susanna's clothes) leaves the company breathless. The humbled count's prayer for forgiveness, and her loving response, build into a radiant hymn before the brilliant conclusion brings down the curtain on the crazy day. *Figaro* is generally agreed to be the most perfect and least problematic of Mozart's great operas. The libretto, despite its complication (to which any synopsis does scant justice), is founded on a carefully constructed intrigue and Mozart draws musical dividends even from a hat, an anonymous letter, and a pin. The advance on the sketched *opere buffe* of the immediately preceding years is astonishing, and must be attributed mainly to the effect on his imagination of the play, ably seconded by Da Ponte's adaptation.

The originality of the ensembles has often and rightly been commented upon. Many of them carry the action forward, not at the "natural" tempo of recitative but under musical control; this makes such moments as the revelation of Figaro's parents to Susanna (the act 3 sextet) both touching and funny, and creates palpable tension when the count comes near to murdering his wife's "lover" (the act 2 trio), although we know the unseen Susanna will enable the page to escape. The arias are no less original for their brevity and directness. They convey, economically and unforgettably, the essential characterization of Bartolo, Cherubino ("Non so più"), the countess, and the count. Figaro and Susanna are presented in ensembles and action arias (his act 1 cavatina, although it is a kind of soliloquy, and "Non più andrai"; her "Venite, inginocchiatevi"). Their central place in the intrigue is confirmed when each has an obbligato recitative (normally a sign of high rank) in the last act; these precede the last arias, soliloquies which deepen Figaro's character (although his cynical denunciation of women is not endearing) and reveal the subtlety and tenderness of Susanna. Mozart's replace- ment of "Deh vieni" in 1789 by "Al desio" is a rare case of his damaging his own work by pandering to a singer.

Modern performances often omit Marcellina's act 4 aria, a stately minuet and melodious allegro of deliberately old-fashioned cut (with coloratura and strings-only orchestration), and Basilio's, an elaborate and inventively composed narration in three sections (andante, minuet allegro). Despite their virtues these pieces of moralizing by minor characters create a sequence of four arias inappropriate so near the denoue- ment, and an excess of minuet tempo.

The only other critical reservation about Le nozze di Figaro concerns the episodic structure of the third act. It comes precisely where Da Ponte had to depart decisively from Beaumarchais (omitting the extended trial scene). The reordering of scenes has no documentary foundation, and can be shown not to represent Mozart's original inten- tion; but the revised sequence avoids two immediately successive entries for the count- ess and works well in the theater. It would have been unmanageable with the original casting, which doubles Antonio with Bartolo; without the countess's "Dove sono," An- tonio must enter immediately after the sextet, in which Bartolo sings. The non sequiturs of act 3, however, count for little in performance and throw into greater relief the in- genious management of its finale. In the great finales of acts 2 and 4, Mozart reached a level which he could never surpass; indeed, he was hardly to equal the B flat allegro of the second-act finale for its mercurial motivic play and the subsequent andante in 6/8 for the synchronization of dramatic revelation with the demands of musical form.

JULIAN RUSHTON

Wolfgang Amadeus Mozart, *Die Entführung aus dem Serail* (*The Abduction from the Seraglio*)

Singspiel in three acts, K384, by Wolfgang Amadeus Mozart to a libretto by Christoph Friedrich Bretzner (*Belmont und Constanze, oder Die Entführung aus dem Serail*), adapted and enlarged by Gottlieb Stephanie the Younger; Vienna, Burgtheater, 16 July 1782.

Pasha Selim, spoken
Konstanze, a Spanish lady, Belmonte's betrothed, soprano
Blonde, Konstanze's English maid, soprano
Belmonte, a Spanish nobleman, tenor

Pedrillo, servant of Belmonte, now supervisor of the pasha's gardens, tenor
Osmin, overseer of the pasha's country house, bass
Klaas, a sailor, spoken
Mute in Osmin's service, silent
Chorus of Janissaries, guards
Setting: The country palace of Pasha Selim, on the Mediterranean coast in an
unidentified part of the Turkish Empire

Act 1

A plaza before Selim's palace, near the sea. A major-key version of the middle section
of the overture (Belmonte's "Hier soll ich dich denn sehen") forms a short introductory aria. Osmin brings a ladder, and begins picking figs; he sings a moral *Volkslied* (lied
and duet, "Wer ein Liebchen hat gefunden": "Whoever finds a lover, let him beware").
When Belmonte speaks, Osmin refuses to answer, directing the later verses at him instead: plausible strangers bring danger to lovers. Belmonte now sings, wrenching the
tempo to allegro, but the wrath of the Turk, enraged by mention of Pedrillo, domi-
nates the ensemble. In a furious Presto, the original G minor yielding to D major, he
drives Belmonte away.

Pedrillo asks Osmin whether Selim has returned. Still not answering, Osmin fumes
about vagabond fops fit only to be hanged ("Solche hergelauf'ne Laffen"). A full binary
exit aria, portentous and often contrapuntal, it flies off the handle in the coda to which
Mozart added "Turkish" music for comic effect. Belmonte reveals himself. Pedrillo assures him that Selim will not force love on Konstanze, but they are in great danger and
Osmin watches everything. Belmonte's heart is beating with anxiety and ardor ("O
wie ängstlich, o wie feurig"); both melody and orchestra are suffused with feeling as
well as detailed imitation of the lover's symptoms.

A march (possibly cut by Mozart, but restored by the *Neue Mozart-Ausgabe*) announces the arrival of the pasha in a boat with Konstanze; the Janissaries greet them
with a vigorous chorus in "Turkish" style. Selim asks why Konstanze remains sad and
promises that her answer will not anger him. In the adagio of her aria Konstanze
relives her past love ("Ach ich liebte, war so glücklich!"); the allegro compresses the
adagio's melodic outline into a vehement protest; all happiness has fled (the adagio text
and mood return in the middle of the allegro). Mozart's sacrifice for Cavalieri brings
coloratura to an inappropriate text ("Kummer ruht in meinem Schoss" [sorrow dwells
in my heart]), but this emphatic utterance tells us that Konstanze is a considerable
character. Selim is angry, but when she leaves he admits that he loves her all the more
for her resistance. Pedrillo introduces Belmonte as an Italian-trained architect; Selim
approves his entry into the household. But Osmin has other ideas. A vivacious trio
in C minor ("Marsch, marsch, marsch! trollt euch fort!"), ending with a faster major
section, forms a comic finale; eventually the Europeans force an entry.

Act 2

The palace garden, with Osmin's house to one side. Osmin is pursuing Blonde, whom
the pasha has given him as a slave; but she will have none of his Turkish ways; tender-

ness, not force, wins hearts ("Durch Zärtlichkeit und Schmeicheln"). Her andante aria is the epitome of Mozartean A major elegance, yet Blonde must glide up to e''''. Osmin indignantly orders her to love him, but she merely laughs, and wards off an assault by threatening his eyes with her nails and reminding him that her mistress is the pasha's favorite (duet, "Ich gehe, doch rate ich dir"). Osmin warns her not to flirt with Pedrillo; she mocks his low notes with her own (to a flat). In a lugubrious andante Osmin declares that the English are mad to allow their women such liberties; Blonde rejoices in her freedom.

At the nadir of her fortunes, Konstanze turns to the most intense style of opera seria, obbligato recitative ("Welcher Wechsel herrscht in meiner Seele") and aria ("Traurigkeit ward mir zum Lose"). In an exquisite adagio Mozart paints her sighing breaths, her halting steps. The aria, its orchestra enriched by basset horns, is a sustained lament in G minor, like Ilia's (*Idomeneo,* act 1) but attaining a new poignancy through its higher tessitura.

Blonde tries to comfort her mistress. Selim threatens not death, which Konstanze welcomes, but every kind of torture. Her aria ("Marten aller Arten": "Every kind of torture awaits me; I laugh at pain; death will come in the end") picks up Selim's threat, but not before a sixty-bar ritornello with obbligato flute, oboe, violin, and cello has unfolded a rich motivic tapestry founded on a march rhythm (with trumpets and timpani). The closing words are given more emphasis by a faster tempo. This magnificent piece, coming immediately after another long aria for Konstanze, is of immense dramatic power, expressing stubborn resistance to coercion from a woman with no hope of deliverance. Selim is baffled; affection and force having failed, he wonders if he can use cunning. (This exit line perhaps prefigured a new intrigue intended for act 3 but not included.)

Pedrillo tells Blonde of Belmonte's arrival. Blonde's reaction, a rondo with a melody from the Flute Concerto K314 ("Welche Wonne, welche Lust"), sparkles with unalloyed delight. Pedrillo musters his courage in a martial D major ("Frisch zum Kampfe!"), but a nagging phrase ("Nur ein feiger Tropf verzagt [Only a cowardly fool despairs]) shows his underlying lack of confidence. He succeeds in getting Osmin drunk (duet, "Vivat Bacchus"), and sends him to sleep it off so that the lovers can meet. Tears of joy are love's sweetest reward; Belmonte's aria of galanterie ("Wenn der Freude Tränen fliessen") is a slow gavotte and then a serenadelike minuet announced by the wind and embellished with wide-ranging passagework.

The escape is planned before the finale (quartet, "Ach Belmonte!"). The first mature Mozart ensemble to incorporate dramatic development begins with a lively D major allegro. Joy gives way to anxiety (andante, G minor); have the women yielded to blandishment? In a faster tempo, Konstanze expresses hurt, Blonde slaps Pedrillo's face, and the voices come together in mingled relief and regret. The men ask forgiveness (allegretto); Blonde withholds it, singing in compound time against the simple time of the others (a device Mozart might have picked up from opéra comique). But eventually misunderstanding is cleared away and the four join in praise of love.

Act 3

The scene of act 1; Osmin's house to one side. Midnight. Pedrillo and Klaas bring two ladders. Belmonte is assured that all is ready, but they must wait for the guards to finish their rounds. Pedrillo advises him to sing; he himself often sings at night and it will not be noticed. In a long andante, featuring clarinets and extended coloratura, Belmonte builds his hopes on the power of love ("Ich baue ganz auf deine Stärke").

Pedrillo gives the agreed signal, a romance ("In Mohrenland gefangen war ein Mädchen"). The opera's second lied, this too refers to the dramatic situation. Its haunting melody, to a plucked accompaniment, rests upon harmonic ambiguity and ends unresolved after four verses when Pedrillo sees a light. Belmonte fetches Konstanze; they hurry off as Pedrillo climbs up for Blonde. Suspecting thieves and murderers, the bleary-eyed Osmin sends for the guard and dozes. Blonde and Pedrillo spot him too late; all four Europeans are arrested. In a brilliant rondo ("O, wie will ich triumphieren"), with piccolo but without trumpets or Turkish music, which Mozart keeps in reserve, Osmin anticipates the delight of torturing and killing his enemies, his lowest bass notes (to D) filled with ghoulish relish.

The interior of the palace. Osmin claims credit for the arrest. Selim confronts the lovers. Konstanze admits guilt in his eyes, but pleads loyalty to her first lover. She begs to die if only his life can be spared. Belmonte humbles himself; he is worth a fine ransom; his name is Lostados. Selim recognizes the son of the enemy who chased him from his homeland. He bids them prepare for the punishment Belmonte's father would certainly have meted out, and leaves them under guard. Belmonte movingly laments his folly in bringing Konstanze to her doom; she blames herself for his destruction, but death is the path to an eternal union, symbolized by the serenely extended arabesques doubled in thirds and sixths (recitative and duet, "Welch ein Geschick! O Qual der Seele!").

Selim asks if they are prepared for judgment. Belmonte says they will die calmly, absolving him from blame. Selim, however, bids him take Konstanze and go. He despises Belmonte's father too much to imitate him; clemency will be his revenge. As he takes dignified leave of them, Pedrillo begs freedom for himself and Blonde. Osmin is overruled; does he not value his eyes? In a *vaudeville* finale, each sings a verse of suitable sentiment, with a moral sung by the ensemble: those who forget kindness are to be despised. Blonde is interrupted by Osmin whose rage boils over into the litany of torture from his act 1 aria, complete with "Turkish" percussion. He rushes off; the others draw the further moral that nothing is so hateful as revenge. A brief chorus in praise of the pasha, in the principal key, C major, brings back the merry "Turkish" style of the overture.

JULIAN RUSHTON

Giuseppe Verdi, *Don Carlos*

Opéra in five acts by Giuseppe Verdi to a libretto by Joseph Mery and Camille Du Locle after Friedrich von Schiller's dramatic poem *Don Carlos, Infant von Spanien;* premiere at the Paris Opéra, 11 March 1867. Revised version in four acts (French text revised by Du Locle, Italian translation by Achille de Lauzières and Angelo Zanardini), Milan, Teatro alla Scala, 10 January 1884.

Philip II, King of Spain, bass
Don Carlos, Infante of Spain, tenor
Rodrigue, Marquis of Posa, baritone
The Grand Inquisitor, bass
Elisabeth de Valois, Philip's queen, soprano
Princess Eboli, mezzo-soprano
Thibault, Elisabeth de Valois's page, soprano
The Countess of Aremberg, silent
The Count of Lerma, tenor
An old monk, bass
A voice from heaven, soprano
A voice from heaven, tenor
Flemish deputies, basses
Inquisitors, basses
Lords and ladies of the French and Spanish court, woodcutters, populace, pages,
guards of Henry II and Philip II, monks, officers of the Inquisition, soldiers.
Setting: France and Spain, about 1560

It is important to bear in mind that, although the 1884 version was first given in Italian, the revisions Verdi made were to a French text: in other words, there is no "Italian version" of *Don Carlos,* merely an "Italian translation." The following discussion will move through the opera by act, marking in italic the version to which various passages belong: 1867 means the version eventually performed at the Parisian première, 1884 the substantially revised four-act version. Where appropriate, French incipits are followed by their Italian equivalents.

Act 1

The forest at Fontainebleau.

1867. An impressive introductory chorus was cut during rehearsals, leaving the opera to start with a brief allegro brillante; offstage fanfares and huntsmen's calls introduce Elisabeth, who (observed by Carlos) gives alms to the woodcutters and then departs.

Carlos, who has come incognito from Spain, has now seen for the first time his betrothed, Elisabeth, and in the brief, Italianate aria "Je l'ai vue" ("Io la vidi") he announces love at first sight. He is about to follow Elisabeth when a horn call tells him that night is falling. Thibault and Elisabeth, lost in the wood, appear, and Carlos offers help, introducing himself simply as "a Spaniard." Thibault goes off for assistance, so making way for the duet that will dominate this brief act. The opening movement, "Que faites-vous donc?" ("Che mai fate voi?"), is formed from a series of contrasting episodes, the tension rising as Elisabeth eagerly questions this stranger about the Infante Carlos whom she is to marry. Carlos presents her with a portrait of her betrothed, which she immediately recognizes as the man before her. This precipitates the second movement, "De quels transports" ("Di qual amor"), a cabaletta-like celebration of their good fortune, based on a melody that recurs through the opera as a symbol of their first love.

The joy is short-lived. Thibault returns to announce that Henry II has decided to give Elisabeth to Philip instead of to his son, so putting an end to the war between Spain and France. The couple express their horror in the restrained, minor-mode "L'heure fatale est sonnée!" ("L'ora fatale è suonata!"), which is immediately juxtaposed with the major-mode offstage chorus of celebration, "O chants de fête" ("Inni di festa"). The Count of Lerma arrives to request Elisabeth's formal approval of the match, a female chorus adding their pleas for peace. Elisabeth reluctantly accepts, and the stage clears to a triumphant reprise of "O chants de fête." Carlos is left alone to bemoan his fate.

1867 Act 2 / 1884 Act 1, Scene 1

The cloister of the monastery of St. Yuste. A solemn introduction for four horns precedes the offstage chorus "Charles-Quint, l'auguste Empereur" ("Carlo, il sommo Imperatore"), a funeral dirge for Charles V. A solitary monk adds his prayer to theirs, but admits that Charles was guilty of folly and pride.

1867. Carlos enters: he has come to the monastery to forget the past. In a solemnly intoned, sequential passage, "Mon fils, les douleurs de la terre," the monk tells him that the sorrows of the world also invade this holy place. The monk's voice reminds a terrified Carlos of the late emperor himself.

1884. Carlos's extended scena explores his anguish at losing Elisabeth and culminates in a revised version of "Je l'ai vue" ("Io la vidi") from the original act 1 (the act entirely omitted from this version). There follows a curtailed conversation with the monk.

1867. Rodrigue, Marquis of Posa, appears and is greeted by Carlos. Posa launches into a description of the battles in Flanders (a first portion of this part of the duet, beginning "J'étais en Flandre," was cut from the 1867 version during rehearsals), and Carlos responds with a lyrical declaration of friendship, "Mon compagnon, mon ami." Carlos then admits his secret love for Elisabeth, now the wife of Philip, his father. Posa reiterates his friendship in a reprise of "Mon compagnon," advising Carlos to forget his sorrows in the battle for Flanders.

1884. The above-described portion of the duet was further condensed and enriched, with a skillful link from the scene with the monk, and with "Mon compagnon" becoming "Mon sauveur, mon ami" ("Mio salvator, mio fratel").

Both. The final section of the duet, the cabaletta "Dieu, tu semas dans nos âmes" ("Dio, che nell'alma infondere"), is a "shoulder-to-shoulder" number reminiscent of Verdi's earliest manner, the tenor and baritone vowing eternal friendship in parallel thirds. In an impressively scored coda, Philip, Elisabeth, and a procession of monks cross the stage and enter the monastery. Carlos and Posa join the chanting monks before a thrilling reprise of their cabaletta brings the scene to a close.

1867 Act 2 / 1884 Act 1, Scene 2

A pleasant spot outside the gates of the St. Yuste monastery. Eboli and the other ladies-in-waiting are not allowed in the monastery, so they amuse themselves outside. The female chorus sets the scene with "Sous ces bois au feuillage immense" ("Sotto ai folti, immensi abeti"), and then Eboli sings her famous "Chanson du voile" (Veil Song), "Au palais des fées" ("Nel giardin del bello"): the two-stanza song with refrain, packed with both harmonic and instrumental local color, tells the story of Achmet, a Moorish king who one evening mistakenly wooed his own wife in the garden. A disconsolate Elisabeth appears, soon followed by Posa, who hands the queen a letter from her mother in which is hidden a note from Carlos. As Elisabeth reads, Posa makes courtly conversation with Eboli; but in the background of their dalliance we hear from Elisabeth that Carlos's letter asks her to trust Posa. At a word from Elisabeth, Posa begins his two-stanza cantabile romance, "L'Infant Carlos, notre espérance" ("Carlo, ch'è sol il nostro amore"), in which he tells how Carlos, rejected by his father, requests an interview with his new "mother." In between stanzas, Eboli wonders whether Carlos's dejection has been caused by love for her, while Elisabeth trembles with confusion. With the completion of the second stanza, however, Elisabeth agrees to the interview; Posa and Eboli walk off together, and the ladies-in-waiting leave.

The ensuing duet between Carlos and Elisabeth, "Je viens solliciter" ("Io vengo a domandar"), is one of Verdi's boldest attempts to match musical progress to the rapid alternations of spoken dialogue: there is little sense of a conventional four-movement form (except perhaps for a cabaletta-style ending), the duet instead passing through a rapid series of contrasting episodes, some sense of strictly musical connection coming from shared motifs. In a controlled opening, Carlos asks Elisabeth to intercede on his behalf with Philip, who will not allow him to leave for Flanders. Elisabeth agrees, but Carlos can restrain himself no further and pours out his love. Elisabeth at first attempts to deflect him, but eventually admits her feelings; Carlos falls into a swoon, and Elisabeth fears he is dying. As he awakens he begins a final, passionate declaration, "Que sous mes pieds" ("Sotto al mio pie'"), but when he attempts to embrace his beloved, she recovers herself and angrily rejects him, telling him sarcastically that to claim her he must kill his father. Carlos rushes off in despair, just as Philip himself appears, angry that Elisabeth has been left alone. He orders her lady-in-waiting, the Countess of Aremberg, back to France; Elisabeth bids the countess a tender farewell in the two-stanza, minor–major romance, "O ma chère compagne" ("Non pianger, mia compagna"). Philip, left alone, gestures for Posa to remain with him.

1867. After a brief recitative, Posa begins the first movement of a duet by describing his soldierly life ("Pour mon pays") and narrating his journeys in war-torn Flanders ("O Roi! j'arrive de Flandre"). Philip stresses the need for political control, and sternly curbs Posa's idealism. The impasse produces a lyrical second movement, the meno mosso "Un souffle ardent," in which the two men are placed in patterned opposition before joining voice in a final section. Posa throws himself at Philip's feet: Philip forgives his rashness, but bids him beware the Inquisitor. The king then confides in Posa, beginning the closing cabaletta, "Enfant! à mon coeur éperdu," with an admission of his troubled personal feelings.

1884. In this radical revision, virtually all trace of the conventional four-movement form disappears from the duet, being replaced by the kind of fluid dialogue we find in Otello. Posa's "O Roi! j'arrive de Flandre" ("O signor, di Fiandra arrivo") is retained, but most of the remaining music is new. Particularly impressive is Philip's advice to beware the Inquisitor, in which solemn chords serve momentarily to halt the musical flow. Philip is more explicit about his fears, going so far as to mention Carlos and Elisabeth; but he closes the duet with yet another sinister reference to the power of the Inquisitor.

1867 Act 3 / *1884* Act 2, Scene 1

The queen's gardens.

1867. Festivities are in progress; Philip is to be crowned the next day. In a further essay in local color, the offstage chorus sings "Que de fleurs et que d'étoiles" to the accompaniment of castanets. Elisabeth appears with Eboli: the queen is already weary of the celebrations and changes masks with Eboli so that she can retire to seek religious consolation. When Elisabeth leaves, Eboli has a brief solo, "Me voilà reine pour une nuit," which recalls the central section of the Veil Song. She writes a letter of assignation to Carlos, hoping to entice him.

The ensuing ballet, entitled "La Pérégrina," tells of a fisherman who happens on a magic cave containing the most marvelous pearls in the ocean. He dances with the White Pearl; gradually the other pearls join in. Philip's page enters to the strains of a Spanish hymn played by the brass; he has come to find for his master the most beautiful pearl in the world. At the climax of the ballet, Eboli (posing as Elisabeth) appears as La Pérégrina: the page's search is at an end. Verdi's music for the ballet, some fifteen minutes long, is the traditional mixture of orchestral sophistication and extreme musical simplicity.

1884. A short, understated prelude is based on the first phrase of Carlos's "Je l'ai vue" ("Io la vidi"); it clearly belongs to Verdi's last manner, particularly in the overt use of thematic transformation and the ease with which it moves between distantly related keys.

Both. Carlos enters, reading the letter of assignation; this briefly sets the scene for the ensuing ensemble, which follows the common Italian four-movement pattern, led off by a condensed series of contrasting lyrical episodes, each punctuated by some dramatic revelation. As Eboli appears, Carlos breaks into a passionate declaration of love, thinking she is Elisabeth. Eboli responds with matching phrases, but the lyrical development abruptly breaks down as she removes her mask. Eboli at first misconstrues Carlos's confusion, and attempts to reassure him: but she soon guesses the truth, and accuses him of loving the queen. At this point Posa arrives, and a brief transitional passage leads to the second main movement, "Redoubtez tout de ma furie!" ("Al mio furor sfuggite invano"), in which the baritone's and mezzo's agitated rhythms are set against the tenor's long, impassioned melody. A brief transition movement during which Carlos restrains Posa from killing Eboli leads to the final stretta, "Malheur sur toi, fils adultère" ("Trema per te, falso figliuolo"), in which Eboli brings down furious curses on the man who has rejected her. She rushes off, leaving Carlos and Posa; they act out a brief coda in which Carlos—after some hesitation—entrusts his friend with some secret papers. The scene concludes with a brash orchestral reprise of their earlier cabaletta, "Dieu tu semas dans nos âmes" ("Dio, che nell'alma infondere").

1867 Act 3 / *1884* Act 2, Scene 2

A large square in front of Valladolid Cathedral. This central finale, the grand sonic and scenic climax of Don Carlos, is formally laid out along traditional Italian lines but, in response to the added resources of the Opéra, is on a scale Verdi had never before attempted. The opening chorus, "Ce jour heureux" ("Spuntato ecco il dì"), is a kind of rondo: the main theme, beginning with a motif formed around scale degrees 1, 3, 6, and 5, and making prominent use of dynamic triplet figures, alternates with a funereal theme to which monks escort heretics to the stake, and with a more lyrical idea in which the monks promise salvation to those who repent. A solemn procession fills the stage, after which a herald announces Philip, who appears on the steps of the cathedral. He is confronted by six Flemish deputies, escorted by Carlos. They kneel before him and, with a solemn prayer for their country, "Sire, la dernière heure" ("Sire, no, l'ora estrema"), lead off a grand concertato movement in which all the principals join, Elisabeth, Carlos, and Posa adding their pleas, while Philip and the monks stubbornly resist. A transitional movement begins as Carlos steps forward, asking to be sent to Flanders. When Philip refuses, Carlos threateningly draws his sword. No one dares intervene until Posa steps forward and demands Carlos's surrender. To a soft, veiled reprise of their friendship cabaletta, Carlos relinquishes his weapon, upon which Philip pronounces Posa promoted to a dukedom. The scene closes with a grand reprise of the opening choral sequence. As the heretics go to their death, a voice from heaven assures them of future bliss.

1867 Act 4 / 1884 Act 3, Scene 1

The king's study. The king, alone with his official papers, sings the famous "Elle ne m'aime pas!" ("Ella giammai m'amò!"). As a complex psychological portrait, the aria has few rivals in Verdi. The king's mood swings from self-pity at his emotional isolation (an arioso accompanied by obsessive string figures and culminating in the passionate outburst of "Elle ne m'aime pas!"), to a somber meditation on his mortality (with mock-medieval "horn fifths" to accompany his picture of the stone vault in which he will lie), to a recognition of his power (a triplet bass melody hinting at the musical grandeur of the preceding concertato finale). But the aria closes with a reprise of its opening outburst: Philip's tragedy, at this point in the drama, is primarily a personal one.

The subsequent duet with the old and blind Grand Inquisitor, "Suis-je devant le Roi?" ("Sono io dinanzi al Re?"), continues the aria's relative formal freedom, its sense that the music reacts immediately and flexibly to the shifting emotions of the dialogue. The opening orchestral idea, with its concentration on low strings, ostinato rhythms, and restricted pitches, sets the scene for this power struggle between two basses. Philip seems in command as he asks the Inquisitor how to deal with Carlos; but, as the controlled opening gives way to freer declamation, the Inquisitor takes over, stating that Posa is the more serious threat and demanding that he be turned over to the Inquisition. Philip resists, but in an imposing declamatory climax the Inquisitor warns him that even kings can be brought before the tribunal. As the opening orchestral idea returns, Philip attempts to restore peace; but the Inquisitor is indifferent and leaves Philip in no doubt as to how the struggle will be resolved.

The *scène et quatuor* that follows (much revised for the 1884 version) is more conventionally structured. In the opening *scène,* set to the kind of lyrically enriched recitative that was now the Verdian norm, Elisabeth rushes in to announce the theft of her jewel case. Philip produces it and invites her to reveal its contents; when she refuses he breaks the lock and finds inside a picture of Carlos. In spite of her protestations, he accuses her of adultery; the queen faints, and Philip summons Posa and Eboli, who arrive to precipitate the formal quartet, "Maudit soit le soupçon infâme" ("Ah! si maledetto, sospetto fatale"). The ensemble is at first dominated by Philip, whose opening statements—fragmentary expressions of remorse—gradually form into a lyrical melody that interweaves with Posa's decision to take action and Eboli's cries of remorse. But towards the end Elisabeth's sorrowful lament takes on increasing urgency and focus.

Philip and Posa leave. Originally the scene continued with a duet for Elisabeth and Eboli, but this was cut during rehearsals for the 1867 première, when the cut extended some way into Eboli's confession; however, Verdi recomposed and expanded this for the 1884 version, in which Eboli first admits her love for Carlos and then, to a bare, almost motifless rhythmic idea in the strings, reveals that she has been the king's mistress. Elisabeth orders Eboli to quit the court, and then departs. Eboli's ensuing aria, "O don fatal" ("O don fatale"), in which she laments her fatal beauty, is cast in a conventional minor–major form, with the major section (in which she bids farewell to the queen) strongly reminiscent in its chromaticism and wide-spaced orchestral sonority of Verdi's last style. In a cabalettalike coda, Eboli resolves to spend her final hours at court in an attempt to save Carlos.

1867 Act 4/1884 Act 3, Scene 2

Carlos's prison. A string introduction of unusual depth and density introduces Posa to the waiting Carlos. Posa bids farewell to his friend in a rather old-fashioned romance, "C'est mon jour suprême" ("Per me giunto è il dì supremo"), and then explains that he has been discovered with Carlos's secret papers. A shot rings out; Posa falls mortally wounded. After telling Carlos that Elisabeth awaits him at the monastery of St. Yuste, he delivers a second romance, "Ah! je meurs" ("Io morrò"), happy that he can die for Carlos's sake. A duet for Philip and Carlos that followed this episode (cut before the 1867 première, though Verdi drew on its material for the "Lacrymosa" of the Requiem) was replaced with a riot scene (subsequently pruned for the 1884 version) in which Eboli appears at the head of a group intent on liberating Carlos. Philip also appears, but the crowd is silenced by the entry of the Inquisitor, who orders all to their knees before the king.

1867 Act 5/1884 Act 4

The monastery at St. Yuste. An impressive and extended orchestral prelude introduces Elisabeth at the tomb of Charles V. Her aria, "Toi qui sus le néant" ("Tu, che le vanità"), is in French ternary form: the outer sections are a powerful invocation of the dead emperor, and their firm, periodic structure stabilizes the number, allowing for remarkable variety and musical contrast during the long central section in which the queen's thoughts stray to memories of the past. Carlos appears for their final duet (from here to the end of the opera, Verdi made a number of important revisions in 1884). The set piece begins with the conventional series of contrasting sections, in the most prominent of which, "J'avais fait un beau rêve" ("Sogno dorato io feci!"), Carlos announces that he has done with dreaming and will now try to save Flanders. The final movement, "Au revoir dans un monde" ("Ma lassù ci vedremo"), a kind of ethereal cabaletta in which the couple bid each other a tender farewell, is similar to the closing duet of *Aida* in its restraint and delicate orchestral fabric. As they say "Adieu! et pour toujours" for the last time, Philip bursts in accompanied by the Inquisitor and various officials. The king tries to deliver his son to the priests, but Carlos retreats toward the tomb of Charles V. The tomb opens and the old monk appears, wearing the emperor's crown and mantle. He gathers Carlos to him and, with a few sententious words, draws him into the cloister.

ROGER PARKER

Alexander Zemlinsky, *Der König Kandaules*

Opera in three acts (1935–36); libretto by the composer, based on André Gide's play *Le roi Candaule* in the German adaptation by Franz Blei. Score reconstructed and instrumentation completed by Antony Beaumont.

King Kandaules, tenor
Gyges, baritone
Nyssia, soprano
Phedros, baritone
Syphax, tenor
Nicomedes, bass
Pharnaces, baritone
Philebos, baritone
Simias, tenor
Sebas, tenor
Archelaos, baritone
The cook, baritone
Trydo, actress

Prologue

King Kandaules and the fisherman Gyges have known each other since they were children. Time and fate have separated them, but their relationship has remained intact.

Act 1

Kandaules is celebrating a feast. The courtiers are discussing the unprecedented event of the evening: Nyssia, the king's wife, will present herself for the first time, and no one but Kandaules has ever seen her without her veil. Kandaules unveils his wife's countenance, and the courtiers are overwhelmed by her beauty. Kandaules gradually begins to realize the scope of his action. "Happiness withers when it is revealed."

An unusually large golden carp is served at the feast. One of the guests nearly swallows a ring lodged in the fish's flesh. The ring carries the cryptic inscription "I hide happiness." Suddenly, a distant glow attracts attention. The house of the fisherman Gyges is burning. Kandaules calls for the fisherman, to find out more about the strange ring. The fisherman comes before the king, and the fascination of their earlier relationship is revived. Kandaules wishes to see the fisherman's wife. Gyges, who imagines his wife to be his alone, learns that she has been unfaithful, and murders her. Kandaules publicly offers Gyges his friendship.

Act 2

Kandaules tells Gyges of his most secret wish. He wants Gyges to see his wife, Nyssia, naked. "Because my happiness, my unconcealed happiness and good fortune, seems to derive its power and passion from others, it often seems to me that it exists only in the knowledge that others have of it, and that I possess it only when others know that I do."

Since he has meanwhile learned of the ring's magic properties—it renders its bearer invisible—he urges his friend to wear it, though Gyges protests. When Nyssia enters the bedroom, Kandaules leaves, and Gyges, invisible, and riveted by her beauty, takes his place. Gyges spends the night with Nyssia.

Act 3

The next morning. Nyssia tells Kandaules that the previous night has been the most wonderful night of love that she has ever experienced. Kandaules cannot bear this truth, and goes looking for Gyges. Torn between love and guilt, Gyges wanders about. He reveals himself to Nyssia as her lover of the previous night, and begs her to kill him.

Nyssia, in vengeful desperation, demands the opposite: she wants Gyges to kill Kandaules. Reluctantly, he obeys. Kandaules dies. Nyssia makes Gyges her husband and king.

presence: culture, vs. hermeneutic culture (Gumbrecht), 109–11, 136; guaranteed by voice, 110; and live performance, 10; and music, 133; production of, 124
press. *See* criticism
prestige, perceived, of opera (Adorno), 28
private: property, in *Kandaules,* 202; vs. public, in *Don Carlos,* 141, 147, 149–50, 154, 159, 161, 173; sphere, in *Kandaules,* 190–91, 198, 202
production: history of, 12–13; means of, suppressed in *Meistersinger,* 57; "open" vs. "closed," 12; as performance text, 11–12
program books: 5–6, 6n12. *See* also *disposizioni szeniche*
property, in *Kandaules,* 197, 202
protection. *See* shelter
protectionism, 17. *See also* conventional stagings
protest. *See* controversy
Proudhon, Pierre-Joseph, 197
psychoanalysis: to elucidate *Don Carlos,* 142; id, ego, superego in *Figaro,* 89; object voice, 111. *See also* Freud, Sigmund; Oedipal scenario; sublimation
public: vs. private, in *Don Carlos,* 141, 147, 149–50, 154, 159, 161, 173; property, in *Kandaules,* 202; sphere, in *Kandaules,* 190–91, 198, 202
Puccini, Giacomo, 179

Quadriga (Brandenburg Gate), 64–65
quilting point, 114

Rabb, Theodore, 25
radical staging. *See* unconventional staging
Rathgeber, Eike, 205
reading: critical, resistance to, 50; failed, 66–67; failure of, in *Meistersinger,* 54; as interpretation, in Wagner, 52–58; paradoxically incompatible with art, in *Meistersinger,* 58; production as, 49; replaced by *Darstellung,* in *Meistersinger,* 55–56; strong vs. weak, 45–46, 59, 66
realism, social, in Sellars productions, 93
Realpolitik: in *Don Carlos,* 143n21, 151n40; in *Kandaules,* 196
recitation, lyrical: in Stuttgart *Entführung,* 126

recordings vs. live performance, 8–11
Regisseur. See director
rehearsal, 24, 33
reiteration, as repetition vs. as revision, 165–66
relation, vs. correspondence, 84
repetition: vs. representation (Attali), 166, 173. *See also* hermeneutic; mise-en-scène
re-presentation, 109–11, 132, 135. *See also* Gumbrecht, Hans Ulrich; presence culture
representation, 109–11, 133: embodied in Kandaules, 195; vs. repetition (Attali), 166, 173. *See also* Gumbrecht, Hans Ulrich; mise-en-scène; presence
Reynolds, Margaret, 79–80
Rheingold, das. See Ring des Nibelungen, der
Rheinmaidens (*Ring*), costume in centenary *Ring,* 21n48
Ricordi, Giulio, 166
Riding, Alan, xivn3
ring, magic, in *Kandaules,* 184, 186
Ring des Nibelungen, der (Wagner)
 1976 centennial production (Chéreau), 17–22, *21,* 77; as "archaeology of Wagnerian mythology" (Foucault), 19; characters in (*see names of individual characters*); hostility toward, 21, 38; importance of, 5, 19; as "palpable deconstructionism," 18n37
Risi, Clemens, 10, 11, 106; on sense vs. sensibility, 123
Robinson, Paul, 151n40; on characters in *Don Carlos,* 30; on family in Verdi, 168n77; on Posa's idealism in *Don Carlos,* 143; on *Realpolitik* in *Don Carlos,* 143n21, 151n40
Rogoff, Gordon, 112n23
Roller, Alfred, 44n17
romance: conventional, in *Don Carlos,* 146–47; Don Carlos's failed attempts to voice, 174; false shelter, in *Don Carlos,* 149; last gasp of, in *Don Carlos,* 154; treacherous, in *Don Carlos,* 143. *See also* love
romanticism: norms of acting, 50; recast as modernist in Kroll *Holländer,* 39
Rosen, David, 166n73
Rosenkavalier (Strauss), 95